Oscar Wilde Revalued

The 1880–1920 British Authors Series

Oscar Wilde Revalued

An Essay on New Materials

& Methods of Research

Ian Small

Number Eight
in the
1880–1920 British Authors Series

ELT Press

of

English Literature in Transition, 1880-1920

University of North Carolina

Greensboro, NC 27412

Number Eight

in the

1880-1920 British Authors Series

Distributed in Europe

by

Colin Smythe, Ltd.

Gerrards Cross

Buckinghamshire

England SL9 8XA

Copyright ELT Press © 1993

All Rights Reserved

Acid-Free Paper ∞

ISBN 0-944318-07-X

Library of Congress Cataloging in Publication Data

92-081205

| *Contents* |

Preface

This review of research on Wilde had its origins some time ago. It was initially commissioned by the Modern Language Association of America as part of a projected review of research on Anglo-Irish literature; the original material was read by Katharine Worth and John Stokes. Both offered helpful advice. Regrettably, however, the MLA project was subsequently abandoned, and the essay on Wilde was put aside until the summer of 1991 when my interest in it was revived through research being undertaken in conjunction with work for the Oxford English Texts edition of the *Complete Works* of Wilde. The particular subject of that research was a census of extant manuscript and typescript drafts of the *oeuvre*, a task undertaken by previous scholars only in a haphazard and piecemeal way.

Around this time ELT Press expressed an interest in publishing as a separate book the section on Wilde which I had written for the MLA project, and thanks to the commitment of its editor, Robert Langenfeld, I have been able to rewrite completely and to enlarge considerably that original essay in the light of my research for the OET edition. This "new" review of research on Wilde has been made possible by a variety of grants and fellowships: from the British Academy; from the University of Birmingham; from the Modern Humanities Research Association, which funded a research associateship at the University of Birmingham; from the William Andrews Clark Memorial Library, the University of California at Los Angeles; and from the Harry Ransom Humanities Research Center, the University of Texas in Austin. I am grateful for the help I have received from Joseph Donohue, Thomas F. Staley, Cathy Henderson, Thomas Wright, Suzanne Tatian, Michael Halls, and Darlene Webb. I am grateful, too, to Merlin Holland for sharing his knowledge of his grandfather's life and work with me. My greatest debts are to Karl Beckson, who read a late draft of this book and made many invaluable suggestions for its improvement; and to David Schwartz, who laboured to make sense of an often muddled manuscript. Nevertheless, any mistakes it still contains remain my responsibility.

One function of the present work is to provide a survey of critical writing on Wilde. My main aim, however, has not been comprehensiveness for its own sake, and where necessary I refer the interested reader to earlier bibliographies, particularly those by E. H. Mikhail, Ian Fletcher and John Stokes. My main ambition is that this essay should be a *vade mecum* for the interested student, postgraduate, or researcher through the morass of work written on Wilde. Thus, for reasons which are discussed at greater length in chapter one, my main emphasis is on post-war critical writing, and particularly on work written since 1970.

Ian Small

Acknowledgements

The author is grateful to the following copyright holders for permission to print manuscript material: Mrs. Imogen Dennis and Ms. Helen Guglielmini; Mr. Merlin Holland; the Early of Lytton; Ms. Jennifer Gosse; Random House UK Limited; Mr. Frederick W. Whitridge.

Abbreviations

The following abbreviations for major libraries are used throughout this work:

BL   British Library
HRHRC   Harry Ransom Humanities Research Center
                University of Texas at Austin
Clark Library   William Andrews Clark Memorial Library
                University of California, Los Angeles

Occasionally the following short titles for the works of Wilde have been used:

Earnest   *The Importance of Being Earnest*
Dorian Gray   *The Picture of Dorian Gray*
Husband   *An Ideal Husband*

Descriptions of Wilde's manuscripts use the following standard abbreviations:

AL   autograph letter
AMS   autograph manuscript
ANS   autograph note
C   Card
L   letter
MS   manuscript
N   note
S   signed
T   typescript

| 1 |

The Myth of Wilde

S INCE 1900 Oscar Wilde has been the subject of some 13,000 articles or books of one kind or another. Or at least so E. H. Mikhail estimated in his 1978 bibliography. Clearly few writers have achieved the distinction of having had so much ink spilled on their behalf. By the same token, however, virtually no major writer in English has been so badly treated for so long by the academic and non-academic critical industries alike. This apparent paradox is easily explained. Mikhail's total, although it sounds impressive, is in fact made up of a great deal of trivia or ephemera, and such material has done little to enhance Wilde's intellectual or literary reputation. At best it has simply been irrelevant to such judgements.

In recent years Wilde has lost none of his fascination, and the number of essays and books about him has continued to grow inexorably. But there has been one significant development since Mikhail compiled his bibliography; in the last fifteen years the *nature* of writing about Wilde has changed almost beyond recognition. Hence the reason for any new review of research is not so much a need to update earlier bibliographies (although much updating needs to be done), but rather a perception that a whole new "Wilde" needs to be recorded.

Until very recently there were none of the basic tools for a proper study of Wilde: no standard—nor even adequate—edition of the collected works, no satisfactory biography, no full census or description of the manuscripts and manuscript resources. In *Anglo–Irish Writing: A Review of Research* (1976)—along with Mikhail's bibliography, one of the few attempts to put Wilde scholarship on a proper footing—Ian Fletcher and John Stokes noted that "in all their dealings with Wilde, the English have been wrong about practically everything." The English may indeed have been in error in their judgement, but their interest in Wilde never waned. For fifty years after his death, Wilde certainly did have a reputation, but it was that of an infamous homosexual rather than a figure worthy of intellectual or academic attention.

Perhaps such notoriety was inevitable, given the public nature of his career, and especially of his trials and imprisonment. However, the consequence of this prurient interest in the life was that although an immense amount of biographical documentation was collected from the 1880s onwards, it amounted to little more than speculation, anecdote, and sometimes malicious misinformation. Moreover such a situation was compounded by the fact that most "critical" accounts (at least until the 1970s) had recourse, in one way or another, to that early body of partial information. In this respect the early biographies are the most biassed; by drawing upon, or by being uncritical of, anecdote and speculation, they were instrumental in creating and then popularizing the "myth" of Wilde.

All of this would be unimportant were it not for the fact that vestiges of the myth remain today even in relatively recent accounts. So revaluations of Wilde as well-known and as thorough as those by Richard Ellmann and Richard Pine continue to read Wilde's life as a "tragedy," his scandals and trials a "fall" occasioned by the hubris of the too-successful socialite. Although these accounts certainly do provide us with new and more reliable information about Wilde (and, in Ellmann's case, an abundance of such information), they still tend to interpret it along traditional lines.

A central aim, then, of this new review of research is to make explicit the changes in direction which have occurred in some Wilde research in the last fifteen years and which will perhaps finally allow the myth of Wilde to be laid to rest. Such a process is needed because the emergence of what may be termed a "de-mythologized" Wilde has taken place piecemeal; the "new" Wilde appears in innovative but scattered research undertaken by a variety of individuals working in isolation or in "marginal" areas such as gender studies, women's studies, textual scholarship, or theatre history. Taken individually, the findings of these critics may not appear to promise much; but taken collectively, they present us with a figure whose career is very different from that of the tragedy described by Ellmann and Pine.

The "new" Wilde is occupied less by the brilliant salon life of the 1890s and much more by hard and sometimes rather prosaic work. Wilde becomes the epitome of the new type of professional writer at the turn of the century, concerned with the unglamorous business of self-promotion, negotiating with publishers, cultivating potential reviewers, and constantly polishing his work. Moreover his interests are now seen to be much more wide-ranging than those associated with the literary and art worlds of the time. The "new" Wilde is preoccupied with issues such as authority, gender, identity, and prison reform; he is seen as thoroughly and seriously engaged with some of the most contentious intellectual issues of his day.

It is not surprising that this changed perception of Wilde has coincided with the emergence of relatively new areas of study within English. Generally speaking, most of the changes which have occurred in Wilde criticism over the past fifteen years have their origins in larger changes which have taken place in the various practices of the discipline. One of the most significant of these changes concerns literary history. For the first seventy years of this century, literary history assumed, but never made explicit, a set of values which marginalized or excluded writers such as Wilde. One of the anomalies of that history is that major but controversial figures of the late nineteenth century, although written about at great length, have rarely been marked out as worthy of serious intellectual attention; they never appeared as central figures in the canon which literary history enshrined. So although Wilde may have been acknowledged as a theoretician of culture, or as a propagandist for art, or as a figure to be accommodated uncomfortably within the history of English bourgeois sexual ethics, he was never accorded the status of "sage" to stand alongside Victorian worthies such as Matthew Arnold or John Stuart Mill. Consistently accused of superficiality and slightness, he was invariably credited only with a kind of clever *haute vulgarisation*—Wilde the "disciple," to use the accepted euphemism, of Pater, of Ruskin, of Godwin.

As a general rule, this situation improved as the century progressed, but serious study of Wilde as a writer (rather than homosexual martyr, socialite, or conversationalist) only really began in the

1970s. As I have suggested, most critical accounts up to this time drew heavily upon biographies (however unreliable they might have been): relatively few emphasized the work rather than the life. So as late as 1973, even a critic as sympathetic as Bernard Bergonzi could assert in *The Turn of the Century* that Wilde was "a tragic celebrity with relatively slender talents" whose work possesses a "largely derivative quality."

However this situation changed dramatically with the advent of the sustained, if sometimes unfocused, critique of the values and assumptions underlying "traditional" literary historiography which occurred in the mid-1970s and 1980s. The details of these processes are very familiar and need no elaboration here. Their specific consequences for the study of Wilde, though, are much less well-known.

In general terms, as the manner in which literary history defined its object of study became problematized, so the relationships between issues such as power, authority, and discourse came to be seen by some as the central concerns of literary history. And this process in turn led to the situation where the categories of the social and the literary, hitherto seen as mutually exclusive, were now no longer held to be so simple or so distinct. This revision of the bases of literary history significantly altered traditional perceptions of Wilde: it allowed the life and the work to read against each other in new and complex ways. Wilde continues to be of general interest to students of gay culture and to social historians, but today such an interest is not at the expense of ignoring his literary work. On the contrary: critics' concern with the replication of ideologies (especially those of sex and gender) in literary works has enabled Wilde's *oeuvre* to be viewed as an exemplary locus of late nineteenth-century politics. For example, a number of writers have perceived in Wilde's critical essays a sustained attempt to resist and subvert the dominant bourgeois and heterosexual ideologies of his time. (It is worth noting in passing that old suspicions concerning the political contexts of Wilde's trials and their relation to possible homosexual scandals in British public life have recently re-emerged.)

As a consequence of such revaluations it has become possible to reintegrate those two figures which, for half a century, were almost distinct "cases" in British and Irish history: Wilde the writer and Wilde the flamboyant homosexual iconoclast no longer exclude each other. The analysis of the relationships between authority, power, and ideology, and of their representations in discourse, has also led to a general interest in what is sometimes termed the "manipulation of meanings" (and hence of categories of thought). Cultural historians since the late 1950s have alerted us to the fact that this phenomenon became increasingly complex with the advent of a mass consumer culture in industrialized societies in the final decades of the nineteenth century. Indeed, literary and theatre historians have long been aware of Wilde's ambivalent relationship with the power of the popular press and the West End theatre in London—the power, that is, of the media techniques of the time—to create "personalities." The work of some recent critics has allowed us to see much more clearly these processes at work, with the result that the premises of past major critical studies of Wilde have been transformed. (Of course, Lloyd Lewis and Henry Justin Smith's *Oscar Wilde Discovers America* [1936] discussed such matters, but with less sophistication and with a different set of emphases.)

The general thesis which up to the 1960s characterized the discussion of many Victorian writers was that of the Victorian "sage" engaging and addressing a range of social issues. Such a thesis tended to exclude Wilde, simply because no simple "position" or "attitude" to the dominant social issues of the late nineteenth century could ever be distilled from his work. However, in the case of Wilde, the notion of the "sage" has now given way to that of the prototypical media "personality" created by, and for, an emerging consumerist culture. Perhaps the relative paucity of serious or informed critical writing on Wilde up to the late 1960s (compared with other Victorian figures, such as Matthew Arnold, or with early modernists, such as E. M. Forster) might have had something to do with a glimpsed or partial perception that such a traditional treatment would have always proved to be inadequate in his case.

The new interest in the relationship between power, authority, and sexuality, *considered as social phenomena*, has also had important consequences for the biographer of Wilde and for the critic who draws upon biography. Wilde's dandyism, his interest in the Decadence, and his homosexuality were topics once addressed only as salacious or entertaining aspects of the life, and thus somehow divorced, except in an incidental manner, from the work. Indeed, Wilde's homosexuality, endlessly discussed from the trials onwards, attracted very little serious analysis: even in the early 1970s, Wendell Harris, in his account of Wilde in the Modern Language Association's *Victorian Prose: A Guide to Research*, could unequivocally assert that "the relationship between Wilde's homosexuality, creative writing and aesthetic theorizing has been wearisomely but largely profitlessly discussed."

Accounts of the transgressive nature of Wilde's "condition" along the lines suggested by W. H. Auden's nasty phrase, the "Homintern Martyr," slowly gave way to an account of its pathology, but even then it was one which was couched in reductive Freudian terms: Wilde the "pariah" became Wilde the "case." However, the discussion of the relationship between gender and power over the past ten years, and the broad interest in uncovering the nature of the relationship between sexual practices and sexual ideology, have gone a long way towards rectifying some of these biases (and perhaps establishing new ones). A particularly significant work in this respect is Peter Gay's encyclopedic and ambitious discussion of Victorian sexuality, *The Bourgeois Experience* (1984–1986). In his second volume, Gay insists that the trials of Wilde momentarily made explicit "the stretches between [Victorian] erotic probity and sinfulness" which were "left vague" in Victorian sexual ethics; and he documents how the press coverage of the trials tended to dwell upon this very issue.

Such a general context provides a useful corrective to traditional views of Wilde's sexuality, in that homosexuality is seen to possess a much greater social significance than was usually allowed. For some critics this leads to a reassessment of Wilde's career in which the "tragedy" of his downfall lies not in his public exposure at his trials, but in his ill-treatment by contemporary society. Hence, Wilde and his works become positive elements in the history of gay rights rather than negative or faintly embarrassing moments in the history of bourgeois literary culture. Important markers in this reassessment of Wilde are represented by the work of British, American, and Canadian critics such as Jonathan Dollimore, Ed Cohen, and Richard Dellamora. Dollimore in particular has examined the relationship between sexual identity and categories of bourgeois thought, arguing that in his critical writing Wilde sees the "notion of individualism [as] . . . inseparable from transgressive desire and a transgressive aesthetic," and that this leads to a "relinquishing" of the notion of an "essential self."

The relocation of Wilde in literary history is not the product of gender studies alone. Other challenges to the assumptions of "traditional" literary history, such as those associated with formalism and structuralism, have also led to a revaluation of his work; Wilde the proto-formalist, and thus the "herald" of modernist iconoclasm, is now a commonplace. So the arguments of Wilde's critical essays are seen by some commentators to rehearse concepts familiar in early twentieth-century modernism; and his complex uses of textual devices in the plays and in *Dorian Gray* are understood as an anticipation of the uses of intertextuality more usually associated with modernists such as T. S. Eliot and James Joyce.

Moreover, further insights into Wilde have even been generated by some of the methods associated with "traditional" literary history. In the area of theatre history, Wilde's plays are now more usually seen in the social and theatrical (rather than simply literary) contexts in which they were produced. As a consequence, the topic of Wilde the practising *playwright*, as well as Wilde the *dramatist*, is now being examined. To take his status as a playwright first: it is now generally assumed that the notion of "texts" and of textual history *has* to include the history of productions. In these cases, simple information concerning the particularities of performances and of audience reaction is as important as general theoretical speculation on the nature of texts and of audiences. So, for example, knowledge of the textual history of *Lady Windermere's Fan* has been enhanced by evidence that Wilde changed elements of the play in direct response to the reactions of his audiences. In addition, theatre historians interested in Wilde as a dramatist have begun to locate him in relation to contemporary dramatic traditions: he is seen as both working within them and reacting to them.

This context has allowed the drama, particularly the society comedies, to be seen as much more radical than was previously thought. So theatre historians such as Russell Jackson, Kerry Powell, Katharine Worth, and Joseph Donohue have shown that Wilde uses contemporary dramatic conventions, but simultaneously subverts their accepted significance. Thus a traditional element of Victorian comedy, that of the matriarch, is in Wilde's hands transformed into an immoral parody of herself—into a Lady Bracknell or into a Duchess of Berwick. Nonetheless, much more still needs to be done in the way of dramatic criticism which pays due attention to issues such as stage-history and theatrical values.

A systematic account of the practices of dramatic authorship in the final years of the nineteenth century is an essential tool for any proper assessment of the nature of Wilde's achievement as a commercial dramatist. Little is known, for example, of the collaborative nature of Wilde's work, although there is abundant evidence that he *must* have collaborated in large measure with George Alexander and Herbert Beerbohm Tree. Issues such as these have been ignored by previous critics who purport to deal with Wilde's dramatic output; but they are essential if the present-day reader is to see Wilde's dramatic and theatrical originality. Nevertheless it has been possible to glimpse Wilde's role as a professional writer engaged with all aspects of the marketing and production of his plays. Moreover, this interest confirms the findings of recent research into the topic of Wilde's journalism. Although hampered at present by a simple lack of appropriate materials, investigations have already revealed the professionalism with which Wilde undertook this particular aspect of his career. The full extent of what Wilde wrote for some periodicals—particularly for the *Pall Mall Gazette*—is not known, and the conditions under which he worked as a journalist have never been examined except in the most general terms. However, suggestions as to how this situation may be remedied are beginning to be proposed by critics such as John Stokes.

A second and large area where the methods of "traditional" literary history have led to new discoveries about Wilde concerns his manuscripts. Recent re-examination of the manuscripts and typescripts of his work held in libraries in Britain and the United States has offered a much clearer overall view of his development as a writer. In particular it has allowed some traditional adverse judgements of Wilde—such as those concerning his plagiarism—to be re-assessed. Wilde's habits of re-using his own work and adapting that of others can be seen as systematic and careful strategy rather than simple laziness or deceit: they are rather to be explained in terms of a confrontation with intellectual and academic orthodoxies. The manuscripts also reveal some aspects of Wilde's intellectual development. In this respect an important recent edition of Wilde's *Notebooks* by Philip E. Smith II and Michael S. Helfand describes early influences in his Oxford years and their significance for his later work. Finally, preliminary research for the Oxford English Texts *Complete Works* has brought to light a number of hitherto unknown or forgotten, but nonetheless important, works and documents by him.

It is probably true to say that there is more interest, certainly more serious interest, in Wilde now than at any time in the century. The significance of the present review lies therefore not simply in its updating of Mikhail's bibliography but in its documenting of a whole new critical vocabulary and methodology.

| 2 |

Biography Reconsidered

A REGRETTABLE but unfortunately correct claim made by Wendell Harris (1973) and later by Ian Fletcher and John Stokes (1976) was that all biographies of Wilde had been characterized by their inaccuracy. Fletcher and Stokes, for example, noted that up to Hesketh Pearson's *The Life of Oscar Wilde* (1946) there was nothing remotely approaching a "competent and professional" life. They observed little improvement in the succeeding thirty years, drawing attention to shortcomings in the biographies by Louis Kronenberger (1976), Sheridan Morley (1976) and, although to a lesser extent, in Montgomery Hyde's work (1975). Wilde's life, they so rightly claimed, readily lends itself to "potboilers": it too easily adapts itself to melodrama, and from there inevitably to fiction.

Unfortunately, the melodramatic and fictional "life" of Wilde is also the popular Wilde. In this respect, one of the most seductive, and hence the most dangerous, "biographical" works to emerge over the past ten years has been Peter Ackroyd's novel, *The Last Testament of Oscar Wilde* (1983). Wilde also figures in other recent fictional works: in Chapman Pincher's *The Private World of St John Terrapin: A Novel of the Café Royal* (1982); in Robert Reilly's *The God of Mirrors* (1986); and in Neil Bartlett's *Who Was That Man?: A Present for Mr Oscar Wilde* (1988). Other, earlier, fictional recreations of Wilde and his milieu are itemized in Fletcher and Stokes (1976), 64-81, and Mikhail (1978) passim. Additional fictional works include Clement Wood, *The Sensualist: A Novel* (1942), Sewell Stokes's

Beyond His Means; A Novel Based on the Life of Oscar Wilde (1955),
Sewell and Leslie Stokes's *Oscar Wilde: A Play* (1938), John Furnell's
The Stringed Lute: An Evocation in Dialogue of Oscar Wilde (1955),
and Desmond Hall, *I Give You Oscar Wilde: A Biographical Novel*
(1965).

Although this "selling" of Wilde on most occasions has meant
trivialization and sensationalism, the main shortcoming of most
biographies has not been their attempt to popularize their subject,
but rather a failure to discriminate between sorts of evidence: at the
simplest level a willingness to take the anecdotal as true, and, at the
most serious, a failure to acknowledge that, given the public nature
of Wilde's life, some information about him was inevitably suppressed or partial. In recent years, however, several researchers,
among them Robert D. Pepper, Joseph Baylen, Robert L. McBath,
Kevin H. F. O'Brien, and, most importantly, Richard Ellmann, have
added significantly to our knowledge of the simple facts of Wilde's
life.

The success of misrepresentations of Wilde in the first part of the
century reveals an important point about his biography. As I noted
in chapter one, Wilde, more than any other figure in literary history
perhaps, comes to the reader with his life already written, in the sense
that the "myth" of Wilde precedes specific knowledge of any actual
details of it. For a man who claimed to have put his genius into his
life and to have stood in "symbolic relations" to his age, such a
situation was probably inevitable. Wilde was one of the first public
figures consciously to manipulate the media in order to create a
public personality. Hence, the first mythologizing and fictionalizing
of Wilde's life was by Wilde himself.

To a certain extent, even Wilde's contemporaries encountered the
man via the myth. From the late 1870s, figures such as George Du
Maurier, W. S. Gilbert and Arthur Sullivan, and Robert Hichens were
instrumental in creating a fiction of Wilde; and, for his part,
Wilde—in, for example, his tour of the United States—was happy to
be a party to that process of mythologizing. This pattern continued
long after Wilde's death; so it is not surprising that we too encounter
the life only via the myth. In a review of Richard Ellmann's biography,
Andrew Shelley (1988) made precisely this point, noting of Wilde that
"his works are really a series of 'exquisite moments' in the myth he

has himself become by now," and observing that in many ways any biography of Wilde is in a sense a retrial: an engagement with, and a refutation of, contemporary reactions to him.

Shelley's comments can be turned into a more general caveat. The student of Wilde's life ought to be wary of the fact that his biographers are never neutral, and indeed rarely try to disguise their lack of objectivity. The moral dimensions of Wilde's career inevitably require the biographer to take sides (and usually it is Wilde's against the forms of established authority which he opposed).

Given the public arena in which Wilde lived, there was, even from the earliest moments of his career, an immense amount of speculation, anecdote, and slander about him. As one would expect, the early biographies are the least impartial. Those by Lord Alfred Douglas and Robert Harborough Sherard, themselves players in the drama they describe, are especially to be distrusted. But they are nonetheless essential to an understanding of the construction of the Wilde myth. All the early biographical material is probably best treated with this caveat in mind. Most of the non-documentary biographical evidence is in the form of recollections or reminiscences, and suffers from all the disadvantages of hindsight—usually pomposity and self-righteousness, the inevitable result of Wilde's acquaintances' attempts at self-justification. The most famous examples are as follows.

Lord Alfred Douglas published four attempts to clarify his relationship with Wilde: *Oscar Wilde and Myself* (1914), *A Letter from Lord Alfred Douglas on André Gide's Lies about Himself and Oscar Wilde* (1933), *Without Apology* (1938) and *Oscar Wilde: A Summing-Up* (1940): all, of course, are partial in the extreme.

Robert Harborough Sherard, Wilde's pathetic champion, also published copiously, but on Wilde's behalf. See particularly: *Oscar Wilde: The Story of an Unhappy Friendship* (1902), *The Life of Oscar Wilde* (1906), *André Gide's Wicked Lies About the late Oscar Wilde in Algiers in January 1895* (1933), *Oscar Wilde, 'Drunkard and Swindler': A Reply* (1933), *Oscar Wilde Twice Defended from André Gide's Wicked Lies and Frank Harris's Cruel Libels* (1934).

None of these works is to be taken on trust, but all testify to the pervasive presence of Wilde in the memory of his contemporaries. Wilde continued to dominate his friends in death as in life. In this respect it is both surprising and disappointing that a proper study of the relationship between Wilde and Robert Ross, his literary executor and lifelong friend, especially as it touches upon Ross's textual decisions about his edition of the *Works*, is still a desideratum. (See, however, Margery Ross, *Robert Ross: Friend of Friends*, 1952, and Maureen Borland, *Wilde's Devoted Friend: A Life of Robert Ross*, 1990.)

Frank Harris's *Oscar Wilde: His Life and Confessions* (1916) is equally partial although much more readable in the sense that the figure of Wilde which Harris draws is a plausible one, but only if plausibility is understood in fictional rather than in biographical terms. The later editions of Harris's work show the persistence of the controversies surrounding Wilde's life in a different way. The 1938 edition carried George Bernard Shaw's "Preface," an equally interesting document in that it reveals a willingness half a century after the event to enter into the moral debate about Wilde. (See Robert Pearsall, *Frank Harris* [1970].) Karl Beckson's Critical Heritage volume on Wilde (1970) reprints important material concerning the relation of Wilde and Harris.

As I have indicated, recollections of Wilde by his contemporaries form a study in themselves. Some of the most significant elements in that study would include the following:

G. B. Shaw.	*Dramatic Opinions and Essays* (1907)
Marc-André Raffalovich.	*Uranisme et Unisexualité* (1896)
Stuart Mason.	*Oscar Wilde: Three Times Tried* (1912)
Grant Richards.	*Memoirs of a Misspent Youth* (1932) and *Author Hunting* (1939)
Ford Madox Ford.	*Ancient Lights* (1911) and *Return to Yesterday* (1931)
André Gide.	*Si le grain ne meurt* (1924) and *Journal* (1949)
Douglas Ainslie.	*Adventures Social and Literary* (1922)
Edmund Gosse.	*The Life of Algernon Charles Swinburne* (1917) (To an extent, Swinburne's recollections are here, as elsewhere, "sanitized" by Gosse)
Ellen Terry.	*The Story of My Life* (1908) and *Ellen Terry's Memoirs* (1933)
Lillie Langtrie.	*The Days I Knew* (1925)
Max Beerbohm.	*A Peep Into the Past* (1923)
Karl Beckson, ed.	*The Memoirs of Arthur Symons: Life and Art in the 1890s* (1977)

Any study would have to take account of a neglected but spirited, and, given the *mores* of the time, extremely courageous account by

Dalhousie Young, *Apologia Pro Oscar Wilde* (1895). A condensed version of this and other material is contained in E. H. Mikhail's *Oscar Wilde: Interviews and Recollections* (1979), a fascinating study made up of contemporary recollections of Wilde drawn from an wide variety of sources.

Other important evidence includes the recollections of Vyvyan Holland in *Son of Oscar Wilde* (1954), *Oscar Wilde: A Pictorial Biography* (1960) and *Time Remembered After Père Lachaise* (1966). Hart-Davis's editions of the *Letters* also contain a wealth of contextualizing information.

Biographical material published early in the century by those who had no real claim or access to documentary, anecdotal or other evidence, continued the dual process of trivializing and mythologizing Wilde's life. But with this caution in mind, the following works will be of use to the student of biography: on Wilde's Irish background, family and boyhood, see Patrick Byrne, *The Wildes of Merrion Square* (1953); Anna, Comtesse de Brémont, *Oscar Wilde and his Mother* (1911); Harry Furniss, *Some Victorian Women* (1923) (on Wilde's mother); Horace Wyndham, *Speranza: A Biography of Lady Wilde* (1951) (but the relationship between mother and son is explained in different terms in Mary Lydon [1981], and in Ellmann's biography); Eric Lambert, *Mad With Much Heart: A Life of the Parents of Oscar Wilde* (1967); and, most reliably, Terence de Vere White, *The Parents of Oscar Wilde* (1967).

The usual way in which Wilde's contemporaries understood his trials and disgrace was to see him as the seducer or corrupter of youth: Wilde was Svengali and Alfred Douglas his victim. Modern versions of the same events tend to reverse this judgement: Douglas becomes the betrayer of Wilde's generosity. Hence Bosie and his family get, in general terms, a bad press. Patrick Braybrooke's *Lord Alfred Douglas: His Life and His Work* (1931) and William Freeman's *The Life of Lord Alfred Douglas, Spoilt Child of Genius* (1948) are improved in all respects by the Marquess of Queensberry and Patrick Colson's *Oscar Wilde and the Black Douglas* (1948) and by Brian Roberts's *The Mad, Bad Line: the Family of Lord Alfred Douglas* (1981).

In contrast to the overarching attempts to mythologize Wilde's career, the American tour tends to be treated as an episode in itself: see Lloyd Lewis and Justin Smith (1936), the relevant parts of Brasol

(1938), Ellmann's biography and the more recent accounts described below.

The main biographies written between those by Harris and by Ellmann all need to be treated with varying degrees of caution. Boris Brasol's *Oscar Wilde: The Man—The Artist* (1938) has some interesting information, but given, as it were, by the way—in, for example, the chronology and in the notes. But it is also cavalier in its treatment of evidence. So, for example, the suggestion that Wilde died of syphilis (see below, Merlin Holland [1988]) is accepted as a simple fact.

The lives by Hesketh Pearson (1946) and H. Montgomery Hyde—*The Trials of Oscar Wilde (1948), Oscar Wilde: The Aftermath* (1963), and *Oscar Wilde* (1975)—were the best biographies of their time; they are all still very readable and helpful in correcting some of the distortions of other biographies. There are, however, clear gaps in them, and not infrequent simple errors of fact. They have since been superseded in many, but not all, respects by Ellmann's work. So, too, but in a much more emphatic manner, have Phillippe Jullian's *Oscar Wilde* (1967), Louis Kronenberger's *Oscar Wilde* (1976) and Sheridan Morley's *Oscar Wilde: An Illustrated Biography* (1976)—works which are now embarrassingly dated.

The amount of biographical material written on Wilde is impressive. A substantial portion of it, however, deals only with particular aspects of his life. So Stanley Weintraub, *Beardsley* (1967) and *Whistler: A Biography* (1974), Leonée Ormond, *George Du Maurier* (1969), H. Montgomery Hyde, *Cases That Changed the Law* (1951) and William T. Going (1958) discuss Wilde's commerce with Beardsley, George Du Maurier, Godwin and Scawen Blunt respectively. Paul Delaney (1978) examines Wilde's friendship with Charles Ricketts, and Daniel Farson (1975) documents his relationship with Florence Balcombe. James G. Nelson (1971) describes his relations with Mathews and Lane, Ricketts, Gray and Beardsley; and Jack Smithers (1939) describes his relations with Leonard Smithers. Wilde's relations with other contemporary figures are detailed in Fletcher and Stokes (1976, 72-3; 1983, 29-31). In particular, see W. B. Stanford and R. B. McDowell, *Mahaffy: A Biography of an Anglo-Irishman* (1971), Stanley Weintraub, *Reggie: A Portrait of Reginald Turner* (1965), Violet Wyndham, *The Sphinx and her Circle* (1963), Jean Delay, *The Youth of André Gide*, and, for its references to the trials, Douglas G.

Browne, *Sir Travers Humphreys: A Biography*. Fuller accounts of the trials are to be found in H. Montgomery Hyde (1948 and 1951), Edward Marjoribanks and Ian Colvin (1932-6), and Derek Walker-Smith and Edward Clarke (1939). Their work is supplemented by Jonathan Goodman's *The Oscar Wilde File* (1986), which reproduces material relating to the trials taken from a variety of sources, although not in any systematic manner.

For further details of anecdotal and biographical minor material, see Mikhail (1978, 116-190) and Fletcher and Stokes (1976, 64-81). Von Eckardt, Gilman and Chamberlin (1987) have some interesting information concerning Wilde's social milieu, although their account of the late nineteenth century tends to be over-schematic.

Many of the details of these and other individual accounts have been subsumed into Ellmann's biography. It is worth pointing out at this stage, however, that Ellmann's use of his sources is frequently uncritical, and their errors sometimes find their way into his work.

Ellmann's biography apart, there have been several other attempts to revalue Wilde's life. However, as I suggested earlier, most continue to utilize and therefore to endorse the Wilde "myth" in one way or another. A good example of such a process is Richard Pine's biography (1983) which divides Wilde's career into four stages: genesis, hubris, nemesis and catharsis: such a reading of Wilde's life is not at all incompatible with the "tragedy" seen both by earlier biographers and more recently by Ellmann. Pine is informative in documenting Wilde's Irishness and his early life in Dublin; and interesting, too, on the importance of John Mahaffy in Wilde's education and development. But nevertheless his emphasis is still upon Wilde as a social figure rather than a writer. He traces the "development" of homosexuality in Wilde and, in keeping with modern concerns with gender, suggests that Wilde presents an exemplary case of late nineteenth-century anti-bourgeois homosexual morality. Unfortunately Pine tells us little about Wilde's relationship with Douglas.

That relationship is much more fully treated in H. Montgomery Hyde's biography of Douglas and it is the subject of his 1982 Tredegar Memorial Lecture (Hyde 1984). Hyde describes his meeting with Douglas in 1931 when Douglas spoke to him of his relationship with Wilde. Hyde reports Douglas's views of his unsuccessful libel action against Arthur Ransome in 1913 and relates Douglas's descriptions of the nature of his and Wilde's sexual relationship, and the details surrounding the typing and publishing of *De Profundis*.

Like Richard Pine, Robert Keith Miller (1982) also gives the general reader a useful account of the life and works. More recently, Norman Page (1991) gives in summary form an outline of the salient details of Wilde's biography. Less concise and less satisfying is a brief, popularizing account of Wilde which bears the unoriginal title of *The Importance of Being Oscar*, written by Leslie Frewin under the pseudonym of Mark Nicholls. (The reasons for such an elaborate disguise are not made clear in the 1986 British reprint of the work under Frewin's real name.) Frewin rehearses very familiar details of Wilde's biography; but his style recalls the excesses of those "potboilers" produced with such monotonous regularity in the early days. Other excursions into biography have certainly been no more successful. As I have noted, Wilde's life has long since presented an irresistible opportunity for the retailers of the familiar; and Anita Roitinger's essay on Wilde's life (1980) draws for the most part upon information which is both readily available and depressingly well-known.

Overshadowing all other studies of Wilde's career is of course the biography by Richard Ellmann. Virtually every page tells us new facts about Wilde. Ellmann moves away from the usual glancing accounts of Wilde's childhood, schooling and subsequent career at Trinity College, Dublin. New information about his relationship with his parents, particularly with his mother (but cf. Mary Lydon [1981], described below), and his career at Portora are given very fully.

For Ellmann, the child is the father of the man, and his Wilde, even in his school days, was already the proto-aesthete. And at Trinity, according to Ellmann, Wilde's aesthetic education was being fashioned: indeed "Wilde can be seen slowly accumulating at Trinity the elements of his Oxford behaviour—his Pre-Raphaelite sympathies, his dandiacal dress, his Hellenic bias, his ambiguous sexuality, his contempt for conventional morality" (32).

In giving a whole new set of emphases to his early life, Ellmann enables us to see Wilde's career as a continuous development. So the pre-Oxford days are described in exacting detail; so too is Wilde's career in the mid-1880s, usually quickly passed over as a stage between the early successes of his Oxford years and of the American lecture tour and the later triumphs of the society dramatist in the 1890s. So much new information about Wilde's early career is in evidence that by the half-way point in Ellmann's biography, Wilde is only 33, still to meet Bosie and still to write a successful literary work. Each moment in Wilde's career is documented with far greater care and in far greater detail than has hitherto been the case. Facts about Wilde's initial reception in New York and the subsequent tour of the States are given in abundance, but for new information about local details, see Robert D. Pepper (1982), and Richard Harmond and G. A. Cevasco (1987). His commerce with London society in the early 1880s and his extravagent self-advertisement are also fully treated. Ellmann also confirms Wilde's career as a mason (cf. Marie Roberts [1986], described below).

Central, however, to Ellmann's account of Wilde is his rehabilitation of the view that Wilde contracted syphilis at Oxford, a claim which Ellmann made initially in lectures, then in print in the *New York Review of Books* in 1984, but one subsequently contested in a letter by Macdonald Critchley to the *British Medical Journal*, and by Merlin Holland (1988). Holland questions Ellmann's claim that Wilde died from tertiary syphilis. He examines and throws considerable doubt on Ellmann's evidence, and argues that the symptoms which Wilde presented in his final illness are not consonant with those of syphilis. Holland suggests that this "fact" like many other "facts" of the biography are simply uncorroborated assertions which have acquired increasing authority with age. In his turn, Critchley argues that Wilde's symptoms were much more consonant with the original diagnosis of meningoencephalitis due to a chronic suppuration of the right ear than with the later diagnosis of syphilis. Patrick Reilly (1989) also provides an account of Wilde's death.

Ellmann had printed other parts of the biography as separate essays: see Ellmann (1987). He claimed quite unequivocally that "homosexuality fired . . . [Wilde's] mind," and Wilde's entries into the homosexual subcultures of London and Paris are described by Ellmann in great detail. Indeed the whole of Wilde's career in France is fully documented. This is a topic which has been taken up by other critics over the past decade: see, in particular, Worth (1983) and Clements (1985). But the passages which describe Wilde's relationship with Douglas, up to the trials and afterwards on the Continent, turn out to be the most revealing. An enormous amount of new information about the relationship is given to us. In particular, the last years in France and in Italy are movingly described, but here compare the differing interpretations of the time spent at Posilippo with Bosie given by Baylen and McBath (1985), upon which Ellmann draws.

All in all, however, Ellmann's biography is not the life of Wilde but the tragedy of Wilde: in this sense he repeats, albeit in a modified form, the figure familiar from almost a century of Wilde mythologizing. Moreover there are also errors in the work, both of fact, and of emphasis: there are simple confusions, such as that between Asquith and Balfour, mentioned by Owen Dudley Edwards in his BBC radio tribute to Ellmann after his death; there are some erroneous details, some of which have been noted by Frank Kermode in his review of the book in the *London Review of Books* (29 October 1987); and there is some disputed interpretation of evidence noted by Paul Chipchase (1987). For example, Ellmann's dramatic description of Wilde's body after his death in 1900 is based on sources discredited for a considerable time. It is worth repeating that these sorts of errors derive not from ignorance or carelessness, but from Ellmann's failure to distinguish between kinds of evidence.

A more substantial criticism has been raised by Joseph Donohue in "Recent Studies of Oscar Wilde." He questions the *nature* of the biography which Ellmann wrote. Donohue suggests that Ellmann's emphasis on Wilde's public success as he embraced homosexuality fails to take account of his success as a dramatist—that is, as a professional man of the theatre: so, Donohue argues,"readers gain only an inadequate sense of Wilde's methods as a writer, of his phenomenal facility, but also of his tireless perfectionism." Detailed corrections of Ellmann's factual errors have been made by Horst Schroeder (1989).

But these criticisms aside, it is clear that Ellmann's work will remain the most authoritative biography for the foreseeable future. Indeed, it has been instrumental in reviving a serious scholarly interest in Wilde.

Some local studies of moments in the life have been significant. Here research into private and public sources has been especially valuable: indeed, as I have indicated, Ellmann incorporated some of this research into his biography. In particular, two documentary studies, those by John Stokes (1983) and by Baylen and McBath (1985) have been revealing. Baylen and McBath print a letter from the British consul for Southern Italy, Eustace Neville-Rolfe, to the Earl of Rosebery detailing the activites of Wilde and Douglas in Posilippo in 1897. Baylen and McBath suggest that Neville-Rolfe, whose homosexuality was known at the time, would have been aware of—and indeed been a party to—Rosebery's alleged homosexuality, especially the scandal surrounding his relationship with Viscount Drumlanrig (Douglas's brother) and the latter's mysterious death in 1894. The authors, following suggestions by Brian Reade (1970) and Vern Bullough (1976), offer some speculation about the alleged connection between the relentless prosecution of Wilde and the possibility of a major homosexual scandal in British public life. In this sense, Baylen and McBath highlight an increasingly fashionable area of interest in Wilde's life—the relationship between sexuality and politics.

Here it is worth noting in passing that Ellmann's discussion of Wilde's homosexuality treats it as a private matter, divorced from contemporary politics. So he uses Baylen's and McBath's research, but ignores the wider political implications which they draw from it. In this respect recent critics, such as Ed Cohen and Richard Dellamora, take issue with the implications of Ellmann's account of Wilde's gayness. See Dellamora's *Masculine Desire*, Ed Cohen's "Legislating the Norm" (1989) and, in the same year, an essay by Lee Edelman which also addresses the topic of identity and sexual difference.

John Stokes (1983) pursues the homosexual context of Wilde's life in the 90s across an equally difficult terrain: he delves into the diaries, scrap-books and manuscripts of George Ives held at the HRHRC. He describes how Ives knew Wilde from 1892 up to the debacle of the trials. According to Stokes, Wilde "in his turn seems to have regarded Ives as an acceptable colleague in the struggles to establish a climate in which the 'New Hedonism,' a new homosexual sensibility, might flourish" (175). Indeed, Stokes points out that Wilde used aspects of Ives's life for details of *The Importance of Being Earnest*. Stokes's painstakingly thorough search for Ives's commerce with the homosexual subculture of London in the 90s points to the possibility of further research in this field (especially among the relatively unknown MSS resources at the HRHRC and the Clark Library).

Wolfgang Maier examines the evidence about Wilde's debts in documents held by the Public Record Office after the bankruptcy proceedings. James D. Griffin reassesses the nature of the relationship between André Gide and Wilde and then the reliability of the Frenchman's recollections of that relationship. Griffin takes issue with a whole line of argument in biographies of Wilde—originating in Sherard's pamphlets (1933 and 1934), through Boris Brasol (1938), Hesketh Pearson (1946), Lewis Broad (1954) and Croft Cooke (1972)—that Gide lied about his relationship with Wilde. Griffin then discusses Gide's correspondence with Wilde, distinguishing between the authentic and forged letters, and concludes that, while the acquaintance between the two writers was not great, "when Gide speaks of days passed with Wilde . . . his perspective must be that of a literary acquaintance, and not a confidant" (169). This very fact makes Gide's admiration for Wilde both impressive and arresting.

Elsewhere Zelda Austen (1983) provides a contrastive study of Wilde's and William Morris's careers in the 1880s, suggesting that Wilde's career and that of Morris may be best understood via a set of antitheses: the Celtic and the Germanic; the Hellenist and the medievalist; the performer and the reformer, and so on. Ruth Z. Temple, in "The Other Choice. The Worlds of John Gray, Poet and Priest," explores the relationships between Marc-André Raffalovich, John Gray and Wilde, and suggests explanations for the antagonism between Raffalovich and Wilde.

On a more miniature scale, Karl Beckson (1983) corrects Wilde's (and Wilde's biographers') misapprehensions about Henry Bevan Isaacson, the Governor of Reading Prison when Wilde was imprisoned there in 1895, and describes Isaacson's career before and after his stewardship of that austere building. Elsewhere Horst Schroeder (1985) describes Wilde's trip to Homburg to take the waters in the summer of 1892. He fixes exactly the date of Wilde's arrival, locates the addresses where Wilde stayed and suggests how the dates of some of Wilde's correspondence at the time might be revised and corrected in the light of this evidence.

In a scrupulously well-documented and well-illustrated essay, but one that is probably better informed about local American than about national British culture, Robert D. Pepper (1982) looks at an earlier moment in Wilde's life, his lecture tour of the States, and in particular his visit to San José in April 1882. Pepper traces Wilde's itinerary in northern California and notes that his lecture in San José coincided with the tour of the Comely-Barton Opera Troupe playing *Patience* in San Francisco in March 1882. Particularly revealing is Pepper's documentation of the depth of local interest which Wilde's tour provoked.

Kevin H. F. O'Brien (1974) also documents an episode in Wilde's visit to north America—his time in Canada; and Mary Louise Ellis (1987) describes "Oscar Wilde in Alabama, 1882." Ophia D. Smith in *Fair Oxford* (1947) gives an account of Wilde's lecture in Oxford, Cincinnati; William Habich (1957) describes "Oscar Wilde in Louisville"; Robert Luttrell McBath Jr. and J. O. Baylen (1980) give an account of Wilde's lecture at DeGive's Opera House in Atlanta, Georgia; and Charles Harmon Cagle (1981) gives details of Wilde's four lectures in Kansas. Forbes Parkhill in *The Wildest of the West* (1951) describes Wilde in Denver.

Further information about the American tour is to be found in Ellmann's biography; but recently Terry L. Meyers in "Oscar Wilde and Williamsburg, Virginia" (1991) points out that Ellmann's suggestion that Wilde lectured in Williamsburg, Virginia, is wrong, and that he in fact lectured in Williamsburg, Brooklyn.

John Unrau (1982) examines the nature of the friendship between Ruskin and Wilde, anticipating and usefully reinforcing Ellmann's information about the influence of Ruskin on Wilde. Unrau cites evidence (in the form of letters from the Revd. J. P. Faunthorpe) that suggests that Oscar and Constance Wilde were better acquainted with Ruskin than has usually been assumed to be the case, and that their friendship survived from Wilde's Oxford days later into his career than is usually supposed. Unrau observes that Ruskin's biographers attempted to suppress knowledge of his acquaintance with Wilde, and he goes on to note that the Faunthorpe letters escaped this general suppression of information following Wilde's conviction and imprisonment in 1895.

Kerry Powell (1986) clears up the confusion over the "invention" of Basil Ward as the model for Basil Hallward. He traces the invention of Ward to a pirated American edition of *The Picture of Dorian Gray* in 1904 and describes how a succession of biographers, including Kronenberger, Sheridan Morley and Montgomery Hyde, have been misled since. Powell suggests that while the "inspiration for the novel came from many directions," the painter who influenced Wilde most forcefully was probably Frank Holl. In a larger study of the relationship between secret societies and creativity, Marie Roberts (1986) notes in passing that Wilde may have been a freemason, information, as I have indicated, corroborated and substantially amplified since by Ellmann.

More suggestive is Kevin H. F. O'Brien's account (1985) of the career of Robert Harborough Sherard and his relationship with Wilde. In a well-documented piece, O'Brien describes Sherard's friendship with Wilde in Paris in the 1880s and the circles in which both Sherard and Wilde moved: indeed, an acknowledgement of the importance of Wilde's commerce with things French is one of the real triumphs of recent biography and criticism. O'Brien is particularly interesting on Sherard's and Wilde's involvement with the mad John Barlas, and on Sherard's dogged and in many ways pathetic championing of Wilde during the trials and his imprisonment.

In one of those ironic coincidences with which academic and publishing life abounds, we have been given in the past decade two biographies of Constance Wilde. Joyce Bentley (1983) writes a short work designed for the popular reader. It draws heavily on a narrow range of well-established sources and occasionally deals in reductive truisms. Anne Clarke Amor's life (1983) is better researched, more adequately documented and finally more thorough. Her grasp upon the relevant issues seems altogether more firm. Yet, as John Stokes (1987) points out, both biographies clearly miss important aspects of the private side of Constance's life: the sale at Sotheby's in 1985 of letters from Constance to Arthur Lee Humphreys (described below) indicates a whole new area of undocumented material to be considered in further accounts of her.

The other members of the Wilde nuclear family are discussed elsewhere. George Sims (1984) describes his acquaintance with Vyvyan Holland, Wilde's younger son. In passing Sims reports details of the sales of Wilde's letters and memorabilia, and mentions the suggestion that Holland's birthday had been entered on his birth certificate as 3 November 1886, rather than his actual birthday, 5 November, to "avoid any humorous connection between the Aesthetic Movement and Guy Fawkes Day" (53)—a detail mentioned also by Ellmann.

Related, perhaps tenuously, to the general idea of family is Mary Lydon's "Myself and M/others" (1981), which among other examples, discusses Wilde's relationship with his mother and locates his jokes about, and representations of, maternity in that context. Lydon quotes Lady Wilde on style and on women and then establishes connections between mother and son by suggesting that the tone of those pronouncements "might be pure Lady Bracknell—or Oscar Wilde. . . . The distinct resemblance adds a nuance, at least, to Oscar's statement about men and their mothers" (9). It is worth reiterating here that accounts of Wilde's relationship with his mother (apart from that by Terence de Vere White) largely ignore her copious correspondence to him, much of which is held at the Clark Library. Related also to the idea of family is Karl Beckson's informed essay of 1983 on Willie Wilde, "The Importance of Being Angry." (See also in this respect Madeleine B. Stern [1953].) Elsewhere Eric Tappe (1986) describes the career of T. Wemyss Reid from editor of the *Leeds Mercury* to general manager of Cassells publishing house in London. Tappe describes how instrumental Reid was in securing Wilde as editor of the *Lady's World* (the title of which Wilde quickly changed to *Woman's World*).

In general terms, recent trends in Wilde biography can be summarized in the following way. The emphasis on uncovering new facts about Wilde has resulted in an explosion of information about him. This information in turn has allowed Wilde's life to be reinterpreted in the context of contemporary cultural and political concerns. However, it is still the case that elements of the "myth" persist (particularly in Ellmann's biography), and have to a large extent structured and interpreted much of this evidence. So, for example, those aspects of Wilde's life and personality which do not fit the myth—his domestic roles as a father, a son, a husband, and his public life as a working dramatist rather than as a socialite—still require attention.

| 3 |

Prologue
to the Letters

U NTIL very recently virtually the only area of study where
Wilde had been at all adequately served was in his letters. Sir
Rupert Hart–Davis produced his excellent and knowledgeable edition
of *The Letters of Oscar Wilde* in 1962. Its collection of over a
thousand items supplemented and succeeded all other earlier collections of the correspondence (such as those by More Adey, details of
which are in Fletcher and Stokes [1976], 61). Hart–Davis's edition
contains an immense amount of contextualizing information: it is a
work of biography in itself and an essential tool for any scholar or
student of Wilde. Indeed it is possible to date the beginning of serious
scholarly attention to Wilde from the date of its publication. *Selected
Letters of Oscar Wilde* (1979), also edited by Hart–Davis, reprints
material from that collection, sometimes in an emended form. In
1985 Hart–Davis supplemented his collected edition with *More Letters of Oscar Wilde*, a further 164 letters taken, he reports, from a
total of over two hundred identified since the publication of his first
collection. Those he left out he claimed were merely "trivial notes,
always undated, often to unidentifiable correspondents"–a claim
which is in fact slightly misleading.

There is a significant number of unpublished Wilde letters at the
HRHRC. These may have been overlooked by Hart–Davis, or they
may have been rejected on the basis of being trivial. Actually they
have several kinds of significance. Some add very minor points of
information to the biography: an undated letter, for example, to

George Ives clearly demonstrates that he was well acquainted with Wilde's subterfuges–"I have said I am going to Cambridge to see you–but I am really going to see the young Domitian," Wilde writes. Other letters, however, provide interesting information about the mundane aspects of Wilde's life, the day-to-day negotiations undertaken as a matter of course by an aspiring dramatist in the late nineteenth century. In addition, there is a very important letter to an unnamed correspondent, but perhaps John Morley, about the corrected proofs of "The Soul of Man Under Socialism" (for details, see below).

Nevertheless Hart–Davis's last collection prints letters taken from every phase of Wilde's career and includes, in the 1880s, correspondents such as Lady Gregory, Walter Hamilton and Herbert Horne. Particularly interesting are those written during the 1890s. In them, our knowledge of Wilde's concern for money and his transactions with his publishers and theatre managers is usefully supplemented. There are, for example, two long letters to George Alexander concerning details of the staging of *Lady Windermere's Fan* and a letter to Beerbohm Tree about the rights over, and the royalties from, *A Woman of No Importance*, which adds to the information about the financial returns of performances of the play that may be gathered from the Beerbohm Tree Collection at the University of Bristol.

The letters of this period to and from publishers provide evidence of how closely Wilde followed commercial transactions and all business matters. Those letters from prison and from the Continent flesh out our knowledge of the final years. Since then other letters have been published: Richard Harmond and G. A. Cevasco (1987) print a previously unpublished letter of Wilde held at the Theodore Roosevelt Association which he wrote soon after his arrival in New York in January 1882. More recently, John Spalding Gatton (1989) identifies two further letters.

Letter writing is, of course, a process which involves at least two parties. In this respect, letters to Wilde have tended to be neglected by editors and scholars alike. In the annotation to both of his collections Hart–Davis does in fact print extracts from some letters to Wilde, but generally speaking there is no equivalent of Richard J. Finneran's collection of letters to W. B. Yeats. The HRHRC has particularly strong holdings of letters to Wilde which have been largely unexamined. They can be divided into two broad categories: those which are part of a sequence and which therefore allow us to make sense of an otherwise enigmatic letter from Wilde; and those from acquaintances, but more usually business connections, which point to, and give useful hints about, missing parts of Wilde's correspondence. In both cases the letters at the HRHRC provide small but significant details of the biography.

Further correspondence which bears some interest for students of Wilde is printed by Mary Hyde in *Bernard Shaw and Alfred Douglas: A Correspondence* (1982), a volume which contains copious reference to Bosie's views of his relationship with Wilde, recollected in letters to Shaw from 1931, when Douglas was 60, up to 1944. More recently, David B. Eakin (1987) discusses Wilde's own correspondence with Douglas.

The selection of letters which follows is by necessity only a sample of the archive material. It is intended to indicate the *range* of evidence available to the interested scholar. A comprehensive edition of the unpublished letters to and from Wilde, with full textual apparatus and explanatory annotation, is clearly beyond the scope and remit of this book. For example, Lady Wilde's letters to Oscar would fill a volume by themselves. For reasons of space, therefore, a few letters to Wilde have been abbreviated, and annotation has been confined to bibliographical information.

Uncollected Letters

ANS to Mr Byrne

Location: Clark Library.
W6721L B995. [1876?].

Magdalen College
Oxford

Mr Byrne,

I am very glad to hear you have let the House. All the Rents &c are to be paid to me direct. And I am responsible for everything. Whatever is due to you for letting the house and the valuation you will please deduct from the rent.

Oscar F.W. Wilde

ANS to Charles Leland

Location: Clark Library.
W6721L L537. [1878–80].

St Stephen's Club
Westminster

Dear Mr Leland,

Will you give me the pleasure of dining with me on Thursday at 8 o'clock *en garçon*. I want to have a talk with you on many subjects.

Sincerely yours

Oscar Wilde

13 Salisbury St
Strand

ALS to Mrs Hunt

Location: Clark Library.
W6721L H942 (bound). Oscar Wilde letters to Mrs Hunt 1880–87.
Letter 3 [post-marked 15 July 1880].

Dear Mrs Hunt,

It is *so* good of you asking me. I am engaged to a lot of places that afternoon and evening but I shall come to you certainly. I am *so sorry* you are all going away.

Yours sincerely

Oscar Wilde

[Letter 8]

Keats House
Tite Street
Chelsea

Dear Mrs Hunt,

I am really very unlucky, and am always engaged when you are good enough to ask me. The loss is mine on this as on other occasions.

Very sincerely yours

Oscar Wilde.

ALS to Miss Boughton

Location: Clark Library.
W6721L B758. [1881].

Keats House
Tite Street
Chelsea

Dear Miss Boughton,

I shall be very happy to come to you on Sunday evening if I can get away from a <u>very aesthetic</u> dinner party to which I am engaged.

Perhaps you will not mind my coming a little late.

Lilies and languors and all!

Very sincerely yours
Oscar Wilde

This letter is *not* for publication

ALS To an unknown correspondent

Location: Clark Library.
W6721L U58. [Dec. 1881?].

9 Charles Street
Grosvenor Square

Dear Harold,

Will you come and lunch with me at St. Stephen's Club tomorrow (Wednesday) at 2 o'c. It's only

(1) 9 minutes from the city. Or will you come here at 5 o'clock to tea.

(2) Lunch will suit me better

(3) Tell me by telegram where to find you and I will go down to city as I want a [illegible word] rug. I go to U.S. on Friday.

Ever yours
Oscar Wilde

ALS To an unknown correspondent

Location: Clark Library.
W6721L U58. [188–?].

Dear Miss Romolu[?] [illegible word]

Allow me to congratulate you on your great success as a reciter. Those who have heard you once, always desire to hear you a second time, and I have no doubt that you have a fine career before you. You seem to me to have all the qualifications necessary for the recitation of poetry and for its dramatic presentation.

Believe me
Sincerely yours
Oscar Wilde.

ALS to Mr Young

Location: Clark Library.
W6721L Y68. [188–?].

Dear Mr Young,

I am so sorry that I cannot go to the theatre tomorrow night after all: I find we have an old engagement to dine out.

I hope however you will come and see me before you go away.

Yours very sincerely

Oscar Wilde

ALS To an unknown correspondent

Location: Clark Library.
W6721L U58. [188–?].

~~Albemarle Club~~
~~13 Albemarle Street W~~
16 Tite Street
Chelsea SW

Dear Frank,

On *Friday* with pleasure at 7.30. But is not the Continental dreary for dinner? Why not that lovely place in King Street, St James'—"Willis's restaurant"—I go there daily, but you have to engage a table beforehand. If you have not tried it, pray do—I know you will like it. It has an excellent chef, and has the advantage of being terribly extravagant.

You must tell me all about Spain. Your letter from there charmed me: *no*, you must tell me all about yourself—You are much more interesting to me than even Spain is.

Ever yours,

Oscar Wilde

ALS to Richard D'Oyly Carte

Location: HRHRC MS Wilde, O; Letters [1882].
[Paper headed: "J. M. Stoddart & Co., / Publishers, / Philadelphia."]

Arlington Hotel
Washington

Dear Carte

You see the unpleasant results of leaving me without a manager—Please don't let it occur again for *both our sakes!* Morse should be always with me: Thanks

Oscar Wilde

LS to Joseph Marshall Stoddart

Location: HRHRC; MS Wilde, O; Letters.
[There is a stamped receipt on the letter: "J.M. Stoddart / Oct / 21/ 1882 / Philadelphia"; also on the letter, in a hand not Wilde's, is: "answrd J.E.B. Oct. 23 '82"].

[19/20 Oct 1882]
Philadelphia

Dear Mr·Stoddard [*sic*],

I hope you will not forget to send me all the reviews of Mr. Rodd's poems—I hear the "Critic" had one and the Times.

Very truly yours
Oscar Wilde
1267 Broadway

ALS to Mr Seaver

Location: Clark Library.
W6721L S442. [1882].

Dear Mr Seaver,

Thank you for your most courteous letter. It would have given me great pleasure to dine with you next week, but I leave on Monday for Philadelphia.

On my return to New York however I hope to avail myself of your hospitable invitation.

Believe me

Dear Mr Seaver

Very truly yours

Oscar Wilde

ACS to Mrs Dion Boucicault

Location: Clark Library.

W6721L B755. [Aug.–Sept. 1883].

46 West 28th Street

Dear Mrs Boucicault,

Thank you very much for your card. I hope you have received your tickets. After Monday I will be freer and should be only too delighted to see you again, and call on you if you allow me.

Believe me

Very sincerely yours

Oscar Wilde

ALS To an unknown correspondent

Location: Clark Library.

W6721L U58. 28 April 1883.

Avril 28

'83

Monsieur,

Je desire tant voir le jour de vermissage à votre salon que j'ose vous faire souvenir de la promesse que vous m'avez si courtoisement fait de m'envoyer une carte d'entrée.

Agréez, Monsieur, l'assurance de mes sentiments les plus distinguées, et de l'admiration infinie que j'ai pour vos oeuvres.

Oscar Wilde

Hotel Voltaire

Quai Voltaire.

ACS to [George Webb?] Appleton

Location: Clark Library.
W6721L A649. [1884?].

16 Tite Street
Chelsea SW

Dear Mr Appleton,

I fear I will not be able to lecture out of town next season, or much in town either, as I am very busy. I will however lecture at Bournemouth in *April* not October.

Sincerely yours

Oscar Wilde

ANS to Mrs Humphrey

Location: Clark Library.
W6721L H926. [188–?].

16 Tite Street
Chelsea SW

Dear Mrs Humphrey

Will you call in. Do you understand?

Sincerely yours

Oscar Wilde

ACS To an unknown correspondent

Location: Clark Library.
W6721L U58. [1880–95?].

"Sur les sujets modernes, faisons des vers antiques"

Oscar Wilde

ANS to Gleeson White

Location: Clark Library.
W6721L W584. [188–?].

16 Tite Street

Chelsea SW

Dear Mr Gleeson White,

I send you a few leaflets about my little book—your pleasant article on the Kakemono I hope to use in January.

Sincerely yours

Oscar Wilde

ALS to Frances Forbes–Robertson

Location: Clark Library.
W6721L H3238. [1885–95].

16 Tite Street
~~New Travellers Club~~,
~~Picadilly W~~

My Dear Frankie,

How unkind of you to be at Mrs Palmer's and not tell me! Why did you do this? I suppose you are right about the Convent Parlour. But we must meet somewhere. Could you and Eric, if he is in town, come to lunch next week somewhere?

I want so much to see again the two wonderful rebels, the two dear friends.

Ever yours

Oscar

ANS to an unknown correspondent

Location: Clark Library.
W6721L U58. [1885–95]. [Mourning stationary].

16 Tite Street
Chelsea SW

Dear Leader,

I enclose the communication you are expecting. Will you write your usual clever pen words and send it to Mrs Humphrey?

Sincerely yours

Oscar Wilde

ALS to an unknown correspondent

Location: Clark Library.
W6721L U58. [1885–1891].

16 Tite Street
Chelsea SW

Dear Sichel,

You may put me down as one of your contributors. I am in the
middle of an article that I will be able to send you this month, I am
glad Time is such a success.

Truly yours
Oscar Wilde

ANS to Hugh Bryans

Location: Clark Library.
W6721L B9151. [27 May 1878; dated by postmark on envelope].

New Travellers Club
Picadilly W.

Dear Hugh,

Lunch *here*—1.30 not Berkley.

Yours
Oscar

ANS to Mrs De La Rue

Location: Clark Library.
W6721L D3392. [1885–95].

16 Tite Street
Chelsea SW

Dear Mrs De La Rue,

My wife is very sorry she is unable to accept your kind invitation,
as her Doctor will not let her dine out for some weeks more, but I
will be very happy to come myself.

Believe me

Sincerely yours

Oscar Wilde

ALS to Luther Munday

Location: Clark Library.
W6721L M965. [1885–95].

16 Tite Street

Chelsea

Dear Munday,

I have received no notice about my subscription. How much is it? If you will let me know, I will send it.

Any Wednesday afternoon you are in Chelsea pray come in and see us at tea time.

Yours sincerely,

Oscar Wilde

ALS to Mr Dighton

Location: Clark Library.
W6721L D574. [1885–95].

16 Tite Street

Chelsea SW

Dear Mr Dighton,

Would you kindly give me the address of Lady Virginia Sandars and of Lady Constance Howard. Miss Corelli's story is very powerful indeed.

Sincerely yours

Oscar Wilde

ALS to Lady Lindsay

Location: Clark Library.
W6721L L748. [1884–95].

Albemarle Club
Albemarle Street. W

Dear Lady Lindsay,

My wife and I hope to have the pleasure of coming to tea tomorrow, but I am very busy and may be detained. I have never seen the sanctum, in which you write, I feel sure, your charming poems. And hope to visit it, if not tomorrow, on some other day.

Believe me
Sincerely yours
Oscar Wilde

ALS to Percy Horne

Location: Clark Library.
Uncatalogued Wilde MS. [1886 Aug 14].

16 Tite Street
Chelsea SW

I fear I have to go out tonight—but I hope to see you soon.

Your poems are most charming, and your choice of epithets exquisite and felicitous. You combine very perfectly simplicity and strangeness.

I have no doubt you will do very lovely work.

Oscar Wilde

ALS to G. H. Kersley

Location: Clark Library.
W6721L K411. [4 Aug. 1886; dated from postmark on envelope].

Albemarle Club,
Albemarle Street. W.

Dear Mr Kersley,

I send you a line from Whitman. I hope you will see him and admire him.

Sincerely yours
Oscar Wilde

ALS to Mrs Charlotte Riddell

Location: HRHRC; MS Wilde, O; Letters [c. 1887].

16 Tite Street
Chelsea SW

Dear Mrs. Riddell,

Will you allow me to add your name to the list of contributors to a monthly magazine I have been asked to edit for Messrs Cassell and Co. the publishers.

I am anxious to make the magazine the recognised organ through which women of culture and position will express their views, and to which they will contribute.

Miss Thackeray, Miss Mulock, Lady Portsmouth, Lady Archibald Campbell, Miss Olive Schreiner, Mrs. Fawcett, Lady Dorothy Nevill, Mrs. Pfeiffer, and others have promised to write, and a short story or article from your pen would add a charm to the magazine.

The magazine will be an illustrated monthly, and the first number will appear under my editorship in November.

I send this to the care of your publishers, as I am sorry to say I cannot remember your exact address.

Hoping you will allow me to count you among my contributors,

I remain
Very truly yours
Oscar Wilde

ALS to Mrs Ewing

Location: Clark Library.
W6721L E956. [Oct. 1887].

16 Tite Street
Chelsea SW

Dear Mrs Ewing,

It will give me very great pleasure if you will write something for the Woman's World. The first number, which appears on Wednesday, will show you the lines on which I propose to conduct the magazine.

I do not propose to have much poetry, if any, but a short prose-article from your pen would I am sure be very attractive.

Is there any French man of letters you would like to write on? Any one you knew, or know, personally. Personal reminiscences are always interesting.

The article should be about 3000 words in length.

Mamma was so sorry to have missed you yesterday but she came with me to see a production of Coppée's 'Le Passant'. The translation was very mediocre, so you missed little by not being [*sic*] seeing it.

When you have decided on a subject pray let me know, and I will let no one else touch it.

With kind regards to your husband. Believe me

Very sincerely yours

Oscar Wilde

ALS to Emily Thursfield

Location: Clark Library.
W6721L T543. [1887].

16 Tite Street
Chelsea SW

Dear Mrs Thursfield,

Will you allow me to add your name to the list of contributors to a monthly magazine I have been asked to edit from Messers. Cassell & Co. the publishers. I am anxious to make the magazine the recognised organ through which women of cultured position will express their views, and to which they will contribute.

Miss Thackeray, Lady Portsmouth, Lady Meath, Mrs Fawcett, Mrs Jeune, Lady Pollock, Mrs Jacob Bright, Mrs Charles Maclaren, Lady Archibald Campbell, Miss Mulock, and many others have promised to write, and I should esteem it a great favour to add your name to the list.

I propose to have articles of about 5000 words in length: would you care to do an article on Pit Women, with illustrations, or would you prefer a literary subject?

I should like you to select your own topic. Do you care for writing monographs? I want one on Mrs Siddons—but perhaps you would prefer something else.

Pray give my kind regards to Mr Thursfield

& Believe me

Truly yours

Oscar Wilde

ANS to Arthur Fish

Location: Clark Library.
W6721L F532. [1888?].

16 Tite Street
Chelsea SW

Dear Mr Fish,

I have not been at all well, and cannot get my notes done. Can you manage to put in something else. I will be down tomorrow.

Sincerely yours

Oscar Wilde

ALS to Marie Singleton [Violet Vane]

Location: Clark Library.
W6721L S617. [1888–1890]. Bound.
[28 Apr. 1888; dated from postmark, but it is not clear whether letters are bound with the correct envelopes. Cf. Hart–Davis who gives different dates for letters he prints from this collection.]

16 Tite Street
Chelsea SW

Dear Mrs Singleton

I will hope to find you at home on Sunday afternoon. I think your article a great success—*the* thing on our Stuarts.

Sincerely yours

Oscar Wilde

ALS to Marie Singleton [Violet Vane]

Location: Clark Library.
W6721L S617. [c. 4 Aug. 1888].

16 Tite Street
Chelsea SW

Dear Mrs Singleton,

I have looked high and low for "L'Immortel," but alas! I fear I have left it at Chambers. I am so sorry.

Sincerely yours

Oscar Wilde

AL to Mrs van de Velde

Location: Clark Library.
W6721L V244. 5 Apr. 1888. [Not in Wilde's hand.]

Woman's World
La Belle Suavage Ludgate Hill
London April 5 1888

Dear Mrs Van de Velde

I have so many manuscripts on hand that I have been unable to publish your story and I am afraid that I can hardly fix any definite date for its appearance. If you care to still leave it with me I will do my best with it. If not I will return it to you.

Yours very faithfully

Oscar Wilde

ALS to Robert Ross

Location: Clark Library.
[ca. 1888].

16 Tite Street
Chelsea SW

My Dear Bobbie,

The kitten is quite lovely—it does not *look* white, indeed it looks a sort of tortoise-shell colour, or a grey barred[?] with velvety dark [illegible word] but as you said it was white I have given orders that it is always to be spoken of as the "white kitten"—the children are enchanted with it, and sit, one on each side of its basket, worshipping—It seems pensive—perhaps it is thinking of some dim rose-garden in Persia, and wondering why it is kept in this chill England.

I hope you are enjoying yourself at Cambridge—whatever people may say against Cambridge, it is certainly the best preparatory school for Oxford that I know.

After this insult I had better stop.

Yours ever
Oscar Wilde.

ALS to Marie Singleton

Location: Clark Library.
W6721L S617. [1888].

16 Tite Street
Chelsea SW

Dear Mrs Singleton,

I will come tomorrow at 4.30 with great pleasure. I think the article will cause immense excitement.

Yours very sincerely,
Oscar Wilde

ALS to Rowland Edmund Prothero [Baron Ernle]

Location: Clark Library.
W6721L E715. [22 Aug. 1890].

16 Tite Street
Chelsea SW

Dear Mr Prothero,

I have sent back revised proof to printers, but find a slip. Will you kindly alter it for me. Page 20. Line 3 from bottom. For "second-rate" read "*commonplace.*"

Faithfully yours

Oscar Wilde

[On verso, but not in Wilde's hand: "Oscar Wilde—22 Aug 1890 has revd. his proof corrected."]

ALS to unidentified correspondent

[Probably John Morley, the editor of *Fortnightly Review*.]
Location: HRHRC; MS Morley, C.D. Misc. Oscar Wilde.

16 Tite Street
Chelsea

Dear Sir,

There is an error of setting in my article, which pray correct at once, if possible.

The passage (p 307) on morbidity, beginning "Perhaps however" and ending with "King Lear" must be transferred to page *308* and put after "*healthy work of art.*" 17 lines from bottom.

It occurs rightly between lines 18 and 17 from bottom—of course as a separate complete paragraph, as it now stands.

Kindly see to this, as it is out of place at present.

Truly yours

Oscar Wilde

ALS to unknown correspondent [Arthur Clifton]

Location: Clark Library.
W6721L C639. [28 Jan. 1891; date from postmark on envelope].

16 Tite Street
Chelsea SW

My Dear Arthur,

The new last line 'Paradise' is charming. 'Vice' does not do—as it is a word tainted in its signification with moral censure—*vitium*: which is faulty.

The evening was charming. I enjoyed it all.

Ever yours
Oscar

ALS to Mrs Gertrude Kellie

Location: Clark Library.
W6721L K29. [1892?].

Lyric Club
W

Dear Mrs Kellie,

I enclose you a note for the acting-manager of the St James'. Any evening you bring it he will do his best to give you best seating.

With kind regards to your husband—that charming singer and poet.

Believe me
Sincerely yours
Oscar Wilde

ALS to an unknown correspondent

Location: Clark Library.
W6721L U58. [1892?].

Dear Sir,

I write in haste to ask your printer to let me have a proof of my poems: if the proofs reach me on Sunday morning I can have them in London on Monday morning. It is too dangerous always to allow poems to appear without a proof.

Yours sincerely
Oscar Wilde

Hotel Voltaire
Quai Voltaire
Paris

ALS to Walter Severn

Location: Clark Library.
W6721L S498. [2 July 1892; date from postmark on envelope].

Lyric Club
W

My dear Walter,

I was so sorry I could not go to you the other day, but I was engaged. Of course, you must come to my play. The early part of next week, on any matinee will be safest for good seating.

Ever yours
Oscar

Please bring enclosed when you go to theatre.

ALS to G.H. Ellnanger

Location: Clark Library.
W6721L E475. [27 May 1893; date from postmark on envelope].

Dear Sir,

It will give me pleasure to meet you, if you will call on me, at 10 St James Place, S W on Friday next at 12 o'clock.

Sincerely yours
Oscar Wilde

ALS to an unknown correspondent

Location: Clark Library.
W6721L U58. [1893?].

The Hotel Albemarle
Picadilly
London

My Dear Gilbert,

If you can, come to supper—but if you are ill don't mind. I am so sorry you are not well.

Always yours

Oscar

ALS to Percy Osborne

Location: Clark Library.
W6721L O81. [1893].

The Cottage
Goring–on–Thames

Dear Percy Osborne,

Enclosed is just returned to me. I was so sorry you did not come over here, and send you this old letter merely to show you that your charming letter was not unregarded.

Let me know where you are, and what you are doing.

Ever yours

Oscar Wilde

MS to Stanhope Ward

Location: Clark Library.
W6721L W2633. [19 Apr. 1893].

Hotel Albmarle
Picadilly, London

Mr Oscar Wilde begs to thank Mr Stanhope Ward for his graceful and interesting gift.

April 15

OW

AN to Charles Kains–Jackson

Location: Clark Library.
W6721L K135. [6 Nov. 1893]. Telegram.

St James St. SW.
Reply paid.
C Kains Jackson, Woodruffe House, Chiswick Mall.

Can you come and see me here tomorrow at eleven wish to consult you professionally on Salomé business.

Oscar Wilde
10 St James Place SW

[On verso:] Reply that C K–J will keep appointment

ANS to Charles Kains–Jackson

Location: Clark Library.
W6721L K135. 10 Nov. 1893. [Not in Wilde's hand.]

10 & 11 St James's Place
SW
10 Nov. 1893

Dear Mr Kains–Jackson,

Could you come here tomorrow (Saturday) at 12 o'clock? I have been very unlucky today in my attempts to find you.

Sincerely yours
Oscar Wilde

AN to C. Kains–Jackson

Location: Clark Library.
W6721L K135. 10 Nov. 1893. Telegram.

Telegram C Kains–Jackson
St James's Street SW   6.00

Reply paid Charles Kains–Jackson.
Woodruffe House Chiswick Mall.

Can you be here at 9.15 tonight very important Oscar Wilde 10 St James Place Please wire reply to 16 Tite Street Chelsea

[On verso:] Absent at author's club HKJ

AN to C. Kains–Jackson

Location: Clark Library.
W6721L K135. 10 Nov. 1893b. Telegram.

Telegram C. Kains–Jackson,
St James's Street S W.   1.40

Reply paid C. Kains–Jackson.
88 Chancery Lane EC.

Can you see me at three o'clock this afternoon if so will come down Oscar Wilde please answer to Willis Restaurant King Street

ALS to Mr Cartwright

Location: Clark Library.
W6721L C329. [1894].

The Haven
5 Esplanade
Worthing

Dear Mr Cartwright

Will you kindly send me my fees for "Lady Windermere's Fan" in Australia: I hear from Brough and Boucicault that they have been forwarded to you.

I hope you have a part in this new play worthy of your distinguished powers of concentration and colour as an actor.

Sincerely yours
Oscar Wilde

ANS to Mrs Patrick Campbell

Location: Clark Library.
W6721L C189 1894.
[10 line presentation inscription from OW to Mrs Patrick Campbell, dated London, '94 and on flyleaf extracted from unidentified volume.]

Mrs Patrick Campbell
in admiration
of her incomparable
art and her
incomparable personality
from
Oscar
Wilde
London
'94

ALS to George Ives

Location: Clark Library.
W6721L I95. [1894?].

10 & 11 St James's Place
SW

So sorry you could not come to luncheon: will you dine at the *Savoy* on Sunday at *8 o'clock*. Alfred Douglas and Egbert Sebright are coming.

Do come
Yours
Oscar Wilde

ALS to Aubrey Fitzgerald

Location: Clark Library.
W6721L F553. [1894; date from postmark and covering letter from recipient].

Albemarle Club
13 Albemarle Street, W
16 Tite Street
SW

Dear Mr Fitzgerald,

My cast for my new play is complete. Otherwise, it would have given me great pleasure to have had you in it.

Should you care to come and see me, I will be at home on Friday at 11.30.

I remember your mother quite well: she used to come to our house in Dublin years.

Yours sincerely,

Oscar Wilde

ANS to G. H. Kersley

Location: Clark Library.
W6721L K411. [1894].

16 Tite Street
Chelsea SW

My dear Kersley,

Kleon might do till we get something better. I dine out tomorrow—but come on Tuesday morning and see me.

Yours

Oscar

ALS to Bram Stoker

Location: Clark Library.
W6721L S8744 [1894?].

16 Tite Street
Chelsea SW

Dear Bram,

Can you come at 12 o'clock? Or if that is too early at 2? I was sorry to miss you.

Sincerely yours
Oscar Wilde

ANS to unidentified correspondent

Location: HRHRC; MS Wilde, O; Letters.
[Letter pasted opposite p. 184 in Paul Wilstach, *Richard Mansfield: The Man and the Author* (NY: Scribner and Son, 1908)].

The Haven
Worthing
Sussex

Dear Sir,

This is my autograph.

Oscar Wilde

Sept
94

ANS to Maurice Gilbert

Location: Clark Library.
W6721L G4655. [1898–1900].
[Recto]
    For *Mr Maurice Gilbert*
    Mr Sebastian Melmoth

[Verso]
Dear Maurice,

Come to the Café de Rohan. I have waiter in till 12 o'clock. We shall breakfast at the Restaurant Lyonnais—Rue de l'Echelle.

ACS to Maurice Gilbert

Location: Clark Library.
W6721L G4655. 2 Apr. [1900].

Dear Maurice,

Arrived at Palermo this morning. Hope you are well.

April 2   OW

ALS to Miss Curtis

Location: Clark Library.
W6721L C978. [189–?].

Lyric Club
W

Dear Miss Curtis,

With great pleasure. Any matinee you like; bring enclosed with you.

Sincerely yours

Oscar Wilde

ACS to Claire de Pratz

Location: Clark Library.
W6721L D424. [26 Feb. 1900].

Telegraphe
Mlle Claire de Pratz
11 Avenue des Chaddeux [?]
[Unintelligible word]
Paris

Many thanks—but I am not at all well. Indeed I write from my bed. Otherwise it wd have been charming to have had tea with you.

Sincerely

Oscar Wilde

Undated Letters

ALS to Emily Thursfield

Location: HRHRC; MS Wilde, O; Letters.

> Raven Hotel
> Shrewsbury.

Dear Mrs. Thursfield,

Thank you very much for your kind invitation of which I will be most happy to avail myself on Friday next: I go to Middlesboro' on Thursday but will return to Newcastle on Friday morning and make my way to Tynemouth.

I look forward very much to seeing you again and, with kind regards to your husband,

> I remain
> Most truly yours
> Oscar Wilde

ALS to unidentified recipient—"Doctor"

Location: HRHRC; MS Wilde, O; Letters.

> 9 Charles St.
> Grosvenor Squ[are]

My Dear Doctor,

With much pleasure—supper after my lecture—that will suit me best—I will come down by *5.30* from St. Pancras—as before: Getting in that is at 5.30 so as to have some time before I lecture—

The invitation of the Club has not yet come. I will formally answer it when it does—with you in the chair it should be most pleasant.

With kind regards to your wife,

> Believe me
> Very sincerely
> Oscar Wilde

ALS to unidentified correspondent—"Edith"
Location: HRHRC; MS Wilde, O; Letters.

My Dear Edith,

I am so overwhelmed with work I fear I cannot join the chorus of your nightingales; but you have my best wishes for your new magazine. All the editors I know have been old and horrid, so a young and charming editor is an era in literature.

I congratulate you.

Your affectionate cousin
Oscar Wilde

ALS to Oscar Browning
Location: HRHRC; MS Wilde, O; Letters.

Woman's World,
Cassell and Company Limited,
La Belle Sauvage,
Ludgate Hill, EC
London 188

Dear O.B.

Certainly: pillage the Americans who are rich, and get your £40. I wd not dream of claiming the prior right.

En revanche—do me the article on the Women Benefactors of Cambridge.—

The Saturday was silly—Give my love to Bobbie—who never writes to me.

Yours
Oscar

ALS to Mr. Morgan
Location: HRHRC; MS Wilde, O; Letters.

16 Tite Street
Chelsea SW

Dear Mr Morgan,

I have lent your MS to a friend whose opinion I was anxious to have about [*sic*] but will return it to you in a couple of days. I see you have a true literary touch as well as a feeling for the best things in art. Your style however seems to me sometimes wanting in reserve, balance, and sobriety—qualities essential to the best prose. These are things that are only attained by long practice. I fear that as it stands it will require revision before it is ready for publication. But you certainly have the artistic faculty.

Very sincerely yours
Oscar Wilde

ALS to Mrs Humphrey

Location: HRHRC; MS Wilde, O; Letters.

16 Tite Street
Chelsea SW

Dear Mrs Humphrey,

I know of no cleverer pen than yours, so I send you enclosed. Will you communicate with Mr. Leader?

Yours truly
Oscar Wilde

ALS to George Ives

Location: HRHRC; MS Wilde, O; Letters.
[Envelope addressed to: George Ives Esq / New Traveller's Club].

New Travellers Club
Picadilly. W

Dear George,

I am charmed to see you are at the Albany—I am off to the country till Monday: I have said I am going to Cambridge to see you—but I am really going to see the young Domitian, who has taken to poetry!

Next week let us meet

Yours

Oscar

ALS to hostess [Ada Leverson?]

Location: Clark Library.
W6721L L661. [1883].

9 Charles Street
Grosvenor Square

Of course I am coming! How could one refuse an invitation from one who is a poem and a poet in one, an exquisite combination of perfection and personality which are the keynotes of modern art.

It was horrid of me not to answer before—but a nice letter is like a sunbeam and should not be treated as an epistle needing a reply. Besides your invitations are commanding: I look forward to meeting Protcus very much—his sonnets are the cameos of the decadence.

Very sincerely yours

Oscar Wilde

Typed Copies of Letters Clark Library

The following letters are taken from a collection of typed copies held at the Clark Library. They therefore have no provenance; but as known manuscripts corroborate the texts of some letters (as with the third letter to Alexander), there seems little reason to doubt their authenticity.

TL. 4 pages to an unknown correspondent [c. 1887]

16 Tite Street
Chelsea SW

Madam,

Will you allow me to add your name to the list of contributors to a magazine I have been asked to edit? The magazine in question is published by Messrs. Cassell & Co., and I am anxious to make it the recognized organ through which women of culture and position will express their views. Lady Dorothy Neville, Lady Archibald Campbell, Lady Pollack, Mrs Francis Jeune, Mrs Henry Fawcett, Lady Ferguson, Miss Thackeray and others have offered to write for it, and I should be very pleased if you would do something; either an article or a short story. I should prefer an article, but a short story about eight pages would also prove attractive. The honorarium for the writers is a pound a page, and the page something larger than a page of the "Nineteenth Century." The magazine will appear in October. Hoping that you will contribute to the magazine, I have the honour to remain,

Yours truly,
Oscar Wilde

TL to J. M. Stoddart [n.d.–1882?]

[. . .] some where and some time—I am not sure where or when[.]

Also I send you an extract from a letter of Swinburne's which I have just received from him about our grand Walt.—"As sincerely can I say that I shall be freshly obliged to you if you will—should occasion arise—assure him of in my name, that I have by no manner of means relaxed my admiration of his noblest works—such parts, above all, of his writings, as treat of the noblest subjects material and spiritual with which poets can deal. I have always thought it and believe it will be hereafter generally thought, his highest and surely most enviable distinction that he never speaks so well as when he speaks of great matters—Liberty, for instance, and Death."

TL to George Alexander [mid–February 1892]

As printed in *Letters*, 308–09. The copy in the Clark Library has preceding two lines:

The Hotel Albemarle
Picadilly, London.

Dear Alexander,

I am still in bed by my doctor's orders or wd. have come down to rehearsal, but will be there to-night for certain.

TL to Leonard Smithers [n.d.]

Hotel d'Alsace
Rue des Beaux Arts
Paris
Sunday

Dear Smithers,

The play has arrived—it really looks quite splendid; I am greatly pleased with it.

I suppose there have been absolutely no reviews? It really is too stupid and too bad. Nor have I seen the fascinating advertisements I should have liked.

I could not remember—did not indeed know—how Mrs Brown–Potter (No. 2)—yours—spells her real name. When you are next in Paris you must bring me a copy to sign for her.

Would you, if you can, ask Arthur Clifton what has become of my Irish property. I was in hopes that my Trustees would withdraw their claim—or come to some terms with me. The place should fetch £3000 if sold—and if I paid 7/6 in the pound there would be over £2000 for me. Something surely could be settled—I am face to face with death and starvation.

Thanks for your promise to let me have something this week.

Yrs

Oscar Wilde

TL to Leonard Smithers [n.d.]

Hotel d'Alsace
Rue des Beaux Arts
Paris

Dear Smithers,

Reggie Turner—2 Clements Inn—tells me he has not yet received his copy of the play—Surely I signed one? I remember it distinctly.

I hope to hear from you to-morrow on financial matters—

Yrs

Oscar

TL to Ernest Dowson [11 June 1897]

Dieppe,
Monday: 11 Juin 97

Dear Ernest,

I must see you: So I propose to breakfast at St. Martin l'Eglise tomorrow at 11.30 and you must come: take a voiture and be there. I want to have a poet to talk to, as I have had lots of bad news since you left me. Do try, like a good chap, to be there, and wear a *blue* tie. I want to be consoled.

Sebastian Melmoth

TL to Ernest Dowson [n.d.]

Villa Giudice
Posilippo
Naples
Monday [Oct. 1897]

Dear Ernest,

Thank you very much for your nice letter—my poem is finished at last—and is now with Smithers. I have added a good deal to it.

What you owe me is between £18 and £20—whichever you choose—I am thinking of telegraphing to you to wire it, or as much as you can afford, through Cook's Agency. They wire money like angels—and cheques and P.O. orders are difficult to cash. If I can find the money I will—for at present I am quite penniless—and Smithers has not behaved well to me at all—I wanted a paltry £20 in advance for my poem—secure on its sale and the American rights—and for three weeks he has put me off with silly promises—never realised of course—I feel it, because when he offered me the entire profits in a moment of dramatic generosity I refused to take his offer and insisted on his sharing half. Also I have refused an offer from "The Musician" to publish the poem as I felt that previous publication of the poem would spoil Smithers' edition. So I made all these sacrifices and at the end he refuses a petty sum in advance. Smithers is personally charming, but at present I simply am furious with him and intend to remain so—till he sends me the money.

I am delighted to hear you finished your novel and are writing stories. I have begun today the tragedy in one-act I told you about at Berneval with the passages about clothes in it. I find the architecture of art difficult now, it requires sustained effort but I must do it.

The Neapolitan papers have turned out to be worst form of American journalism. They fill columns with me and write interviews of a fictitious character. I wish the world would let me alone and really I thought that at Naples I should be at peace. I dare say they will tire of this nonsense soon.

I hope you will do a good thing with "Aphrodite" and that when you make lots of money, you will be able to find time to come to Naples —which I know you would like. The museum is full as you know of lovely Greek bronzes—the only bother is that they all walk about the town at night. However one gets delicately accustomed to that—and there are compensations.

Yours
Oscar Wilde

TL to Ernest Dowson [n.d.]

Cafe Suisse
Dieppe [1897]
Wednesday 6:30

Dear Ernest,

I write a little line, whose only excuse is its entire illegibility, to tell you how charming you are (at Berneval) and how much I like *your* friend and *mine*, the dear Achille. He is a most noble and splendid fellow, and I feel happy to have his esteem and friendship.

Tonight I am going to read your poems—your lovely lyrics—words with wings you write always—it is an exquisite gift—and fortunately rare in an age whose prose is more poetic than its poetry. Do come soon and see me.

The youthful costermonger returns on Friday with the price of a pony and cart in his pocket. I have given him a costume idea, but I hope he will survive it—the effects up to this, are not so promising as I could wish. But he means well.

His calling you Ernest was awful. It is the effect of vegetables on the mind.

I am now going to write poetry, as soon as the "coster" leaves us. Poor fellow, I hope he will be all right.

You and Achille and Achille's friend and I must *all* be at Berneval together. I am making arrangements.

Give to Achille my sincere friendship, you have it, and other things, always.

S.M.

TL to an unknown correspondent [n.d.]

Clumber
Nr Worksop

Dear Henriette,

I was a little annoyed with you for repeating to Alice something Mamma had said to you. It gave Mamma a great deal of bother. However, that is long ago. We are too old friends to quarrel.

Constance and I must come some Saturday evening to see your mother.

Yours faithfully
Oscar Wilde

TL to George Alexander [July 1894?]

[The text is a fuller version of that printed by A.E.W. Mason and subsequently in *Letters*, p. 359.]

16 Tite Street
SW

My dear Aleck,

Thanks for your letter. There really is nothing more to tell you about the comedy beyond what I said already. I mean that the real charm of the play, if it is to have charm, must be in the dialogue. The plot is slight, but, I think, adequate.

Act I. Evening party. 10 p.m.

Lord Alfred Rufford's rooms in Mayfair. Arrives from country Bertram Ashton his friend: a man of 25 or 30 years of age: his great friend.

Rufford asks him about his life. He tells him that he has a ward, etc. very young and pretty. That in the country he has to be serious, etc. that he comes to town to enjoy himself, and has invented a fictitious younger brother of the name of George —to whom all his misdeeds are put down. Rufford is deeply interested about the ward.

Guests arrive: the Duchess of Selby and her daughter, Lady Maud Rufford, with whom the guardian is in love—fin-de-siecle talk, a lot of guests—the guardian proposes to Lady Maud on his knees—enter Duchess—

Lady Maud. "Mamma, this is no place for you."

Scene: Duchess enquires for her *son Lord Alfred Rufford*: servant comes in with note to say that Lord Alfred has been suddenly called away to the country. Lady Maud vows eternal

[f. 2:]

fidelity to the guardian whom she only knows under the name of *George* Ashton.

(P.S. The disclosure of the guardian of his double life is occasioned by Lord Alfred saying to him "You left your handkerchief here the last time you were up" (or cigarette case). The guardian takes it—the Lord A. says but "why, dear George, is it marked Bertram—who is Bertram Ashton?" Guardian discloses plot.

Act II

The guardian's home—pretty cottage. Mabel Harbord, his ward, and her governess, Miss Prism, Governess of course dragon of propriety. Talk about the profligate George: maid comes in to say "Mr George Ashton."—governess protests against his admission. Mabel insists. Enter Lord Alfred. Falls in love with ward at once. He is reproached with his bad life, etc. Expresses great repentance. They go to garden.

Enter guardian: Mabel comes in: "I have a great surprise for you—your brother is here"—Guardian, of course, denies having a brother. Mabel says "You cannot disown your own brother, what ever he has done." Finally Lord Alfred arrested for debts contracted by guardian: guardian delighted: Mabel, however, makes him forgive his brother and pay up. Guardian looks over bills and scolds Lord Alfred for profligacy.

[f. 3:]

Miss Prism backs the guardian up. Guardian then orders his brother out of the house. Mabel intercedes, and brother remains. Miss Prism has designs on the guardian—matrimonial—she is 40 at least—his consternation.

Act III

Mabel and the false brother. He proposes, and is accepted.

When Mabel is alone, Lady Maud, who only knows the guardian under the name of George, arrives alone. She tells Mabel she is engaged to Maud—scene naturally. Mabel retires. Enter George, he kisses his sister naturally. Enter Mabel and sees them. Explanations, of course. Mabel breaks off the match on the ground that there is nothing to reform in George: she only consented to marry him because she thought he was bad and wanted guidance — He promises to be a bad husband—so as to give her an opportunity of making him a better man; she is a little mollified.

Enter guardian: he is reproached also by Lady Maud for his respectable life in the country: a J.P.: a county-councillor: a churchwarden: a philanthropist: a good example. He appeals to his life in London: she is mollified on the condition that he never lives in the country: the country is demoralising: it makes you respectable. "The simple fare at the Savoy: the quiet life in Piccadilly: the solitude of Mayfair is what you need, etc."

[f. 4:]

Enter Duchess in pursuit of her daughter—objects to both matches. Miss Prism, who had in early days been governess to the Duchess, sets it all right, without intending to do so—everything ends happily.

Result   Curtain
Author called
Cigarette called
Manager called

Royalties for a year for author

Manager credited with writing the play. He consoles himself with bags of red gold.

Fireworks

Of course this scenario is open to alterations: the third act, after entrance of Duchess, will have to be elaborated: also the local doctor, or clergyman, must be brought in, in the play, for Prism.

Well, I think an amusing thing with lots of fun and wit might be made. If you think so, too, and care to have the refusal of it—do let me know—and send me £150. If, when the play is finished, you think it too slight—not serious enough—of course you can have the £150 back—I want to go away and write it—and it could be ready in October, as I

[f. 5:]

have nothing else to do—and Palmer is anxious to have a play from me for the States "with no real interest"—just a comedy.

In the meanwhile, my dear Aleck, I am so pressed for money, that I don't know what to do. Of course I am extravagant, but a great deal of my worries comes from the fact that I have had for three years to keep up two establishments—my dear Mother's as well as my own—like many Irish ladies she never gets her jointure paid—small though it is—and naturally it falls on me—this is of course quite private but for these years I have had two houses on my shoulders—and of course, am extravagant besides—you have always been a good wise friend to me—so think what you can do.

Kind regards to Mrs. Aleck.

Ever,
OSCAR

Letters to Wilde

As I indicated in chapter one, we have very little information about letters to Wilde, yet many of the main research libraries have a large number of such letters waiting to be explored by critics. The most important is a lengthy correspondence from Lady Wilde to Oscar, dating from 1876, when Wilde left Dublin, to Lady Wilde's death in 1896. The letters are full, and Wilde carefully preserved them. They are now at the Clark Library.

Other unpublished letters to Wilde will prove valuable in two distinct ways. At their most prosaic, they will clarify details of known facts about the biography. So there are letters to Wilde, usually from unidentified correspondents, the principal value of which lies in their relation to certain letters by Wilde which have already been published. In some cases they simply allow that correspondence to be dated. On other occasions, they reveal letters hitherto published individually to be seen as part of a larger sequence. So, for example, an unidentified letter at the HRHRC adds a fuller context to one of Wilde's published letters, which in its turn allows his correspondent to be identified as the minor nineteenth-century poet and anti-colonialist, Wilfrid Scawen Blunt.

The letter from Wilde (which Rupert Hart–Davis prints) is as follows:

[? July 1883]

9 Charles Street

Dear Mr Blunt,

It will give me great pleasure to come down to you on Saturday week, and look at your horses, and talk about sonnets.

Please present my compliments to Lady Anne, and believe me most truly yours

Oscar Wilde

There is an extant corresponding letter which is clearly the invitation to which Wilde's letter is the reply (the text is below). Seeing both halves of the correspondence allows the identity of Scawen Blunt and the date of his letter to be established; it also dots a small "i" in the biography of Wilde. A snippet of information such as this, taken in isolation, is of course of no great importance; but collectively such fragments allow the full dimensions of Wilde's social acquaintance to be glimpsed.

The kind of insights which such snippets provide is better illustrated by another unpublished letter in the HRHRC collection—from Robert Buchanan to Wilde:

My dear Oscar Wilde,

I ought to have thanked you thus for your present of *Dorian Gray*, but I was hoping to return the compliment by sending you a work of my own: this I shall do in a very few days. You are quite right as to our divergence, which is temperamental. I cannot accept yours as a serious criticism of life. You seem to me like a holiday maker throwing pebbles into the sea, or viewing the great ocean from under the awning of a bathing machine. I quite see, however, that this is only your "fun," & that your very indolence of gaiety is paradoxical, like your utterances.

Buchanan was a controversial figure who had made a reputation as a virulent critic of most of the values Wilde stood for. To discover Wilde initiating a friendly exchange of books and letters with Buchanan is therefore interesting. Of course, attempts by Wilde to curry favour with potential reviewers by sending them complimentary copies of his work was not unusual. Rather it is the reputation of Buchanan which makes this letter noteworthy.

Twenty years earlier Buchanan had become notorious for his vituperative journalism attacking what he saw as a vicious and degenerate trend in contemporary literature. The targets of his invective on that occasion were Dante Gabriel Rossetti and Algernon Swinburne in particular, and the embryonic Aesthetic Movement in general. A decade later, following the publication of Rossetti's *Ballads and Sonnets* and the revised *Poems*, Buchanan's arguments were revived by a number of like-minded critics.

The Picture of Dorian Gray was a novel which, in the eyes of those critics, seemed to fulfill Buchanan's warnings. It was a book hardly likely to appeal to a man of Buchanan's sensibilities, and Wilde's approach to him is therefore very engaging. It might be seen to be an act of uncharacteristic naïveté, but a much more likely explanation is that Wilde, ever the opportunist, was simply attempting to enlist an ally, or at the very least attempting to forestall overt criticism from a potential opponent. The practice of mutual log-rolling—that is, of averting hostile criticism by enlisting one's friends as potential and therefore favourable reviewers—was well known among late nineteenth-century authors, and Wilde himself often indulged in it. Here, however, Wilde is taking the process one step further by attempting to make a friend of an enemy.

Unpublished letters to Wilde are a useful resource for the scholar for another and more important reason. The ways in which Wilde's life has been troped have inevitably involved neglecting some of the mundane aspects of his career, particularly many details of his career as a *writer*. So, for example, the importance of his early attempts to place all of his work with Macmillan, revealed in the Macmillan archive, has been virtually ignored. So too have the day-to-day negotiations undertaken as a matter of course by any aspiring dramatist in the late nineteenth century. Often significant information about such matters is contained in letters to Wilde. In them, Wilde can be seen as a working dramatist who collaborated in all aspects and at all points in the production of his plays.

In this respect a passage from a letter from his fellow-dramatist Charles Haddon Chambers is particularly revealing: "I am going to do the little gold nugget story almost at once. The *motif* charms me. But ought I to use your plot as my own?" (For full text, see below.) The significance of the letter is *not* to be found in Chambers's log-rolling attempt to recruit Wilde and Charles Hawtry to promote his own play *The Collaborators*; rather it exists in the throwaway postscript which sheds further light on what critics have long commented upon, Wilde's apparent unconcern with originality. Chambers's letter, however, shows in a more practical way that a disregard for the authorship of ideas or plots was not unique to Wilde. In such instances it is possible that Wilde may have been typical rather than exceptional.

Other unpublished letters to Wilde may also throw further insight into the commercial opportunism of the English theatre in the 1890s.

So a letter from the drama critic William Archer from 1894 (for text, see below) reveals a readiness to enlist Wilde's good offices in promoting a new journalistic venture, for in modern terms Wilde was, by the mid-1890s, extremely good copy. Archer was about to begin a theatre column for the *Pall Mall Budget*, and he wrote asking Wilde for advance information about a play he knew Wilde had written and for confirmation of its title (the play turned out to be *An Ideal Husband*):

> I am going to do for the *Pall Mall Budget*, in a somewhat tentative fashion, a sort of weekly *causerie* on things theatrical. . . . Is it the case that Lewis Waller is going to produce a play of yours at the Haymarket during Tree's absence? And is it possible for you to give me any inkling of the nature of the play, or to let me announce its title?

At the time Wilde was of course at the height of his powers and was thus a natural target for those journalists wishing to create and exploit a media personality. Letters such as these will allow the details of the lives of commercial dramatists and journalists of the time to be seen more fully.

As I indicated in "Prologue to the Letters," the selection of letters below is only a sample of the material available. It is worth reiterating, then, that for reasons of space some letters to Wilde have been abbreviated, and annotation has been confined to bibliographical information.

Letters to Wilde at HRHRC

ALS Lord Houghton to Wilde

MS Wilde, O. Recip.

24 Addington[?] St
May 20th [1877]

Dear Mr Wilde,

Thank you for your sonnet which is touching and peaceful but [?] not true. My life of Keats shows that he was anything but unhappy & he was [illegible word] with unusual rapidity. The medallion is very like him and having been put up by enthusiastic friends, it would not do to destroy or displace it.

I am

Yours sincerely

Houghton

Give my best regards to Mr Mahaffy.
I [illegible word] him & [two illegible words] when he went to London.

ALS William Michael Rossetti to Wilde

MS Wilde, O. Recip.

Marine House
Gorleston
Great Yarmouth
3 Aug. 1877

Dear Sir,

I was much obliged to you for your letter, & the magazine wh. [*sic*] accompanied it containing your interesting little article about the grave of Keats. Ought to have answered before now, but was occupied & am just now away from home (56 Euston Sq, London), but shall be back directly.

No doubt English people ought to erect a statue to Keats & I shd be glad to lend my modest cooperation to any such project. I don't however see any particular opening for it at present. Will confide also that I feel more especially interested in Shelley than in Keats: I did some while ago—when the Byron statue was first projected—put into print a strong suggestion that advantage might be taken of the movement so as to combine a Shelley with a Byron memorial, but it led to nothing. All three must get their statues some day, & assuredly will.

Believe me, Dear Sir,

Yours very faithfully,

W M Rossetti

ALS Edmund Yates to Wilde

MS Wilde, O. Recip.
The World
A Journal for Men and Women

1, York Street
Covent Garden
London, WC
Tuesday 20 May 1879

Dear Mr. Wilde,

I am very sorry that I shall not be able to use your poem in the June number, and I hope you will allow it to stand over until July. I have an eight page poem of Mrs Singleton's on a subject of the day "Killed at Isondula," and a two page poem of Mr Scudamore's, which has been in my hands for three months, and this is all the verse I can afford space for in one number. You shall have proof of "The New Helen" as soon as possible.

Faithfully yours
Edmund Yates

ALS Charles G. Leland to Wilde

MS Wilde, O. Recip. 4 Oct. 1879.
Address: 22 Park Sq. E.

Concerning an engagement and Walter Besant's wish to propose
Wilde for the Savile Club. Leland urges Wilde to join:

> I have pledged myself you will outgrow Pessimism and all morbid
> nonsense, and after your youthful fashionable fermentation come
> out a clear-headed, vigorous, healthy manly writer. That is the
> style of men you will meet with us—at least we *aim* at it.

ALS Matthew Arnold to Wilde

MS Wilde, O. Recip.

Pains Hill Cottage
Cobham, Surrey
July 9th [1881]

Dear Mr Wilde

Your volume and note were put into my hands as I was leaving the
Athenaeum last night. I have but glanced at the poems as yet, but I
perceive in them the true feeling for rhythm, which is at the bottom
of all success in poetry; of all endeavour, indeed, which is not
factitious and vain, in that line of expression. I shall read the book
attentively when I get a moment of that of which we all have too
little,—leisure. I see you have found out the force of what Byron so
insisted on:—that one must shake off London life before one can do
one's best work.

Your note has very kind,—too kind,—expressions about me and
what I have done. I have not much to thank the *public* for; but from
my fellow workers, both in poetry and in prose, I have met with
kindness and recognition such as might satisfy any man.

Sincerely yours,
Matthew Arnold

ALS Wilfrid Scawen Blunt to Wilde

MS Wilde, O. Recip.

10, James Street
Buckingham Gate
July 13 [1883]

Dear Wilde,

Will you come to me at Gabbut [?Crabbet] on Saturday the 28th July for Sunday to see my horses and meet some of my friends—

Yours truly

Wilfrid Scawen Blunt

turn over

My address is
Gabbut Park
Three Bridges
Sussex
and the 4.p.m. train from Victoria will be met.

ALS James Payn to Wilde

MS Wilde, O. Recip. n.d.—"22 Sept." [1886?]

The Cornhill Magazine
Smith Elder & Co
Sept. 22

Dear Sir,

We do not publish translations in the Cornhill or I should have been glad to hear from you.

Yours truly

James Payn

ALS W. E. Gladstone to Wilde

MS Wilde, O. Recip.

Hawarden Castle
Chester
Nov. 1, 88

Dear Mr Wilde,

From the printed memorial, and I am[?] afraid from the painful circumstances which you mention, I should as a reader suppose Lady Wilde's claim to be a very good one: but I am sorry to say I am not in a condition to sign the paper as I have found it necessary to make a rigid rule against taking part in any memorial of this nature, and to act by [illegible word] letter of my own in cases which I happen to have personal knowledge. Much regretting this obstacle I remain

Very faithfully yours,
W E Gladstone

ALS Richard Le Gallienne to Wilde

MS. Le Gallienne, R. Letters. [11 Nov. 1888].

85, Oxton Road
Birkenhead
11. xi, '88.

My dear friend,

This is but a little script to tell you how rich you have made me with your two sweet letters, & also to thank you for your further generosity in turning so ready an ear to my "foolish whisper" . . .

Yea! dear Poet, let me have that Dream for my own, if so it be your pleasure—& although I have no such casket for its enshrinement as Heine coveted for the songs of his beloved die Mouche[?], still you know full well that love will not fail to make for it some dainty ark.

The thought that you sometimes recall me is sweet as a kiss & it is blessed to know that but a little while & I shall be with you once more. For, I come up to town for a week on the 15th of December—the first three days will be dedicate to the Moloch of my business examination, but the remainder will be my own. On one of these I trust we may meet. I shall have news to tell you in which I think you will rejoice with your true-lover,

Richard Le Gallienne

ALS W. E. Henley to Wilde
MS Wilde, O. Recip.

[Illegible] House
Chiswick W
25/11/88

The "prose of France," my Oscar, is also my fancy point. Flaubert indeed is prose of France, but not genuinely French prose, the which (so far as I can [illegible word] myself to myself) I didn't accuse you of coming off in.

That, however, is nothing to the point. The point is that, as I think, you've assimilated your Flaubert to an extent that seems to me quite wonderful. His style to you is what rhyme is to *some* poets. . . .

W. E. H.

ALS Sir T. Wemyss Reid to Wilde
MS Wilde, O. Recip.

"The Speaker"
115, Fleet Street
London EC
24 Jan. 1890

My dear Oscar Wilde,

Of course I am going to use the admirable wisdom of your sage; but the world is so little prone to take a good teacher upon trust that I must ask you to back him with your name. You do not object to that I trust. Otherwise all the nonconformists will rage furiously against me, & my life will not be safe in the hands of any shop-keeper who reads the *Speaker*.

Yours ever sincerely
T. Wemyss Reid

ALS Frank Harris to Wilde

MS Wilde, O. Recip.

The Fortnightly Review Office
11, Henrietta Street
Covent Garden, WC
10 February 1890

My dear Wilde,

Our lunch today has made me wish that you would write an Article for the March *Fortnightly*. Can you do this within 8 days?—An Article on Literature or any Social Subject as paradoxical as you please.

Sincerely
Frank Harris

ALS Alexander Macmillan to Wilde

MS Wilde, O. Recip.

Macmillan & Co.
Bedford Street
Covent Garden
London
16 June 1890

My dear Wilde,

Thank you for letting me see your story, which I read through yesterday. George is not here today, so I cannot give it him, but as you want it back so soon I think I ought not to keep it any longer & am returning it by hand with this note.

It is a weird tale & some of the conversation is most brilliant. I am afraid however that it would not do for us to publish. We have done very little in the way of such strong situations, and I confess there is something in the power which Dorian Gray gets over the young natural scientist, & one or two other things which is rather repelling. I dare say you do not mean it to be. I am sure it is not for us, & I do not like to keep it any longer.

Yours very truly
Alexander Macmillan

ALS Wilfrid Meynell to Wilde

MS Wilde, O. Recip. n.d. [late August 1890].
[See *Letters*, p. 274]

~~The Weekly Register~~
~~43, Essex Street, Strand,~~
~~London.~~
Palace Court House
Bayswater Hill W
Saturday

Dear Mr Oscar Wilde,

I wish you would pronounce ex cathedra (on a postcard) upon the *he* & *him* question raised in my article on Newman in this week's *Athenaeum*.

Believe me,
Very truly yours
Wilfrid Meynell

ALS Henry Irving to Wilde

MS Wilde, O. Recip. n.d. ("18" [Feb 1891?]).
[See *Letters*, pp. 285–86]

Royal Lyceum Theatre
Strand
18—18

Dear Oscar Wilde,

[My?] thanks for your[?] first play which I have read with great interest.

How wise [?] of you to have it presented [?].

I read you the last [rest of letter illegible]

Yours sincerely
Henry Irving

ALS Robert [Williams] Buchanan to Wilde

MS Wilde, O. Recip.

Merkland
25, Maresfield Gardens
South Hampstead
Aug. 5. 1891

My dear Oscar Wilde,

I ought to have thanked you thus for your present of *Dorian Gray*, but I was hoping to return the compliment by sending you a work of my own: this I shall do in a very few days. You are quite right as to our divergence, which is temperamental. I cannot accept yours as a serious criticism of life. You seem to me like a holiday maker throwing pebbles into the sea, or viewing the great ocean from under the awning of a bathing machine. I quite see, however, that this is only your "fun," & that your very indolence of gaiety is paradoxical, like your utterances. If I judged you by what you deny in print, I should fear that [you] were somewhat heartless. Having seen & spoken with you, I conceive that you are just as poor & self-torment-ing a creature as any of the rest of us, and that you are simply joking at your own expense.

Don't think me rude in saying that *Dorian Gray* is very very clever. It is more—it is suggestive & stimulating, and has (tho' you only outlined it) the anxiety of a human <u>Soul</u> in it. You care far less about <u>Art</u>, or any other word spelt with a capital, than you are willing to admit, and [therein?] lies your salvation, as you will presently dis-cover. Though here and there in your pages you parade the magnifi-cence of the Disraeli waistcoat, that article of wardrobe fails to disguise you. One catches you constantly *in puris naturalibus*, and then the Man is worth observing.

With thanks & all kind wishes

Yours truly

Robert Buchanan

Oscar Wilde Esq.

ALS Elkin Mathews to Wilde

MS Wilde, O. Recip.

The Bodley Head
Vigo Street
London W
Oct 24 1891

Dear Sir

Poems

I would undertake to issue your volume of Poems on the following terms, viz:-

To instruct printer to supply Title-page with my imprint for 230 copies.

On receipt of Artist's Design for Cover at cost of £5.5.0. Block to be prepared from same the cost of which as well as that of Title-page Binding and Advertising to be first charges on the amount received for copies sold.

The cost of advertising not to exceed £5.5.0.

For my commission I agree to take 20% on the net published price, it being agreed that the book shall be brought out as a net one, the price to be fixed when bound.

After the above charges have been met the Balance to be remitted Quarterly, the first Balance to be struck Six Months after the date of publication.

I am, yours faithfully,

Elkin Mathews

Oscar Wilde Esq.

ALS Herbert Beerbohm Tree to Wilde

MS Wilde, O. Recip.

Queen Down Warren
Near Sittingbourne
12 Dec. 1891

My dear Wilde,

I returned your play which I read with great interest and which I considered dramatic and stirring. It would of course require a deal in the way of rewriting, and I have two elaborate productions before me.—I think, if you will allow me to criticise, that the dialogue is, here and there, somewhat redundant, and the heroine's passions struck me as too fluctuating—for *theatrical* purposes. But there is great force and picturesqueness in it all.—I see there is talk of a new play by you.—My wife and I were reading several of your articles, among them "Pen, Pencil & Poison," and again "the Decay of the Art of Lying"—I think they are the most brilliantly written things of our time:—it was a real joy to read them.—

I hope we may soon meet and discuss things in general and your play in particular.

Yours sincerely

Herbert Beerbohm Tree

P.S. I send you a copy of the lecture I delivered last Thursday.
HBT

ALS Elkin Mathews to Wilde

MS Wilde, O. Recip.

> The Bodley Head
> Vigo Street
> London W
> 25 Feb. 1892

My dear Sir,

Poems

I hope by the time this letter reaches you that Mr. Ricketts will have received specimen cases. I saw one today done up in the darker cloth, and the gold design looked splendid. I would strongly urge you to select this cloth "colour 11⁺ plain" as it is distressing to see pale coloured binding get dirty after very little use. The binders tell me that (presuming 230 were sent) the 230 copies would fall short by *10* on account of soiled, injured and missing sheets. They have rendered me a list of the latter.

I regret that I was out when you called some days ago—but you see that the matter will now be steadily pushed on to a conclusion.

I am yours faithfully

Elkin Mathews

ALS John Lane to Wilde
MS Wilde, O. Recip.

June 8 1893
The Bodley Head
Vigo Street
London

Dear Mr Wilde,

Here is a specimen page of "Lady Windermere's Fan" which I trust will meet with your early approval. We are badly in want of Act I. Please let us have it soon. I have this day seen Beardsley and arranged for 10 plates and a cover for 50 guineas!

Yours always

John Lane

ALS Edmund Gosse to Wilde
MS Wilde, O. Recip.

29, Delamere Terrace
Westbourne Square.W.
15 12. '93

My dear Mr Wilde,

It is very kind of you to send me "Lady Windermere's Fan," the brilliant merit of which is only enhanced by the absence of stage disturbance. I have just read it through, & I think more highly of it than ever.

We might still have a drama, if they would only close the play-houses.

Very truly yrs
Edmund Gosse

ALS John Hare to Wilde

MS Wilde, O. Recip. [11 Apr. 1894?]
[See *Letters*, pp. 348–50 and 426, and Wilde's allusions in *De Profundis*]

April 11[?]

3, Park Crescent
W.

Dear Wilde,

I cannot give you a definite answer till Thursday—but I may say at once that my feeling is to [?claim] by April and accept from July, [?finding] it *immediate* production [illegible word]. I [illegible word] Mrs[?] [illegible word] poor and unattractive, failing this production it immediately to follow Pinero—You must remember that the fault is not mine that your play was not produced long ago, had it been ready by the time you agreed then it could have been produced to follow "Diplomacy"—& you can hardly expect me now to surrender a comedy that suits me as well in many respects, simply because other managers [illegible word] from [illegible word] play [illegible words] from temporary difficulties—If you will come here and see me on Thursday at 12 o'cl—I will either return you your manuscript or definitely settle its production at the Garrick.

Sincerely
John Hare

ALS William Archer to Wilde

MS Wilde, O. Recip.

40, Queen Square. W.C.
29 May 94

My dear Wilde,

I am going to do for the *Pall Mall Budget,* in a somewhat tentative fashion, a sort of weekly *causerie* on things theatrical. It will not be a *news* column, but when interesting news comes in my way, I shall of course be glad to make use of it. Is it the case that Lewis Waller is going to produce a play of yours at the Haymarket during Tree's absence? And is it possible for you to give me any inkling of the nature of the play, or to let me announce its title? If so, you will be doing me a favour; if not, & if my proposed *causerie* comes to anything, *ce sera pour une autre fois.*

> In either case
> I am
> Yours very sincerely,
> William Archer

ALS Richard Le Gallienne to Wilde

MS Wilde, O. Recip.

> ~~Mulberry Cottage~~,
> ~~Boston Road,~~
> ~~Brentford.~~
> c/o Grant Allen, Esq
> Hind House[?]
> Haslemere
> 19, June, '94

My dear Oscar,

I have sent for your acceptance a copy of my "Prose Fancies"—that the word of the prophet might be fulfilled, which in an old but treasured letter of yours says:

"your prose shd be very good, for you have distinction"! Forgive so egotistical quotation. I wd quote a better author—if I knew one.

> Yours ever sincerely
> Richard Le Gallienne

ALS (Sir) George Henry Lewis to Wilde

MS Wilde, O. Recip.
Messrs Lewis and Lewis

10 & 44 Ely Place
Holborn EC
London
7 July 1894

Dear Mr Wilde,

I am in receipt of your note. The information that you have received that I am acting for Lord Queensberry is perfectly correct, and under these circumstances you will at once see that it is impossible for me to offer any opinion about any proceedings you intend to take against him.

Although I cannot act against him, I should not act against you.

Believe me
Yours faithfully
George Lewis

Oscar Wilde, Esq.
16 Tite Street
Chelsea S.W.

ALS Lewis Waller to Wilde

MS Wilde, O. Recip.

The Walsingham House
Picadilly. W.
Aug. 18th 94

Dear Wilde,

Tree consents to Mrs Pat Campbell—now we want her consent—please see her as soon as possible & read play to her—or if not convenient I will.

Yours sincerely
Lewis Waller

ALS Lady Maud Beerbohm Tree to Wilde

MS Wilde, O. Recip. n.d [1894].

77 Sloane Street
SW

My dear Mr Wilde,

Thank you very much for my book, & for the sweet flattery of your pretty inscription! I am *very* proud & glad to possess it & very proud & glad to be concerned in its production—I mean in its production as a stage-play—in its production as a book alas! I am nothing. Oh! why did I not introduce some ineffaceable "gag" so that some word of my own *own* might have become immortal?

What a delicious bit of book it makes—a foz to hold—
Very many thanks, & kindest regards—

Yours always sincerely,

Maud Beerbohm Tree

ALS C. Haddon Chambers to Wilde

MS Wilde, O. Recip. n.d

St George's Club
Hanover Square
Friday

My dear Oscar,

I send you "The Collaborators."

I think you will agree that if Hawtrey and Penley were to play it the result would be fine.

If you come to that conclusion and can, without any trouble to yourself get Hawtrey to read it I shall be delighted.

Very sincerely yours

C. Haddon Chambers

P.S. I am going to do the little gold nugget story almost at once. The *motif* charms me. But ought I to use your plot as my own?

ALS Montmorres to Wilde
MS Wilde, O. Recip. n.d.

~~THE ARTIST~~
~~14, Parliament St.~~
~~Westminster.~~
24 Radcliffe Road
South Kensington SW

Dear Mr Wilde,

You may perhaps have heard that I have undertaken the Editorship of the "Artist." I write to ask a favour of you: may I once more "interview" you in quite a private way to learn your opinion on "an ideal mode of life." I do hope you will be able to grant my request. I have the vividest recollection of a very pleasant "interview" some two years ago.

I trust that we are shortly to be charmed by another of your plays.

Very truly yours
Montmorres

Correspondence to Wilde
Clark Library

ALS George A. Macmillan to Wilde

M1665L W6721. 11 June 1878.

Macmillan & Co
London, June 11, 1878

My dear Wilde,

Miss Fletcher called here this morning & said she was going to write to you today so you will know her address from herself. I had not seen her before.

I'm quite delighted to hear of your success in the Newdigate. My people here don't care much for publishing prize poems, so I am afraid that though of course I should have been glad to oblige you, we cannot undertake yours. I think I should advise your getting it printed in Oxford, especially as you want it out quickly. What is the length of it? Tell me when it is out, as I am anxious to see it.

Whenever you think of writing something on a larger scale we shall be happy to hear of it.

Are you not to be in town this season? If you are up by any chance on July 3rd we should be very glad if you could accept the enclosed invitation. You would be sure to meet a lot of interesting people.

Look me up when you do come to town.

& Believe me

Yours very truly

George A. Macmillan

ALS Oscar Browning to Wilde

MS Wilde L91: 3; [Various] [File of 7 letters—one incomplete—to Oscar Wilde].
[Letter 1:]

King's College
Cambridge
Feb 18 1880

My Dear Wilde,

I shall be delighted to give you a testimonial but I once did one for a friend and was answered by the Duke of Richmond that no testimonials can be received for anyone who has not reached the age of twenty five. I do not know if you have attained that mature majority. If you tell me that you have I will write to the Duke at once. I need hardly say that any political influence which you can bring to bear on the Duke and his Private Secretary will be of great avail.

Believe me

Ever yours

Oscar Browning

ALS William Blackwood to Wilde

PR5819 P851. cop. 2

45, George Street
Edinburgh
4th June 1889

Dear Sir,

I am glad you are agreeable to my publishing your story "The Portrait of Mr W.H." in a new series of "Tales from Blackwood" after it has appeared in [the] Maga[zine]. I am having it set up and am endeavouring to arrange for using it in my July number. As you are desirous of having the honorarium now I have the pleasure of enclosing your cheque of £25—in acknowledgement of it, which in the circumstances is somewhat beyond Maga[zine]'s usual scale. The Printers estimate it will run to about 18 pages & I expect to send you proof in January.

Yours truly

William Blackwood

Oscar Wilde Esq.

ALS Dion Boucicault to Wilde

B7553L W6721. 22 Apr. 1894.

Lyceum Theatre
Sydney
April 22nd / 94

My dear old friend Oscar—My time has been so occupied since my arrival from New Zealand that I have had no leisure moment to sit down and scribble you a few lines. I received your letter with delight. You have been informed rightly, I am very grey, but I think it is rather becoming—so I shall not dye my hair as you suggest. I am very sunburnt with my trip so that I am a fit subject for a study in black & white.

I hear you have a cottage at Goring. Please see there is a room prepared for me on my trip to England. I hope to arrive somewhere about the end of July. I prefer a room looking on to the river, and should like it, please, furnished in the Eastern way, that style of decoration setting off to the greatest advantage my peculiar form of beauty. I have not been able, in this benighted land, to secure a copy of "Salomé"—so have one beautifully bound & preserved in a cedar casket perfumed with attar of roses—awaiting my arrival.

I am sending you a photograph of myself, which please cherish.

I produce *Lady Windermere's Fan* in about a month's time here—you shall have all the papers, and photographs of the scenes & principal characters forwarded to you. Here's to its success. Why should I write that? A play by Oscar Wilde cannot fail. His name alone is one to conjure with. In the lexicon of his youth there's been no such word as "fail."

You ought to send me your photograph—I have only one taken centuries ago. You hear I look old and grey. I hear you have found the *elixir vitae*—the secret of perpetual youth and are looking younger yearly. How is it done? Please forward recipe.

Ever affectionately yours

Dot

address
c/o Allen & Allen

167 Philip St
Sydney
NS Wales

ALS John Lane to Wilde

L265L W6721. Sept. 1894.

Sept 7 94.

Dear Mr Wilde,

Mr Matthews, it appears, has had some correspondence with you *re* the distribution of your books on our dissolving partnership. You wrote quite frankly to the firm that you wished me to retain the Plays & that you wished Mr Matthews to publish Mr W.H. I was perfectly agreeable to that arrangement, but it now appears that Mr Matthews has again communicated with you on the subject & he declines to have Mr "W.H." at "any price" but he wants the "plays." Since I have pointed out that if he takes the plays he must also take Mr W.H. He declines both.

For my part I am perfectly willing to publish your plays, & Mr W.H. provided I see & approve the latter before it is printed, but I am sure that you as a man of the world would not expect me or any other publisher to issue a book he had never seen.

Can we not meet, talk the matter over & settle things?

Yours very truly,

John Lane

AL John Lane to Wilde

L265M3 D7582. 21 Sept. 1894.

Dear Sir,

We have considered your letter in all its bearings and have come to the following decision.

Mr Lane will carry out the firm's agreement with you with regard to your 3 plays, Salomé & the Sphinx and Mr W.H. We are agreed that

Mr Lane shall accept all responsibilities assumed by the firm in the agreement. There can be no grounds however for your complaint against the firm with regard to the lapse of time since the agreement for this book was entered upon as we have never received the M.S. If you will send it to Mr Lane he is prepared to deal with it immediately.

Draft of letter sent by the firm
to Oscar Wilde 21 Sept 1894

AL More Adey to Oscar Wilde

W6721 A233L. W6721. [1896]b.
[Draft fragment of a letter with notes in Adey's hand; for Wilde's response, see *Letters*, p. 515.]

. . . Miss S has heard from a lady whom I believe to be Cyril's godmother who has been with Mrs W for about 6 months, that Mrs W was anxious for O to promise . . . I wrote to Miss S offering to see O & obtain this from him, Mrs W has probably seen my letter offering to see O: I advise O to make this assurance, if possible in writing, but I strongly urge him to refuse if asked to enter into any legal agreement to give up his rights over his children. He need not mention this warning but act upon it!

AL More Adey to Oscar Wilde

A2332 N911. [1896?]. [Notes and Drafts in More Adey's hand concerning financial settlement, divorce proceedings and custody of children.]

. . . We want you to write to your wife saying much what you said to More, namely that you wished her to have her own money to bring them [the children] up upon as she liked, that you would not interfere with them, and that you would not of course live with them on your release. We want you also to add that you are willing to join with her in appointing a guardian for them on her death, if she will chose someone who will not bring them up either to hate or despise their father & that is all you ask. We hope that if you do this you may avoid being legally deprived of guardianship, and may retain enough influence over your wife to practically prevent the education of your children in ways which you would not approve.

ALS Herbert Beerbohm Tree to Wilde
T786L W6721. 17 Feb. 1900.

Her Majesty's Theatre
17 Feb. 1900

Dear Wilde,

Pray excuse my delay in answering your letter—the fact is that "A Woman of No Importance" has only once been given by Mrs Waller—I understand that I am bound to pay any fees to the Trustees in Bankruptcy. Anyhow, I have received no payment from her. I spoke to Alexander about you the other day, and he told me that he owed you some fees and that he would be glad to settle them—I told him I was sure they would be welcome—I am indeed glad, and we all shall be, to know that you are determined to resume your dramatic work, for no one did such distinguished work as you—it has been rumoured that you had already finished your play—but I suppose this was not true.—I do most sincerely hope that good luck may come to you and that your splendid talents may shine forth again.

I have a lively remembrance of your many acts of kindness and courtesy—and was one of those who devoutly hoped that misfortune would not submerge you.

With best wishes, I remain

Yours sincerely
Herbert Beerbohm Tree

ANS Clifford Millage to Wilde
M6441L W6721. 5 Nov. 1900.
The Daily Chronicle

59 Rue de Maubeuge
Paris
12 Salisbury Square
London EC

5 Nov. 1900

My dear Sir,

I should be happy if you could make a rendez-vous at your *earliest* convenience as I should like to know something about your piece "Mr & Mrs Daventry" in your interests & in my professional capacity. I know that your address was in the Rue André des Arts but failed to find it.

Yours faithfully

Clifford Millage

ALS Dion Boucicault to Wilde

L91: 3 MS Wilde; [Various] [File of 7 letters—one incomplete—to Oscar Wilde]; n.d.
[Letter 2:]

51 Victoria Sq
Wednesday

My dear Oscar,

Your play reached me last night.

I read it this morning. The *charpente* of the work is good and dramatic—I mean the spinal column.

Vera

+

The Czarewitz

The catastrophe is new & good—But the ribs and the limbs do not proceed from the spinal column.

Your other characters—

Your subjects of dialogue

which occupy 5/6 of the play—are not *action*—but discussion.

The *interest*—lies with V & the C—and all that does not further that interest—develop and increase is improper—however good it may be.

You asked me to be candid—I have been so.

You have dramatic powers but have not shaped your subject perfectly before beginning it. You have seen three incidents:

1 The adherence of the Czarewitz and her rescue of the Nihilist

2 The assassination of Czar

3 The sacrifice of Vera & its manner

But between these incidents as *dialogue*—not action—a chain of *incidents*, should lead from one to the other.

Your action stops for dialogue—whereas dialogue should be the necessary outcome of the action exerting an influence on the characters.

Ever yours

Dion Boucicault

ALS Marion Morris to Wilde

L91: 3 MS Wilde; [Various] [File of 7 letters—one incomplete—to Oscar Wilde]; n.d.
[Letter 3:]

48 Wellington Road
St Johns Wood N5

Dear Mr Wilde,

I am going to bother you—now I suppose you will not read any further! It is the penalty you pay for being influential and great. I am neither so I want to borrow some of your powers. Mr Mackay whom you saw act at Goring, is very anxious to know if you would be so very kind as to give him a letter of introduction to Mr Hare. Mr Forbes Robertson would have spoken for him, but he has never seen him play anything & told him that a few words from you would go so much further. He is *so* anxious to get [illegible word] being diffident; he would not even write to you himself!

Please forgive one for troubling you, when I have no right to & if you could, give Mr Mackay the benefit of your influence with Mr Hare.

Believe me

Yours sincerely

Marion Morris

I don't think I shall ever go on the stage because I shall wait till *you* give me a part to create!

| 4 |

Manuscripts

EDITORS and critics alike have been aware for some time of the complexity of Wilde's compositional practices. From the early 1880s onwards his extensive borrowing has been frequently noted, initially and most famously perhaps in the rejection of his volume *Poems* (1881) by the Oxford Union, with the barbed comment by Oliver Elton that it was the work of a "number of better known and deservedly reputed authors." This allegation of plagiarism has continued to the present day; recently, however, a number of critics have begun to question the adequacy of such a characterization. The occasion for this re-examination was an unforeseen consequence of the work of some textual editors.

The attempt to establish stemmata for the society comedies revealed that Wilde "borrowed" from his own work much more extensively than from all other authors. Moreover, this "borrowing" was too systematic and knowing to be the result of expedience or external pressures of work. Clearly the term "plagiarism" obscures rather than illuminates such processes. It is therefore becoming increasingly obvious that a detailed knowledge of Wilde's manuscripts is necessary not only for the text-editor but also for the literary critic. In this sense it is to be expected that much recent editorial work will be able to generate significant critical insights.

One interesting example relates to Wilde's reputation as a fountain of *bons mots* and epigrams. An examination of some of the earliest drafts of his plays reveals that he began with a series of witty phrases, jokes, or puns; in the compositional processes they may have been shuffled around—between characters, or even between plays—but the original phrases, jokes, or lines remained intact.

A particularly compelling example of this devotion to the discrete phrase or line rather than the word as the smallest unit of composition is to be found in the drafts of the poem "Pan." In three of the drafts of that poem Wilde's revisions consist not in changes to either stanza structure or to individual lexical items, but principally in a wholesale reshuffling of lines (with, it has to be said, little regard to the consequent changes in the sense of the poem). The drafts of "Pan" also illustrate another and better-known feature of Wilde's compositional practices (discussed below), that of the substitution of a word by its antonym. This view of Wilde as a writer concerned with local effects is not new; less well-known, however, is the sureness of his narrative and dramatic sense. So the scenario for *The Cardinal of Avignon* in the holograph of More Adey held at the William Andrews Clark Memorial Library (printed by Mason and reproduced below) reveals how elaborately plotted Wilde's plays were. That scenario reveals Wilde to be manipulating an unpromising narrative in order to create a sequence of situations with a potential theatrical and dramatic richness.

There has yet to be a comprehensive census of the extant manuscripts and typescripts of Wilde's works. The dispersal of the manuscript and typescript drafts of those works after the bankruptcy proceedings following his conviction in 1895 has made such a census necessary, but unfortunately it has also made it virtually impossible to execute fully. Any account of the manuscripts will inevitably now be incomplete; moreover, any census will encounter two other kinds of complications.

In the first place, the holdings of some major institutions, both in the UK and in the USA, are not fully nor adequately described in their respective catalogues. Indeed, Wilde's compositional practices, his habit, that is, of radically but irregularly re-drafting material, have made any cataloguer's job extremely difficult. It is quite clear that what purport to be drafts of texts comprise only *parts* of texts, composed at quite different times and at quite different stages of revision, but subsequently bound together by collectors or librarians. The full extent of this contamination of the known drafts of Wilde's work has yet to be properly surveyed. However, in at least one case, that of the manuscripts of *A Woman of No Importance*, it is already been established that they have been incorrectly collated.

The second complication in compiling a comprehensive census is that there are many drafts of Wilde's works in the hands of private collectors, and they are therefore relatively inaccessible. Moreover, while the existence of some private collections are familiar to the scholarly community, there are a large number of manuscripts whose locations are unknown.

With these caveats, what follows, while it is the most comprehensive account of the disposition of Wilde's manuscript and typescript materials yet undertaken, is of necessity incomplete. As a consequence the census is arranged in two ways. The first section describes the known extant manuscripts of individual works. The second section details the same material but according to its location in the appropriate major research libraries.

Works Identified by Title

The Plays

Current work on the Oxford English Texts *Complete Works of Oscar Wilde* will attempt to construct as completely as possible stemmata for all Wilde's dramatic output. In some cases this procedure will involve publishing manuscripts for the first time. However, editorial work already completed has begun to reveal the complex nature of Wilde's compositional practices. So, for example, there have been several recent individual studies of the drafts of some of the dramatic works: Jackson (1980); Small (1980); Shewan (1982 and 1983); Small and Jackson (1983); Berggren (1987); Glavin (1987 and 1988); Lich (1987); Small and Jackson (1987); Lawler (1988); and Reed (1989). Taken together they show how thorough-going and systematic Wilde's revisions to his work were: they give the lie to his humorously misleading claim that he functioned solely by the mystery of *sprezzatura*. Indeed, the general design of the plays may have been conceived with brilliant rapidity, but it is now clear that the details of plotting and the final shape of the dialogue were evolved over a period of meticulous and laborious revision. In fact comparison

of the drafts of the plays shows that Wilde had a variety of compositional practices: they include the moving of whole blocks of dialogue
(and in particular jokes) from play to play, or the setting aside of
material, even names of characters, for later use. In such a comparison, his continual self-plagiarism is also made clear.

Identifying these processes is complicated by the fact that, as I have
indicated, the progression of manuscript and typescript drafts for each
act of a play was often irregular, and that some stages in the process
are not represented by material currently extant or available. In this
respect, an important addition not only to our knowledge of Wilde's
unfinished pieces, but also to the problems of establishing stemmata,
was made by Rodney Shewan (1982) who, in a painstaking piece of
dramatic reconstruction, identifies, describes, and then reproduces
the manuscript of *A Wife's Tragedy* held in the Clark Library. A
further piece of reconstruction was recently made by Small and
Jackson (1987). Their report on a cache of theatre scripts of *A Woman
of No Importance* at the Herbert Beerbohm Tree archive in the Bristol
Theatre Collection at the University of Bristol has allowed the
construction of a full stemma for that play, perhaps the only dramatic
text of Wilde for which such a recreation of the processes of composition will prove possible.

A second issue which bears upon the texts of Wilde's plays concerns a general editorial problem—namely, what constitutes the
copy-text for a performed play. This question has been most cogently
addressed by Shakespeare editors in a debate about the relationship
of the quarto to the folio texts. Broadly speaking, the issue which
bears most fully upon the editing of Wilde's work is the question of
whether an editor should take as copy-text a published (and therefore
necessarily later) text of a play, or whether he or she should attempt
to recover the text of one or more of its performances. In the latter
case, it has to be borne in mind that establishing a performance text
demands that attention be paid to the uniqueness of a performance,
and therefore to the necessarily unstable nature of all performance
texts. In this respect recent arguments surrounding the editing of the
two *King Lear*s suggest ways in which future editors of, for example,
The Importance of Being Earnest, might be able to proceed—more
specifically, how they might take account of the differences between,
say, the first performance text and that represented by the Leonard
Smithers 1899 first edition. As long ago as 1971 Joseph Donohue

argued that priority should be given to the text of the former rather than the latter, and he outlined a strategy for its recovery.

In connection with the notion of performance texts, and the idea of Wilde as playwright rather than dramatist, it is worth pointing out that Rupert Hart–Davis's volume *More Letters* described material which provides the basis for a fuller account of Wilde's dealings with the theatre managers for whom he worked. A number of these letters are from Wilde's managers, and they are useful in a variety of ways; most interestingly they reveal the way financial pressures inevitably impinged upon his creative life. Others show his attempts to enlist himself as an agent in the production of his plays; his activities range from offering to use his influence to advertise his work in the press, or more practically, attempting to assemble as strong a cast of actors as possible.

A more detailed study of the practices of dramatic authorship—contracts, working conditions, and so forth—in the late nineteenth century is still, however, a prerequisite of further accounts of Wilde's methods of composition. So, for example, the recent discovery by Peter Raby of the original scenario for *The Importance of Being Earnest* shows Wilde's principal preoccupations to be financial. Most importantly, an account of the conditions for authorship will help provide an important corrective to the romantic myth inaugurated by Wilde himself suggesting the effortless improvisation of his creative genius.

Because they are dramatic texts and were thus reproduced more often and more carefully, both for public performance or for rehearsal, the manuscripts and typescript drafts of the society comedies have survived best and their history is thus most fully documented.

Lady Windermere's Fan

For *Lady Windermere's Fan*: the British Library holds the first manuscript draft entitled "Lady Windermere's Fan"; it also holds the Licensing Copy of the play in the Lord Chamberlain's collection. A manuscript of Act III of the play was sold at Christie's in New York as part of the sale of the Prescott Collection in 1981 (for details, see the Prescott sale catalogue, Christie's, New York, 6 February 1981). The Pierpont Morgan Library holds an autograph MS of Act III in 16 leaves. The Clark Library holds a second, later manuscript draft entitled "Lady Windermere's Fan" (probably used for a revival of the work), a typescript draft entitled "A Good Woman," and a later typescript draft entitled "Lady Windermere's Fan"; the HRHRC holds a typescript entitled "A Good Woman." For details of the stemma of the play, see Small (1980).

A Woman of No Importance

For *A Woman of No Importance*: an early autograph sketch book containing working notes for the play was included in the Prescott sale described above. The British Library holds the following: a fuller, heavily corrected later manuscript draft entitled "Mrs Arbuthnot"; a typescript with manuscript revisions also under the title "Mrs Arbuthnot"; a later typescript, also with manuscript revisions, again under the title "Mrs Arbuthnot," bound with the early typescript (MS Add. 37945: the earlier draft is ff.1–91, the later ff.92–178). The Lord Chamberlain's collection at the British Library has the Licensing Copy of the play.

The HRHRC has a typescript draft of the play entitled "Mrs Arbuthnot"; the draft has manuscript revisions and additions (only some of which are in Wilde's hand) to both recto and verso, not all of which reproduce adequately in photocopy or microfilm. Some of these MS additions are stage directions from Wilde to Herbert Beerbohm Tree; others are Tree's comments upon and interpretation of moments in the play. Taken together, these revisions constitute an interesting dialogue between manager and author about the play, and are evidence that some of the dramatic effects of the plays were the result of collaboration. The Clark Library also has a typescript draft with manuscript revisions of *A Woman of No Importance*. The Herbert Beerbohm Tree archive in the Bristol Theatre Collection, the University of Bristol, has Tree's varied and numerous typescripts of the play, some with manuscript revisions and all free from the confusions brought about by haphazard collecting. The material includes property lists, prompt copies, actors' parts, diagrams of sets as well as the actors' parts and the prompt-copy for Charles Hartley's 1904 provincial tour of the play. For the stemma of the play see Small (1983) and Small and Jackson (1987).

An Ideal Husband

For *An Ideal Husband*: the British Library holds a manuscript draft, including two drafts of Act II; a typescript draft with manuscript revisions, and the Licensing Copy of the play (in the Lord Chamberlain's Collection). A manuscript of Act IV and a typescript of Act III were included in the sale of the Prescott Collection. The Clark Library holds an early notebook typescript draft of the play with manuscript revisions and a separate draft of Act IV. It also holds page-proofs of the first edition published by Leonard Smithers, with Wilde's manuscript revisions and two MS notebooks which contain an early working draft of the play. The Pierpont Morgan Library holds a typescript of Act III with revisions by Wilde. The Harvard Theatre Collection holds a typescript with manuscript revisions of Act I; and a further typescript of the same act, with revisions in a hand other than Wilde's, marked as a prompt-book. The New York Public Library at Lincoln Center holds a typescript used by Daniel Frohman; it has manuscript stage-directions in Act IV. For an account of the (incomplete) typescript of the play held at the Texas Christian University, see Lich (1986). For a stemma of the play, see Lich and Jackson (1983).

The Importance of Being Earnest

For *The Importance of Being Earnest*: as already indicated, the Clark Library holds the first scenario of the play. The Arents Collection in the New York Public Library holds Acts I and II of the only known manuscript draft; Acts III and IV are in the British Library. All four acts are transcribed in volume I of Sarah A. Dickson (1956). Ruth Berggren (1987) printed the four act version of the play; see Editions, below. The Arents Tobacco Collection also holds a typescript draft of Acts I, III and IV, reprinted in volume II of Dickson's edition; also a typescript (typed by Winifred Dolan) of the play revised by Wilde for the 1899 Smithers' first edition. The British Library holds the Licensing Copy of the play, under the title *Lady Lancing: A Serious Comedy for Trivial People by Oscar Wilde*. The New York Public Library at Lincoln Center (Burnside Frohman Collection) holds a typescript of the four-act version of the play (dated 31 October 1894); and the Harvard Theatre Collection holds George Alexander's typescript copy of the play with his manuscript alterations. The Arents Collection in New York Public Library holds the Frohman typescript, the basis for the first American production. A four-act typescript dated 8–25 October 1894 was included in the sale of the Prescott Collection. The page-proofs of Smithers' 1899 first edition of the play, with Wilde's autograph revisions, are in the HRHRC. For a stemma of the play see Jackson (1980).

Salomé

For *Salomé*: what is probably the earliest extant MS is that held in the Bodmer Library at Geneva. It is written in French in Wilde's hand in a bound notebook on 57 leaves, mostly recto, with some additions on facing verso. Another early draft is that held at the HRHRC. It is dated November 1891, Paris. The Rosenbach Foundation in Philadelphia holds a later manuscript version written in two notebooks of British origin (that is, revised on Wilde's return from Paris). The New York Public Library holds a manuscript of the play of dubious provenance. The HRHRC MS carries with it a letter of probity asserting that both the New York Public Library and Clark Library texts are forgeries. Clyde de L. Ryals (1959) describes the changes made by Pierre Louÿ s to Wilde's final fair copy in French and particularly to Wilde's use of the subjunctive; other changes by Louÿ s, not of a grammatical nature, are subsequently scored through in Wilde's hand. For further information about Wilde's transactions with Louÿ s, and the printing of the first French edition (which Wilde appears to have financed himself), see the section on Letters, above. The page-proofs, corrected by Wilde and others, are at the Clark Library.

Other Plays

For *Vera; Or, the Nihilist; The Duchess of Padua; A Florentine Tragedy; A Wife's Tragedy;* "Beatrice and Astone Manfredi": an early manuscript draft of *Vera* (under its original title of *Vera of the Nihilists*) is held at the Clark Library; and another early draft is held at the Beinecke Library at Yale. The Clark Library holds a copy of *Vera* with corrections made for the 1883 New York performance. For *The Duchess of Padua*: the Clark Library holds a MS fragment and a heavily annotated and corrected complete MS, together with material relating to the American production of the play. The BL has one of only four extant copies of a privately printed facsimile of a signed MS of *The Duchess of Padua*, dated 15 March, 1883, with Wilde's corrections. Fragments of *A Wife's Tragedy* (see Shewan 1982, described above), and "Beatrice and Astone Manfredi" are held at the Clark Library. For an account of some of the unpublished Wilde material at the Clark Library see also John J. Espey, in Ellmann and Espey (1977) and the relevant sections in this work. For *A Florentine Tragedy*: the HRHRC holds an MS draft of fragments and workings written in a notebook. It is an early sketch of the play with no *dramatis personae*, no attribution of speeches, no parts, and no act or scene divisions. As with the early drafts of the other plays, there are speech fragments but no dramatic structure. The Clark Library holds two MS fragments of the play. Princeton University Library possesses manuscripts of Act II of *The Cardinal of Avignon*, and a manuscript of the scenario of *The Dutchess of Padua*; and two pages of a draft of that play.

The Fiction

For The Picture of Dorian Gray: a manuscript draft of the periodical publication and a typescript of chapter 3 are held by the Clark Library. A version of chapter 4 of the novel is held at the New York Public Library. The Pierpont Morgan Library has the signed MS of the first version of the novel, now on exhibition under glass. It also has an autograph MS in ten pages of chapter 5.For an account of the relationship between the MS, and the two printed versions (the periodical and the first book edition) see Lawler (1988). The location of the manuscripts for the other fiction is not easy to ascertain. The HRHRC holds a TMS with autograph corrections of a translation of "The Remarkable Rocket' ("La Remarquable Fusée": traduction d'Alexandre Renolds). The Clark Library holds a portion of the original autograph MS of "The Fisherman and his Soul." The Bodmer Library has a MS of "The Fisherman and his Soul," beginning with page 4.

Criticism, Lectures and Reviews

Intentions

For *Intentions*: the Berg Collection in New York Public Library holds an incomplete twenty-page holograph of "The Decay of Lying," under the title "On the Decay of Lying"; a holograph first draft of parts of "The Decay of Lying" under the original title of "The True Function and Value of Criticism," together with a letter from Wilde relating to a correction in the typesetting, are held in the Hyde Collection, New Jersey; and the Clark Library holds a complete and revised later manuscript version of the same essay which, while it is not printer's copy for the periodical, is the latest known MS draft of the work. There is no known extant manuscript material for either "Pen, Pencil and Poison" or "The Truth of Masks." For "The Portrait of Mr W.H.," the Rosenbach Foundation in Philadelphia holds a MS. Wilde's commonplace books are held by the Clark Library and have now been published (see Smith and Helfand [1989]). The Clark Library also holds an exercise book used by Wilde for his Greek and Latin studies, and other notebooks, all as yet unpublished.

Lectures and Reviews

The Beinecke Library at Yale holds versions of lectures. The Clark Library holds four manuscripts and typescript versions of "Art and the Handicraftsman," and four manuscript fragments and the corrected typescript of "The English Renaissance of Art." The Clark also holds a manuscript fragment of a lecture on house decoration and fragments of essays on Chatterton and Hellenism. A more substantial draft of the last piece was in the possession of the late H. Montgomery Hyde; it is now in the Hyde Collection in New Jersey. The Clark also holds an unpublished draft review of Dante Gabriel Rossetti's poems; a typescript of Robert Ross's transcription of Wilde's essay on "Hellenism" (now published: see Wilde, 1979) and on "Greek Women"; a manuscript fragment of an early article on dress design (published in the *Pall Mall Gazette* in 1884); and manuscript fragments of epigrams and aphorisms. The Clark also holds the manuscript of an early unpublished review of Henri–Frédéric Amiel's *Journal Intime* and Lord Beaconsfield's letters, entitled "Amiel and Lord Beaconsfield." The Pierpont Morgan Library has an unpublished review of J. A. Symonds's *Studies of the Greek Poets* in 45 leaves, and a MS containing undergraduate translations from Lucretius and Tacitus. It should be reiterated that Wilde's journalism has received relatively little attention, and until the relevant volume of the Oxford English Texts edition of the *Complete Works* has identified the extent of his journalistic writing, all attempts to locate and identify manuscripts will be provisional.

De Profundis

An autograph manuscript and a typescript of *De Profundis* is held by the British Library. The Ross Collection in the Bodleian Library holds a transcript of the text. The Clark Library holds a typescript made by Stuart Mason. For an account of the composition and typing of the letter, see Hart–Davis (1962). The Clark Library possesses a considerable body of material relating to the publication of various parts of the work in the first half of this century.

Poems

Manuscript versions of the poems are held by a number of institutions. The Beinecke Library at Yale, the New York Public Library, Princeton University Library and the British Library all hold manuscripts of the poems. The Clark Library in particular has numerous manuscripts of poems, published and unpublished. These include complete or fragmentary manuscripts of the following: "Amor Intellectualis"; "La Belle Gabrielle"; "The Burden of Itys"; "Choir boy (and other fragments)"; "Easter Day"; two MSS of "Endymion"; "Helena"; "Libertatis sacra fames"; "The Little Ship"; "Love Song"; "Pan: a Villanelle." The HRHRC also holds a variety of MSS of the poems, both published and unpublished: "And Many an Afghan Chief"; "Lily-Flower"; an autograph MS and a printed version (John Luce and Co., London and Boston, 1909) of "Pan: A Villanelle"; and "Désespoir." It also holds a MS in Alfred Douglas's hand of Wilde's "The New Remorse" which bears the title "Oscar Wilde's Best Sonnet." The punctuation differs significantly from both the first publication as "Un Amant de Nos Jours" in 1887 and in *Poems* (1908). (See Appendix 1.) The Beinecke Library at Yale holds a MS of "The Star-Child," as does the Huntingdon Library. A draft of "The Sphinx" is held by the British Library; three further drafts are held by the Clark Library.

Recent sales of manuscript material have made it possible to identify the whereabouts of some previously unknown MSS drafts. The sale of the Prescott Collection, in addition to the items mentioned above, included the following: an Oxford notebook; Stuart Mason's copy of the Tite Street sale; various manuscript drafts, including that of "The Rise of Historical Criticism," "L'Envoi" for *Rose Leaf and Apple Leaf*, "Lecture to Art Students," and the preface to *The Picture of Dorian Gray*; manuscript notes of "Personal Impressions of America"; Wilde's annotated copy of the *Nicomachean Ethics* ; and various letters. There have been other sales since: H. R. Woudhuysen (1986) describes the most important, that at Sotheby's on July 10–11. He gives details of the memorabilia, visiting cards, photographs and the like, sold on that occasion. He also describes the only known water-colour painted by Wilde and then the more substantial literary remains included in the sale: an unpublished poem ("Heart's Yearnings"); Carlos Blacker's copy of a working typescript of *De Profundis* (exhibiting variants from the published text and corrected by Stuart Mason); an autograph manuscript of "The Harlot's House," with variants of the published text; and two unpublished letters. The catalogue for a previous sale at Sotheby's (22–23 July, 1985) describes (and prints extracts from) what appear to be love-letters from Constance Wilde to the London bookseller, Arthur Lee Humphreys, during the period immediately preceding Wilde's trials and imprisonment. Other sales have included Constance Wilde's autograph book, sold at Sotheby's in London in July 1986; a letter from Wilde to Leonard Smithers selling the rights to *Lady Windermere's Fan* and *A Woman of No Importance,* sold at Christie's in New York in November 1985 (see the *Times*, 25 November 1985); Wilde's copy of Walter Pater's *Imaginary Portraits,* sold at Sotheby's in London in December 1984; and his Savoy Hotel bills, sold at Sotheby's in London in July 1984.

Epigrams

See "Manuscript Holdings by Library. University of California," below.

Manuscript Holdings by Library

British Library

BL Add. MSS. 37942. "The Sphinx." 10 ff. Final autograph draft with designs in pencil by Charles Ricketts.

BL Add. MSS. 37943. *Lady Windermere's Fan.* First draft in four acts. 100 ff.

BL Add. MSS. 37944. "Mrs Arbuthnot" [*A Woman of No Importance*]. First draft in 210ff.

BL Add. MSS. 37945. "Mrs Arbuthnot" [*A Woman of No Importance*]. Two typed versions with autograph corrections. 178 ff.

BL Add. MSS. 37946. *An Ideal Husband.* Drafts of the four acts, with two versions of Act II. 312 ff.

BL Add. MSS. 37947. *An Ideal Husband.* Typed copy with autograph, corrections. 96 ff.

BL Add. MSS. 37948. "Lady Lancing." [*The Importance of Being Earnest*]. Early drafts of Acts III and IV. 191 ff.

Bristol Theatre Collection
University of Bristol

Various drafts of *A Woman of No Importance*, once the property of Herbert Beerbohm Tree. The material comprises the following:

HBT 18(a)/1. Property list and prompt copy with autograph revisions of *A Woman of No Importance* with diagrams of sets.

HBT 18(a)/2. Carbon copy of typescript of HBT 18(a)/1 with autograph corrections in pencil.

HBT 18(a)/3. Typescript of *A Woman of No Importance* incorporating autograph corrections to HBT 18(a)/2.

HBT 18(a)/4. Carbon copy of HBT 18(a)/3 with notes in pencil and diagrams in black and red ink.

HBT 18(a)/5. Carbon copy of typescript with autograph corrections of *A Woman of No Importance.* Incorporates autograph corrections made to HBT 18(a)/1. Clearly a working copy of the play. Text has stage directions and business and bears the inscription "As revived at His Majesty's Theatre May 22nd 1907."

HBT 18/1. Four acts of *Mrs Arbuthnot,* marked "prompt copy"; with five actors' parts for *Mrs Arbuthnot* used in rehearsal. Notes by Tree including memoranda for alterations. Eleven further actors' parts.

HBT 18/2. Carbon copy of typescript from HBT 18(a)/5.

HBT 114. Thirteen actors' parts and prompt copy of *A Woman of No Importance* for Charles Hartley's 1904 provincial tour.

HBT 122. Typescript with autograph corrections entitled *Mrs Arbuthnot*. Marked "2nd." on cover.

HBT 129. Typescript entitled *A Woman of No Importance*. An unmarked copy which incorporates autograph corrections made to HBT 122.

Harry Ransom Humanities Research Center
University of Texas

[Untitled poem]. Unpublished ALS "And many an Afghan Chief ...."

Written for James E. Kelly; removed from a drawing of Oscar Wilde and a young boy.

> And many an Afghan chief who lies
>   Beneath his cool pomegranate trees,
> Clutches his sword in fierce surmise,
>   When on the mountainside he sees
>
> The fleet-foot marri scout who comes
>   To tell how he has heard afar
> The measured roll of English drums
>   Beat at the gates of Kandahar.
>
>   Oscar Wilde
>   Written for James E. Kelly
>   Jany 14th '82

"Lily-flower." Unpublished AMS 1878.

One folio, written on lined paper (has "lazy. —" below left of Wilde's signature).

> A ring of gold and a milkwhite dove
>   Are goodly gifts for thee,
> And a hempen rope for your own love
>   To hang upon a tree.

[The New Remorse]. AMS copy in the hand of Lord Alfred Douglas entitled "Oscar Wilde's Best Sonnet" (see Appendix 1).

PAN; a double villanelle and DESESPOIR, a sonnet.

Printed booklet of poems with AMSS; the MS of "Pan" is not that printed here or in Ross (see Appendix 2).

La Remarquable fusée. Traduction d'Alexandre Renolds.

TMS with autograph corrections in green ink. (In the HRHRC catalogue the attribution is to a Lord Heron—"Traduit de l'anglais par Lord Heron.") n.d.

[A Florentine Tragedy]
AMS/draft fragments and workings; written in a notebook, bound in limp roan, 43ff., paper watermarked D.K. & Co., London. Early sketch of the play in pencil, with revisions and emendations in ink. Pencil notes made at different times. Two sorts of revisions made in pen. No *dramatis personae*; no attribution of speeches; no parts; no act or scene divisions. Contains four small pen and ink sketches. Like the early drafts of other plays, there are speech fragments, but no dramatic structure. Lines, phrases and speeches embodied in the finished play.

"A Good Woman" *[Lady Windermere's Fan]*
TMS with A revisions; 71ff. [1892]. All acts typed at Mrs Marshall's Type Writing Office, 128 Strand. Text very similar to the Licensing Copy.

Act I No corrections. No emendations to verso.

Act II Corrections in Wilde's hand; additions to appropriate verso. Additions to stage directions *not* in Wilde's hand; additions to business in text. Corrections in pencil and in ink in Alexander's and Wilde's hand. Particularly heavy revisions to verso of ff. 15, 16, 17, and 18.

At the point where the Duchess of Berwick refers to Australia, Alexander adds "Keep this in" and later "<u>in</u> <u>in</u> <u>in</u>" (each time double underlined and circled).

Act III contains Wilde's corrections on verso of ff. 5, 7, 8; and Alexander's alterations to stage directions. Corrections are of two sorts—in pencil and in ink.

Act IV contains Wilde's MS corrections throughout, particularly on verso of ff. 1 and 9.

Salomé; drame en un acte
AMS with A revisions.

Notebook dated November 1891, Paris; black cloth covers.

Holding carries a letter of probity, stating that the Rosenbach MS is longer, written in two notebooks of British origin. The HRHRC MS is written in one notebook purchased near Wilde's address in Paris when he was working on the play.

"Mrs Arbuthnot" [A Woman Of No Importance]
TMS with A revisions in several hands; identifiable are those of Wilde and Beerbohm Tree. 129ff. in six books. All acts typed at Mrs Marshall's Type Writing Office, 128 Strand.

One draft of Acts I, II and IV; three copies, in different states, of Act III, one containing a paste-up of MS fragments.

Act I Corrections only infrequently in Wilde's hand.

Plans for stage set on verso of f.17.

Act II (first copy): passages marked for deletion and revision mainly in Wilde's hand in both pen and ink; in ff. 16–19 passages marked for deletion in Wilde's hand and "I don't think so" on f. 16 also in his hand, an indication perhaps that the draft was being read by different individuals on different occasions.

Act II (second copy): mainly unattributable deletions. At one point Wilde writes "Mrs. Tree must not emphasize here too much" (Maud Tree was playing Mrs Allonby). Ff. 15 and 16 are in manuscript in two hands, neither of which is Wilde's. These folios are formed from passages taken from different sheets of paper, pasted together to form one sheet, one of which is Haymarket Theatre notepaper. This copy ends at f. 16 and is unfinished.

Act II (third copy): has the same manuscript corrections as the second copy. Deletions and revisions not in Wilde's hand and in two sorts of pencil.

Act III contains Wilde's corrections to verso and recto, and stage directions to Tree concerning the speech of Lord Illingworth about youth: "Tree not emphasise this." Business over the name of Harford marked for deletion in Wilde's hand—"Cut writing." Verso has the direction: "With more emphasis." At f. 15 verso, opposite "Hester. Are you quite alone, Mrs Arbuthnot?," Tree writes "This is a bombshell/ said suddenly." At f. 17 verso: Wilde writes (over Mrs Arbuthnot's long speech) "No gesture at chair," relating perhaps to HBT stage directions suggested by Tree.

Act IV has a rough stage plan on verso of title page, and stage directions which are *not* in Wilde's hand. Throughout the act passages marked for deletion are in brown pencil, and the revisions in Wilde's hand are on the facing verso.

[*Translation from Turgenev*]: "A Fire at Sea."
AMS in ink in 25 folios, with ff. 1–5 missing. Bound in green. MS corrections in ink and in pencil. Anonymously printed as "A Fire At Sea" in *Macmillan's Magazine*, liv, no. 319 (May 1886), 39–44, and not reprinted. See Mason p. 111.

The Importance of Being Earnest
Bound page-proofs corrected in Wilde's hand (and others). 160 pp. Dated December 1898. Contains details of print-run: 1000 copies, 100 printed on large paper, both numbered. *Dramatis personae* corrected in MS (not Wilde's hand). In general corrections pay attention to emphasis; so, for example, Thomas Cardew's address is corrected from "the Glen, Fifeshire, N.B." to "the Sporran, Fifeshire, N.B." Corrections dated from 11.11.98 to 19.11.98. See Jackson (1980).

Pierpont Morgan Library

MA 3576. An early holograph draft of Act III of *Lady Windermere's Fan* written in a notebook in sixteen leaves.

MA 3579. Typescript, with extensive autograph revisions, of Act III of *An Ideal Husband*, stamped at Mrs Marshall's Type Writing Office, 24 January 1894. Accompanying note states that the typescript post-dates manuscript drafts of the act at the Clark and British Libraries, but predates the typescript draft at the British Library.

MA 883. Signed AMS of the original periodical version of *The Picture of Dorian Gray* in 264 leaves. The Clark typescript was prepared from this manuscript.

MA 3149. AMS of ten pages in a copybook of chapter 5 of *The Picture of Dorian Gray*.

MA 737. "Latin Unseen." A holograph of translations made by Wilde while an undergraduate at Oxford of Tacitus's *Annals*, 3: 26, and Lucretius's *De Rerum Natura*, 4: 749-76.

MA 3574. AMS in forty-five leaves. Identified by the catalogue as an essay and review of J. A. Symonds's *Studies of the Greek Poets*, but incomplete.

Princeton University Library

WIA-WILK. AMS in 7 pp. A fragment of a notebook containing translations from Hugo and Mallarmé.

CO213. AMS of "Hélas" in one leaf.

CO213. AMS draft of a prose piece entitled "The Master" in 5 leaves.

RTC01. Three undated AMS of epigrams, two of one page, and one of four pages.

RTC01. AMS dated 1891 in one page of a poem "To My Friend Luther Munday."

RTC01. Two pages from a draft of *The Duchess of Padua*.

RTC01. AMS in fifteen pages of the scenario of the *Cardinal of Avignon*.

RTC01. A folio notebook of 61 leaves, perhaps the beginning of Act II of *The Cardinal of Avignon*.

RTC01. AMS in five pages of the scenario of *The Duchess of Padua* (under the title of the *Duchess of Florentine*, as submitted to Mary Anderson.

William Andrews Clark Memorial Library
University of California

Wilde W6721M. C697. [1887–1900].
Collection of 80 letters, essays, poems, and plays: all forgeries by Fabian Lloyd, the son of Constance Wilde's brother, Otho Lloyd.

Wilde W6721Z. C6975. Boxed.
Collection of papers relating to the publishing history of works of Wilde. 128 items. Mostly material related to the publishing history of the works after Ross's edition.

In October 1909 John W. Luce published *The Poems of Oscar Wilde*, the first volume in the American edition of Ross's first collected edition of the works of Wilde. The plates for the volume were taken from the Methuen edition published in London in the previous year. The only difference in the American edition was the inclusion of two further poems, "Désespoir" and "Pan." The Prospectus for the Boston edition contained a note from Ross dated 11 November 1909 which was subsequently printed in the volume of poems. There is an undated manuscript note by Ross (*PR5811 F08B), which is a draft of his letter for the Prospectus:

> This collection of Wilde's poems contains "Ravenna," the volume of 1881 in its entirety, the "Sphinx," and the "Ballad of Reading Gaol." Of the Uncollected Poems published in the Uniform Edition of 1908 a few, including the Translations from the Greek and the Polish, are omitted. Two new poems "Désespoir" and "Pan," which I have recently discovered in manuscript, are now printed for the first time.
>
> Robert Ross

A further item (*PR5811 F09L) contains a copy of the Prospectus for the Luce edition. Mason notes that for the purposes of copyright, the text of the two poems were set up and published simultaneously as a pamphlet. A copy of the Luce pamphlet is held at the HRHRC. Mason notes that an early version of "Pan" was published in a periodical also entitled *Pan* edited by Alfred Thompson in September 1880, well before the appearance of *Poems* (1881). This earlier version is significantly different from the later Luce edition: whatever manuscript Ross discovered, it certainly was not that of the 1880 text. But neither printed version is the same as the MS "Pan" held at the HRHRC. Fong (1978) discusses the various versions of the poem (p. 257). He does not note, however, that Wilde's compositional procedures here—the cancelling of lines and their subsequent and re-insertion into later drafts, the substitution of a word for its antonym, and so on—seem to mimic on a miniature scale what is known about the composition of the plays.

Another item (*PR5819 P851 cop 2) contains an auction catalogue for Sotheby, Wilkinson and Hodge dated 27 July 1911:

> A Collection of Autograph Manuscripts, Printed Books, Newspaper Cuttings, & c., By and relating to Oscar Wilde. The Property of a Gentleman.

Many of the lots were later included in the sale of material belonging to Robert Ross, C.S. Millard and Vyvyan Holland (the Dulau sale) sold to the Clark Library in 1928. Lot 200 refers to the following:

> Translation from Ivan Tourgenieff, MS. on 24½ pp. (lacking the first five pages and pages 12 and 13), apparently unpublished.

(This MS is now held in the HRHRC [see above].) A further item (marked *PR5828 K54L) contains a copy of George Herbert Kersley, "'The Yard': Memories of the House of Cassell," *Sunday Times*, 19 Sept. 1920, a memoir of Wilde at *Woman's World.*

Wilde W6721M3. A516. [1886?]. Bound. Finzi 2417.
"Amiel and Lord Beaconsfield." Unpublished AMS in pencil in 7 leaves. Not in Mason. Review occasioned by publication of translation of Amiel's *Journal Intime* and correspondence of Lord Beaconsfield (Benjamin Disraeli) in 1885. MS appears to be a fair copy.

Wilde W6721M1. A524. [187?]. Finzi 2418.
["Amor Intellectualis"]. AMS fragmentary early drafts of last stanza of poem in 2 pp. See Fong, p. 83 and p. 537.

Wilde W6721M3. A784. [1882]. Bound. Finzi 2419.
["Art and the handicraftsman"]. AMS in 3 leaves. Autograph fragments for a lecture, partly written in Philadelphia in 1882. Fair copy. The text is not continuous, and is a version of last page of essay published in Ross's *Miscellanies, Collected Works* (1908), XIV, 308.

Wilde W6721M3. A784. [1882]a. Bound. Finzi 2420.
["Art and the handicraftsman"]. Original AMS fragment in 8 leaves; on paper headed "J.M. Stoddart/ Publishers/ Philadelphia." See *Miscellanies, Collected Works* (1908), XIV, 305, line 34 to 307, line 18. Original title of work is erroneously given on MS as "The English Renaissance of Art."

Wilde W6721M3. A784. [1882]b. Bound. Finzi 2421.
["Art and the handicraftsman"]. Incomplete typescript draft of 7 pages with AMS emendations. The spelling of some words (e.g., "labor") is American, and so this copy was almost certainly made in the USA. Corresponds to Ross's *Miscellanies, Collected Works* (1908), XIV, 252, line 20 to 254, line 27.

Wilde W6721M3. A784. [1882]c. Bound. Finzi 2422.
["Art and the handicraftsman"]. Typescript 13 pages with AMS emendations out of a total of 44. It corresponds to Ross's *Miscellanies, Collected Works* (1908), XIV, as follows: f.14—pp. 252–54; ff.30–31—pp. 266–68; f.33—pp. 268–69; f.35—pp. 270–71; ff.37–41—pp. 272–75; ff.41–43—pp. 305–308.

Wilde W6721M2. B369. [188–]. Finzi 2423.
[*Beatrice and Astone Manfredi*]. Photostat of autograph page of play. One leaf. Appears to be a fair copy.

Wilde W6721M1. B438. [1876?]. Bound. Finzi 2424.
AMS "La belle Gabrielle" [An unpublished poem from the French]. AMS in 2 leaves.

> [Love] could I charm the silver breasted moon
> To lie with me upon the Latvian hill. . .

Appears to be a fair copy. See Fong. pp. 168–69, 419, 551.

Wilde W6721M1. B949. [187–?]. Finzi 2425.
AMS ["The burden of Itys"]. Three line fragment of an early draft. One leaf. MS is marked "189–?" in error.

Wilde W6721M3. C2673. [1896 Nov.].
[*The Cardinal of Avignon—a sketch*] MS of 5 leaves in holograph of More Adey. Verso of fifth folio reads:

> Sketch of Senario [sic]
> of The Cardinal of Avignon
> by Oscar Wilde
> Copied by More Adey Nov/96
> by permission of Wm Wilde

and:

> "Sent to Dick [Richard Mansfield]
> 18 April 1894
> received reply 17 May 1894."

Paper headed "11, Upper Phillimore Gardens,/ Kensington,/ London. W./" on right and "Telegrams/'Spadino' London" on left. (Printed in Mason, pp. 583–85.)

[f.1]

The Cardinal of Avignon

by

Oscar Wilde

The play opens in the palace of the Cardinal at Avignon. The Cardinal is alone and somewhat excited for he has received news that the Pope is sick and about to die. "What if they were to elect me Pope?" he says this giving the keynote of his inordinate ambition. Nobles and Princes enter and the Cardinal who knows the vices and pleasures of each one, solicits and obtains promises of their votes, by promising each of them the fulfilment of some of their personal aims and desires. They exeunt and the Cardinal says "Will God place me on such a pinacle [*sic*]?" and he has a fine speech with regard to the Papacy. A servant enters and says a lady wishes to see him. He refuses—but the lady, a beautiful young girl, the ward of the Cardinal's, enters. She upbraids him for refusing to see her and a very pretty and affectionate scene occurs between them. In the course of the conversation the girl says "You have spoken to me of many things, but there is one thing you never told me about, and that is Love." "And do you know what Love is?" "Yes, for I love!" Then she explains to the Cardinal that she has plighted her troth to a handsome young man who some time since came to the Cardinal's Court and has been made much of by the Prelate. The Prelate is much upset and makes her promise not to mention this conversation to her lover. When his ward has left him the Cardinal is filled with rage and sorrow: "And so my sin of 20 years ago has risen up against me, and come to rob me of the only thing I love"—The young man is his son.—

[f.2]

The scene now changes to some gardens at the rear of the Palace. The Cardinal's ward and her betrothed are together. They have a passionate love scene. The young man mindful of what they both owe to the Cardinal, asks his betrothed whether she has told the Cardinal of their betrothal. She also mindful of her promise, says: "No."—He urges her to do so as soon as possible. At this point there enters a pageant and suddenly a masque of death appears. This alarms the girl who sees in it a presage of some coming woe. Her lover scouts the idea saying: "What have you and I with our new-born love, to do with Death? Death is not for such as you and I." The pageant comes to an end, and the lovers part; the girl in leaving drops her glove. The Cardinal comes out of the Palace, picks up the glove and at the same time sees the young man. He is furious: "So they have met."—He is determined he will not lose the only thing he loves and so in the course of conversation he tells the young man, who desires to be told of his father, that years ago a mighty prince on his death bed entrusted his two children to the Cardinal's care. "Am I one of those children?" "You are." "Then I have a brother?" "No, but a sister." "A sister! Where is she? Why do I not know her?" "You do know her; she is the girl to whom you have betrothed yourself!"—The young man is horror and grief stricken. The Cardinal, without however betraying his own relationship, urges him to pluck this impossible love from his heart and also to kill it in the heart of the girl. She now re-enters and the Cardinal explains that her lover finds he has made a serious mistake and does not love her sufficiently to wed her. This portion of the play winds up with a powerful scene between the two lovers, the young man rigidly carrying out the promise exacted from him by the Cardinal. The scene now changes back to the interior of the palace as at the opening of the play. The Cardinal is alone and is already repenting of the deed of yesterday. He is miserable.

[f.3]

A struggle is going on within him between his ambition and his love. He is desperately in love with his ward, and at the same time he doubts whether with such a sin on his soul, God will raise him to the papacy. Trumpets are heard. Nobles and Princes enter. The Pope is dead and he has been elected Pope in his place. He is now the Pope. The Nobles & c after making obeisance, exeunt. The Cardinal is radiant: "I who was but now in the mire am now placed so high, Christ's Vicar on earth & c & c." A fine speech. Now his ambition conquers. He sends for the young man. "What I told you yesterday was simply done to test you. You and your betrothed are no relations. Go, find her and I will marry you to her tonight before I ride away to Rome." At this moment the huge doors at the end of the hall are thrown open and there enter friars bearing a bier covered with a pall, which they proceed to set down in the centre of the hall, and then exeunt, without speaking a word. Both men intuitively feel who is the occupant of the bier. The young girl has killed herself in despair at the loss of her lover. The Cardinal opens the doors and says to the soldiers outside: "Do not enter here whatever you may hear until I walk forth again[.]" He then re-enters the room and draws a heavy bolt across the doors. The young man then says: "Now I am going to kill you." The Pope answers: "I shall not defend myself, but I will plead with you." He then urges upon the young man the sanctity of the papal office & c & c; and represents the horrible sacrilege of such a murder. "No, you cannot kill the Pope." "Such a crime has no horror for me, I shall kill you." The Pope the[n] reveals to him that he is his father, and places before him the hideous crime of patricide. "You cannot kill your father." "Nothing

[f.4]

in me responds to your appeal. I have no filial feelings. I shall kill you." The Pope now goes to the bier and draws back the pall and says: "I too loved her[.]" At this the young man runs and flings open the doors and says: "His Holiness will ride hence tonight on his way to Rome." The Pope is standing blessing the corpse, and as he does so, the young man throws himself on the bier between the Pope and the corpse and stabs himself. The soldiers, Nobles & c re-enter and the Pope still stands blessing—

Curtain

Wilde W6721M1. C545. [1874/8]. Bound. Finzi 2426.
["Choir boy" and other fragments of unpublished poems. MSS. 5 pp. The poems are:

"The choir boy";

["Sweet I went out in the night"];

["There is no peace beneath the moon"] the first verse of which is repeated in "Lotus leaves" (Ross, pp. 241); see Mason pp. 82–83. The first version of "Lotus leaves" appeared in *The Irish Monthly* (Feb. 1877).

["See! the gold sun has risen!"].

See Fong (1978), pp. 24, 30, 28, 51.

Wilde W6721M3. C734. [188–?]. Boxed. Finzi 2427.
Commonplace book. [A collection of notes on various topics]. A bound AMS notebook of 133 pages. See Philip E. Smith II and Michael S. Helfand, eds., *Oscar Wilde's Oxford Notebooks* (1989).

Wilde W6721M3. D278. [1913]. Finzi 2428.
De Profundis. Typescript made by C.S. Millard of the "Unpublished extracts of De Profundis." A collation of newspaper extracts, typescript and holograph passages. Many autograph corrections.

Wilde Temp MSS 30552S. [11 Jan. 1984].
De Profundis. Typescript transcription containing several variants from Hart–Davis's transcription. Paper has American watermark. No MS emendations.

Wilde E 91. 142 MS Wilde. [From Sotheby's sale of 13 Dec. 1990].
"The Suppressed Portion of De Profundis." Typescript, marked up
with changes and annotations in an unidentified hand, but which
corresponds to the text printed by Hart–Davis (1962). Contains an
ALS from Alfred Douglas to Murrough O'Brien dated 13 Oct. 1939
which outlines the circumstances under which Douglas would agree
to the publication of the "suppressed portion":

> 1 St Ann's Court
> Nizell's Avenue,
> Hove 2, Sussex

> . . . A great many of the things that OW said about me in the letter are,
> not only demonstrably, but *admittedly and obviously*, untrue. E.g: when
> he says that he never wrote a line when he was in my company, whereas
> the plain truth is that from the moment when I met him till he died he
> never wrote anything at all when I was away from him. The one exception
> being this unpublished part of De Profundis, which is *a letter to me!*

Wilde W6721M3. D758. [188-?]. Finzi 2429.
[Draft review of D.G. Rossetti's poems]. Unpublished AMS in 5
leaves. Probably early 1880s. There is no argument; instead only
fragments of a review in the form of scattered observations, much in
the manner of other early draft material. About Rossetti: "he has the
perfect articulateness of the real artist"; "like another great leader of
the romantic school he has become a classic in his own lifetime";
"the strength and splendour of his own dominant personality."

Wilde W6721M2. D829. [1881–3]. Bound. Finzi 2430.
The Duchess of Padua. AMS 122 leaves. Together with contract (in
holograph) of the agreement between Wilde and Hamilton Griffiths,
manager of Mary Anderson. Also correspondence about Anderson's
decision to delay staging of the play. In ink; with deletions and
emendations. The text is incomplete and without full stage directions.

Title page reads:

> The Duchess of Padua
> a tragedy in five acts
> written for Mary Anderson
> by
> Oscar Wilde.

Very different from item *PR5817 D821, the first printed edition of the play. Clark Library has an autographed copy of that edition bearing the following:

> Written in Paris in XIX Century
> Privately printed as manuscript.

The edition contains full stage directions, with Wilde's estimates of the lengths of each act, and is dated 15 March 1883. The copy text for this version is not the MS of the play held at the Clark.

Wilde W6721M2. D829. [1882?]. Finzi 2431.
The Duchess of Padua. MS in 2 leaves; characters' names and a fragment of dialogue. Four-line fragment written on lined paper taken from a notebook. Seems evidence of an early draft of play. Distinct from previous item.

Wilde W6721L. G646. [1878?]. Bound. Finzi 2431a.
"Easter day." Fair MS copy of sonnet sent to *Good Words.* First published, however, in *Waifs and Strays,* 1 (June 1879). MS is dated "Rome 1877," but Fong (p. 381) notes that on Easter day in 1877 Wilde was in Brindisi en route for Greece. MS has variations from printed versions of poem. See Fong, p. 71 and pp. 527–28. Filed with copy of letter to *Good Words* offering poem for publication:

> 1 Merrion Square. N
> Dublin

Mr Oscar Wilde begs to enclose two sonnets for publication in "Good Words" if approved of.

If accepted Mr Wilde would be very much obliged if they were printed on a full half page, *without the intersecting line,* which destroys the appearance of a sonnet very much.

Mr Wilde would not like them both to appear in the same month, as there is a slight similarity of rhyme in them.

The other poem referred to is "Sonnet (Written after hearing Mozart's 'Dies Irae' sung in Magdalen Chapel)." See item W6721L G646 [1878?] Bound—"Sonnet (Written after hearing Mozart's 'Dies Irae' sung in MagdalenChapel)" described below; the publishing history of the poem is noted by Fong, pp. 381–82, and 528–29.

Wilde W6721M1. E56. [187–?]. Finzi 2432.
["Endymion"]. MS, one leaf of fragments of two stanzas and jottings.

Wilde W6721M1. E56. [1876?] Bound. Finzi 2433.
["Endymion"]. AMS in 5 pp; 4 recto, 1 verso. Early manuscript fragments on different sorts of paper, probably at different moments in poem's composition. Last folio has *"Verona"* at foot. Corresponds to lines 29–42 of printed poem. See Fong, p. 545.

Wilde W6721M3. E58. [1882?]. Finzi 2434.
["The English Renaissance"]. Manuscript fragment with corrections of lecture delivered at Chickering Hall, NY, 9 Jan. 1882. MS in 3 leaves on lined paper, torn from notebook. A clean, perhaps fair copy. See Ross's *Miscellanies, Collected Works*, (1908), XIV, 252, line 20 to 254, line 6.

Wilde W6721M3. E58. [1882]a. Bound. Finzi 2435.
["The English Renaissance"]. AMS in ink with MS corrections: portion (in 17 leaves) of lecture delivered at Chickering Hall, NY, 9 January, 1882. Pagination is from 105–121; corresponds to Ross's *Miscellanies, Collected Works*, (1908), XIV, 270, line 25 to 275, line 18. Page 118 is in a different ink, and belongs to a different MS, perhaps a fair copy.

Wilde W6721M3. E58. [1882 Feb. 9]. Finzi 2436.
["The English Renaissance"]. A typed version of a stenographic report of the lecture by the *Buffalo Courier* (NY), 9 February 1882. Not identical with the version published by Ross. Begins at Ross's *Miscellanies, Collected Works*, (1908), XIV, 249, line 12; first page transcribed here is not in Ross. Final pages of transcription contains material taken from "Art and the Handicraftsman," showing that Wilde was considerably changing his lectures as his American tour progressed.

Wilde W6721M3. E58. [1882]. Bound. Finzi 2437.
["The English Renaissance"]. Original typescript with AMS manuscript corrections and deletions. Typescript paginated from 8–49, corresponding to Ross's *Miscellanies, Collected Works*, (1908), XIV, 248, line 2 to 275, line 8. Omits pp. 243–47 and final three paragraphs of the text of Ross's version of the essay. In addition there are numerous local variants.

Wilde W6721M3. E64. [189–?]. Finzi 2438.
[Epigrams]. MS with corrections on one lined folio, numbered "8," taken from a notebook. Contains the following (only some of which were published):

It is perfectly scandalous the way people go about nowadays saying things against one behind one's back that are absolutely and entirely true.

Credit is the only thing a gentleman should live on.

Those who pay their bills are soon forgotten.

One's buttonhole may be allowed to be romantic in feeling, but one's necktie should be distinctively most classical in both style and treatment.

The old should be neither seen nor heard.

To become a work of art is the object of living.

Pleasure is what we take from others, Duty what we expect from others, and Genius what we deny to others.

What is called insincerity is simply a method by which we can multiply our personality. One should never be useful. Only the uncivilized are useful.

Wilde W6721M3. E64. [189–?]. Finzi 2439.
[Epigrams and aphorisms]. MSS with corrections. 8 leaves. On pages taken from a notebook, but not that of previous item. Heavy deletions and emendations. Some entries are deleted in their entirety. Contains the following (only some of which were published):

Beautiful and affected manners will rob virtue of half its grossness.

Most women are so artificial that they have no sense of art. Most men are so natural that they have no sense of beauty.

The smallest affectation will rob virtue of half its grossness.

If one tells the truth one is sure, sooner or later, to be found out.

Those who see any difference between soul and body have neither.

The criminal classes are so close to us that even the policeman can see them. They are so far away from us that only the poet can understand them.

It is only by the continual contemplation of one's own perfection that one can hope to become perfect.

Dullness is the coming of age of seriousness.

Whenever the necessities of life are cheaper than the luxuries of life the community becomes uncivilized. Bread should be always dearer than flowers.

When at the end of each year the English make up their national ledger, they balance their stupidity by their wealth, and their vices by their hypocrisy.

Foolish people say that one would sacrifice anybody for the sake of an epigram, but the world goes to the altar of its own accord.

There is nothing to be said in favour of anyone's principles. There is much to be said in favour of everyone's prejudices.

Philanthropic people lose all sense of humanity. It is always their distinguishing characteristic.

In old days men of letters wrote books and the public read them. Nowadays books are written by the public and nobody reads them.

Those who love once only in their lives are the really shallow lovers.

The English are the most extraordinarily hardworking race. They are the only nation now left in Europe that takes the trouble to be hypocritical.

To be really mediaeval one should have no body. To be really modern one should have no soul. To be thoroughly Greek one should have no clothes.

Ambition is the last refuge of the failure.

Very young people imagine that money is everything. When they grow older they know it.

One should never makes one's *début* with a scandal. One should reserve that to lend an interest to one's maturer years.

Beer, the Bible and the seven deadly virtues have made our England what it is.

The public are quite charming. The only offensive thing about them is their brass-band. Journalists are the brass-band of the public.

There are as many publics as there are personalities.

It is very sad nowadays that there is so little useless information.

One should spend one's days in saying what is incredible, and one's evenings in doing what is improbable.

It is perfectly monstrous the way people go about nowadays saying things against one behind one's back that are absolutely and entirely true.

When a woman marries again it is because she detested her first husband. When a man marries again it is because he adored his first wife. Women try their luck. Men risk theirs.

I like men who have a future and women who have a past.

Religion is the fashionable substitute for Belief.

A great Empire has been forced upon the English. They have carried their burden as far as the Stock Exchange.

Everything is a poison. But there are two kinds of poisons. There are the poisons that kill, and the poisons that keep alive. The last are the more terrible.

There is something really tragic about the enormous number of young men there are in England who start life with perfect profiles, and end by adopting some useful profession.

Women marry in order to find peace, and take lovers in the hopes of having excitement. In both cases they are disappointed.

Shallow sorrows and shallow loves live on. The loves and sorrows that are great die by their own plenitude.

Good resolutions are simply cheques that men draw on a Bank where they have no account.

In old days people had a great respect for grey hairs. Now they have a great respect for dyed hair. That shows a distinct advance.

Most women are so artificial that they have no sense of art. Most men are so natural that they have no sense of Beauty.

Dandyism is the assertion of the absolute modernity of Beauty.

In the development of the intellectual life it is only those who know where they are going that ever lose their way.

The journalist is always reminding the public of the existence of the artist. That is immoral of him.

The journalist is always reminding the artist of the existence of the public. That is indecent of him.

Many movements begin with the appearance of the Disciples, and end with the arrival of the Founder.

Miracles always happen. That is why one cannot believe in them.

It is much more difficult to talk about a thing than to do it.

The intellectual stagnation of the English as a race is a proof of the fatal influence of a permanent income on Thought.

In mad and coloured loves there is much danger. There is the danger of losing them no less than the danger of keeping them.

Man can only worship his inferiors. That is the intellectual weakness of all cosmogonies[?] and the emotional strength of all religions.

Death and vulgarity are the only two facts in the nineteenth century that one cannot explain away.

The things about which one feels absolutely certain are never true. That is the fatality of Faith, and the lesson of Romance.

Art has a soul, but man has not.

I can believe anything provided it is quite incredible.

No crime is vulgar. But all vulgarity is crime. Vulgarity is the conduct of other people.

An artist can create a passion. But no one, except a sentimentalist, can repeat an emotion.

The tragedy of the poor is that they have no real passion for pleasure.

When a play that is a work of Art is produced on the stage what is being tested is not the play but the stage.

When a play that is not a work of art is produced on the stage what is being tested is not the play but the public.

In the presence of a work of art the public should applaud and the journalist be silent.

The applause of the public is the only thing that keeps one from sleeping.

The real value of the disciple, is that at the moment of one's triumph he whispers in one's ear that after all one is immortal.

Wilde W6721M3. E78. [1886?]. Bound. Finzi 2440.
[*Essay on Chatterton*]. AMS notebook, partly in ink, partly in pencil. About 70 pages of manuscript, liberally interspersed with printed clippings from biographies of Chatterton by Daniel Wilson and David Masson. Apparently intended for publication in *The Century Guild Hobby Horse*. See Mason, pp. 13–14. The lecture ends with a poem by Rossetti, not Wilde; see Roger Lewis (1990).

Wilde W6721M3. E96. [1873?]. Bound. Finzi 2441.
[*Exercise book used for Greek and Latin studies at Trinity College, Dublin*]. MS in 19p. Mostly jottings about Latin grammar and idioms. Occasional translations of lines.

Wilde W6721M3. H286. [9 Dec. 1904]. Finzi 2442.
Fantaisies decoratives. Decorated MS transcript by Walter Ledger. With similar transcript of "The Harlot's House." Both presented to C.S. Millard.

Wilde W6721M3. F537. [1891]. Bound. Finzi 2443.
["The Fisherman and his Soul"]. MS in 4 leaves on lined paper torn from notebook in what appears to a fair copy; pages numbered from 31–34. Few MS corrections. Clark index claims that the manuscript is the concluding portion of the original autograph MS; in fact it corresponds to first edition of *House of Pomegranates* (1891), 93–96; and to Ross, *House of Pomegranates, Collected Works*, X, 96, line 10 to 99, line 16.

Wilde W6721M2. F633. [1893]. Bound. Finzi 2444.
[*A Florentine Tragedy*]. MS in 13 leaves. Pencil and ink on lined paper, with pencil and ink corrections. First two folios are unnumbered; remaining folios are Ross's copy-text for 1908 *Collected Edition* (vol. II), and run as follows: ff. 1–7 are printed as pp. 85–94; ff. 20–23 are printed as pp. 109–114. The MS is mentioned by Mason, p. 465. Of the two remaining folios, Mason prints one and the first part of the first speech of the second. It is not in Ross's edition, and seems to be a fragment of an alternative opening for the play:

[f.1]

   Bianca, a beautiful woman, is kneeling before an image of the Madonna. She is simply but beautifully dressed.

[f.2]

Enter by Window, Guido

Guido—   Last night it snowed in Florence, but tonight
            It rains red roses. Nay, my gentle dove,
            Why do you lure the hawk to follow you, visit
            And then grow timorous? Do you know my name?

Bianca —   Too well. Too well.
            You are that terrible Lord, whom men call love,

                    homely
            And I a common burgher's unloved wife.
            It is enough that I have looked on you.

Guido —No, by St James, but it is not enough.

Bianca —Tell me your name. Nay do not tell your name.
            Love having many names has yet but one.
            I am content, so I may touch your cheek,
            Or smooth these tangled blossoms.
                        How fair you are!
            Fair as that young St. Michael on the wall
            Of Santa Croce where we go and pray.
            Your throat like milk, your mouth a scarlet flower
            Whose petals prison music, and your eyes
            Wild woodland wells in which dark violets see
            Their purple shadows drown.
                        Our Florence lilies
            Are white and red, but you have lily and rose
            Yet in one garden.

Wilde W6721M2. F633. [1893]a. Bound. Finzi 2445.
[*A Florentine Tragedy*]. MS in 5 leaves. Pencil and ink on lined paper
with pencil and ink corrections. The first, unnumbered folio—the
setting of the play—is reproduced by Mason, p. 463; but the MS which
he reproduces is not that of the remaining folios. The second folio is
a pencil draft of what could be an opening scene. Among other lines
it contains the following:

                Then do not go till dawn:
                    Ah! what is that?
                How swiftly come the feet

> Simone is my name;
> A merchant of this city here.
> This is my wife Bianca.

The final three folios are numbered 10, 11, 12, and are part of the MS described above. They correspond to Ross's edition as follows:

> f. 10 corresponds to p. 99, line 9 to p. 98, line 2 (to the break in the text in Ross's edition); ff. 12 and 13 correspond to p. 99, line 16 ("Oh would that death. . .") to p. 102, line 4 ("her virtues as most women have.").

Wilde W6721M3. F811. [188?].
[Fragment] Begins "Elder-tree, there stands a neglected grave." MS one leaf, in ink on lined paper; it appears to be a fair copy:

> Elder-tree, there stands a neglected grave. The grass grows thick and rank around it, and the weeds have covered it all over. No bird ever sings there, and even the sunbeams seem to avoid the spot. Yet in that lonely grave the most beautiful woman in the world lies asleep. Her throat is like a reed of ivory, and her mouth is like a ripe pomegranate. Like threads of fine gold are the threads of her flowing hair, and the turquoise is not so blue as her blue eyes.

Wilde W6721M3. F811. [Dec. 1891]. Bound. Finzi 2446.
[Fragment of a draft reply to the critics of *A House of Pomegranates*]. MS in 4 leaves, with emendations and corrections. Printed by Mason, pp. 368–69.

Wilde W6721M3. F811. [1882]. Finzi 2447.
[Fragment of the original manuscript of a lecture delivered in Philadelphia]. MS in one leaf. [Recorded as missing 5 August 1981.]

Wilde W6721M2. L157. [1892?]. Boxed. Finzi 2448.
A Good Woman [*Lady Windermere's Fan*]. Four acts in four notebooks; typescript with corrections and additions in Wilde's hand. For place in stemma of play, see Small (1980).

Wilde W6721M3. G793. [1873]. Bound. Finzi 2449.
AMS notebook bearing title in Wilde's hand of "Greek Proverbs collected from the fragments of Comic dramatists both of old and new Comedy." Dated "Michaelmas 1873, Trin[ity] Coll[ege]." Mostly in Greek; with notes and parts in Latin. Also notes on metre, Greek

vocabulary, notes jotted in English, Latin translations, and notes from philosophy lectures showing that Wilde was reading Alexander Bain, George Grote, and John Stuart Mill on formal logic, particularly on the nature of propositions.

Wilde W6721M1. H286. [April 1881]. Bound.
["The Harlot's House"]. AMS in 4 leaves in ink. Copy of part of poem, together with jottings. Fragmentary manuscript in Wilde's hand, differing from the published version. See Fong, p. 285 and p. 593. MS does not correspond to extract of sale catalogue bound with it.

Wilde W6721M1. H286. [9 Dec. 1904]. Finzi 2450.
["The Harlot's House"]. 13p. Decorated MS transcript by Walter Ledger.

Wilde W6721M1. H474. [1874?]. Bound. Finzi 2451.
"Helena" [An unpublished poem]. MS in one leaf. The last six lines were later incorporated into "Camma":

> Helena
> ~~Cléopatre~~
> Cornish[?]

> They say the Corinth moon was amorous
> Of so much beauty, that the evening star
> Stayed all night long upon its silver ear
> To listen to those sweet lips tremulous
> With broken music, that the boisterous
> Rude English seas forgot to fume and fret
> When on its sands Verona's lovers met,
> And that the nightingale grew envious[.]
> Yet methinks I'd rather see thee play
> That serpent of old Nile whose [illegible word]
> Made Emperors drunken—Come sweet Egypt shake
> Our stage with all thy wildest [ ] nay
> I am grown sick of mimic passions, make
> The world[?] thine Actium, me thine Antony.

See Fong, p. 271, and pp. 579–81.

Wilde W6721M3. H477. [187–?]. Finzi 2452.
["Hellenism"]. MS in 6 leaves. Original MS fragment of an essay on Hellenism. See Mason, p. 67, and Montgomery Hyde (1975) p. 32n.

The major portion of the original (ff. 1–9) was part of Montgomery Hyde's collection (and is now the property of Lady Eccles); a photocopy of it is included here with MS ff. 10–15, although the two fragments do not follow on from each other. Also: a typescript of both the Clark fragment and of the Montgomery Hyde fragment. The essay was privately published in 1979.

Wilde W6721M3. I19. [1872]. Bound. Finzi 2453.
["The idea of the good"]. [Greek lecture notes from Trinity College, Dublin.] MS in 10 leaves from a lined notebook. Notes taken from lecture(s) on Plato, Socrates and pre-Socratic philosophy.

Wilde W6721M2. I19. [1893]. Bound. Finzi 2454.
An Ideal Husband. Possibly the first MS draft of the play; in 2 AMS lined notebooks. Acts I & II are in notebook 1; Acts III and IV are in notebook 2. Both have heavy deletions, revisions and additions in Wilde's hand. The second book is inscribed:

> June 19 93
> Bosie present
> The Cottage,
> Goring

and contains a list of characters and a rough scenario.

Wilde W6721M2. I19. [1893–4]. Bound.
An Ideal Husband. Act IV in AMS and typescript. First 7 leaves are in typescript, clearly from Mrs Marshall's Type Writing Office; so are pp. 21–23 and 27–30. The remaining pages comprise 6 small sheets of lined paper in Wilde's hand and 6 folio sheets also in Wilde's hand; pp. 27 and 28 are typed facsimiles initialled by Richard Glaenzer. See Jackson (1983).

Wilde W6721M2. I19. [19 Feb. 1894]. Bound. Finzi 2455.
An Ideal Husband. Typescript of play in 102 leaves; four acts in four notebooks, from Mrs Marshall's Type Writing Office. All have heavy corrections and additions on recto and on facing verso in Wilde's hand. See Jackson (1983).

Wilde *PR5818 I19. Finzi 2456.
An Ideal Husband. By the author of *Lady Windermere's Fan.* London. Leonard Smithers and Co. Proof sheets with revisions and additions

in pen in Wilde's hand. There are substantial additions on pp. 18, 121, 162–67.

Wilde W6721M3. I38. [188–]. Finzi 2458.
[Index and autograph notebook]. One leaf. AMS of titles of poems and page numbers; in a photostat copy.

Wilde W6721M2. L157. [1892?]a. Boxed. Finzi 2459.
Lady Windermere's Fan. Typescript of play in 71 leaves. Four acts in four books, with duplicate copies of acts II, III, and IV. All copies typed at Mrs Marshall's Type Writing Office; first four dated 15 Nov. 1894; duplicate copies undated. Acting copies with lists of props for each act and length of each act. All drafts are without any MS emendations, suggesting that they could be copies for revivals, etc. Also 2 leaves TLS from J. Schwartz to H. Richard Archer, with explanation about dating of typescript.

Wilde W6721M2. L157. [1892?]b. Bound. Finzi 2460.
Lady Windermere's Fan. MS acting version of play in 93 leaves. Fair copy on lined paper in a notebook, in unknown hand, of a late version of the play, probably relating to the 1902 revival. Extensive business, etc. has been marked up.

Wilde W6721M3. L471. [1882]. Boxed. Finzi 2461.
["Lecture on House Decoration"]. Holograph MS of part of lecture given on American tour. Fair copy in ink in 5 leaves. Incorporated into "Art and the Handicraftsman" in *Miscellanies, Collected Works* (1908), XIV, 302–303, beginning at "But don't treat it [your marble—Ross] as if it is ordinary stone"; and ending at "like snows which the sunset has left cold."

Wilde W6721M1. L695. [187–?]. Finzi 2462.
["Libertatis sacra fames"]. Early AMS draft in 2 pages. Jottings and early fragments of poems. See Fong, p. 576.

Wilde W6721M1. L778. [1878?]. Finzi 2463.
"The little ship." [A poem]. AMS in two leaves, with corrections in Wilde's hand. See Fong, pp. 43–44.

Wilde W6721M1. L897. [1876?]. Bound. Finzi 2464.
"Love song." [An unpublished poem]. AMS on one leaf, fair copy of first 2 ½ stanzas. Jottings and titles on verso. See Fong, pp. 36–38, and pp. 508–509. See also MS Clark W6721M1. T974. [1874/8].

Wilde W6721M2. W872. [1893]. Boxed. Finzi 2465.
Mrs Arbuthnot [*A Woman of No Importance*]. Typescript of play in 87 leaves. Corrections in Wilde's hand, many of which are on verso. See Small (1983).

Wilde W6721M3. M835. [1884]. Bound. Finzi 2466.
["More Radical Ideas upon Dress Reform"]. AMS in six leaves with deletions and emendations. MS fragment of draft of article published in the *Pall Mall Gazette* (11 Nov. 1884). See *Miscellanies, Collected Works* (1908), XIV. The MS is, however, very different from the printed version.

Wilde W6721M2. N911. [189–]. Bound. Finzi 2467.
[Notebook containing fragments of dialogue used in Act III of *An Ideal Husband* and other jottings]. AMS in ink in eleven pages. Fragments of dialogue in blocks, such as:

Lord Caversham:
    Tom, how old are you?

Lord Goring:
    I'm forty-five, father. . . But my best friends tell me I don't look a day more than forty-six. So you see I must have been living a very respectable life.

Notebook also contains plans of acts:
    For Act I:
    1 Lord Goring alone
    2 Lord Goring and Lord Caversham
    3
    4 Bagles[?]
    5 Mrs Cheveley
    6 Sir Robert
    7 Sir Robert and Lord Goring
    8 Goring alone
    9 Goring and Mrs Cheveley

For Act II:
   Young and Sir Robert
   Young and Lady Chiltern
   Lady Chiltern and Sir Robert—
   letter
   Scene
   Lady C alone—<u>letter</u>
   Enter Violet

Wilde W6721M3. N9111. [1874/6]. Bound. Finzi 2468.
[Notebook kept at Oxford containing entries dealing mostly with philosophical, historical, and literary subjects]. AMS of 84 pages in a lined notebook in ink. See Smith and Helfand (1989).

Wilde W6721M2. N9111. [1894]. Bound. Finzi 2469.
[Notes of aphorisms and dialogue used in *A Woman of No Importance* and *The Importance of Being Earnest*]. AMS notebook.

Wilde W6721M3. N9112. [1874/6]. Cased.
[Notebook on philosophy]. AMS 18ff. in ink in notebook. Jotted remarks on philosophical issues and lectures. Discussed by Smith and Helfand (1989).

Wilde W6721M3. N911. [18—].
[Notes and draft fragments of poems]. MS in six pages; jottings in pencil and ink.

Wilde W6721M3. N111. [1874/6]. Bound. Finzi 2470.
[Notes on the *Ethics* of Aristotle]. Bound AMS notebook of 23 pages in ink. Exercise book used by Wilde at Oxford, about one-third full of notes on book VI of Aristotle's *Ethics* and on Euclid.

Wilde W6721M1. P187. [1880]. Bound. Finzi 2471.
"Pan: a villanelle." [Unpublished poem]. AMS in ink on 11 leaves. Contains fragments of "Pan": see Fong, p. 257 and p. 570 for details. MS also contains fragments of other poems including an early and unknown AMS draft of 'Theocritus':

   [f.7]

      O singer of Persephone!
      Hast thou forgotten Sicily.

Young Hylas keeps a goat for thee
    For thee the [ ] wait

Simaetha calls on Hecaté
    And hears the wild hounds at the gate.
Hast thou forgotten Sicily.

All night upon the line [illegible word]
    The [ ] [illegible word] fishers wait

And still in boyish rivalry
    Young ~~Lacon~~ Daphnis challenges his mate.

    It [ ]

All night upon the
    Poor Poly bewails his fate

Also f. 9:

This is the land of corn and vine
    Set in the purple of the seas
But where is lovely Proserpine

The brown cones drop from off the pine
    The elm is filled with [illegible word] bees

He needs no Tyrian buskins fine
    His feet are purple with the lees

Amid the quiet pasturing kine
    The milk white bull is [illegible word] at ease
This is the garden of the vine
    But where is lovely Proserpine —

The laughing girls dance in line
    Like [ ] Pleiades

Also f. 6:

Villanelle

O sweet if sad Euripedes
Child of the Salaminian seas

Ah surely the Pierian bees
Brought food to the [illegible word] Helen[?]

Now beneath the cypress trees
I [illegible word] song & singing done

Dost thou sleep well in Macedon

Or dost thou lack the [illegible word]
Of [illegible word] the Athenian sun.

Wilde W6721M3. P568. [1882, 10 May]. Finzi 2472.
["Philosophy of decorative art"]. [A lecture delivered on 10 May 1882 in Philadelphia]. Photostat in one leaf of an article published in the *Philadelphia Inquirer*, 11 May 1882. See Mason, p. 488.

Wilde W6721M3. P572. [188–?]. Finzi 2473.
["Phrases and Philosophies"]. AMS in 3 lined leaves: two are smaller leaves originally laid in the printed work. On paper torn from notebook, with deletions and corrections; some entries scored through entirely.

Moralists spend their lives in warning people against the sins of which they have grown tired. The active moralist is a tired Hedonist. At least, he should be.

A ~~grand passion~~ great romance is the privilege of people who have absolutely nothing to do. That is the ~~great~~ use of the idle classes in a country.

Pathos leaves the artist unmoved. But Beauty, real Beauty, can fill his eyes with tears.

The commonest thing is delightful if one only hides it.

It is a vulgar error to suppose that America was ever discovered. It was merely detected.

Being natural is simply a pose, and one of the most irritating poses I know.

There is a fatality about good resolutions. They are invariably made too soon.

One can always be kind to people about whom one cares nothing. That is why English family life is so pleasant.

~~[T]he only thing that can console one for having no money is extravagance.~~

~~A truth ceases to be true when more than one person believes in it.~~

In the well-thumbed lexicon of the journalist there is no such word as success.

Religions die when they are proved to be true. Science is the *débris* of dead Religions.

Sympathy with suffering is the joy of one leper meeting another leper on the road.

Every now and then England ~~finds~~ discovers that one of its sores shows through its rags and shrieks for the nonconformist. Caliban for nine months in the year it is Tartuffe for the other three.

It is absurd to talk of the intellectual superiority of man to [].

Nothing that actually occurs is of the smallest importance.

~~One should pass one's whole life in looking for temptations. Etc.~~

~~One should so live that one becomes a mode form of fiction. To be a fact is a failure.~~

Wilde W6721M3. P576. [188–?]b.
["Phrases and philosophies for the use of the young"]. MS in two leaves. On lined paper torn from a notebook, although not the same paper as above. Numerous holograph corrections and deletions. Some published in *The Picture of Dorian Gray* and *The Chameleon*.

There is only one thing worse than being talked about. That is not being talked about.

The capacity of finding temptations is the test of the culture of one's nature. The capacity of yielding to temptations is the test of the strength of one's character.

Only the weak resist temptation.

~~Industry is the root of all ugliness.~~

To treat the serious things of life very trivially, and the trivial things of life very seriously, is the only true Philosophy of life.

Manliness has become quite effeminate. Only women are manly nowadays.

~~Maleness is a condition of perfection.~~

The beautiful mistake of the young is in imagining that Life is a passion, not a philosophy. The horrible mistake of the old is in imagining that Life is a passion, not a philosophy.

Everything is of use to an artist, except an idea.

A truth ceases to be true when more than one person believes in it.

Only the real masters of style ever succeed in being obscure.

The aim of art is not to give pleasure, any more than it is to give pain. The aim of art is to be Art.

Only mediocrities prosper. Only the hopeless improve. The artist revolves in a cycle of masterpieces, the first of which is no less perfect than the last.

~~Ambition is the last refuge of the failure~~.

Art has a soul, but man has not.

One touch of nature will make the whole world kin. Two touches of nature will ~~destroy~~ ruin any work of art.

In old days men of letters wrote books and the public read them. Nowadays books are written by the public and read by nobody.

Wilde W6721M3. P676. [189–]. Bound. Finzi 2474.
[Phrases, aphorisms and fragments of verse]. Lined AMS notebook. At one end of the book are AMS fragments of verse in pencil for 9 pages. Some lines are fragments from a verse drama—at one point from *A Florentine Tragedy*:

Simone:

> It may not be:
> This world is full of voices: everything
> That is in nature has it separate tongue.
> When blood is shed the gentle earth cries out.

[SPACE]

Bianca:
Then let us cast him into

[SPACE]

Simone:

> Of what avail?
> Rivers will speak of hidden things, and reeds
> Flute our most dearest secrets to the wind
> Until it wanders wailing.

At the other end of the notebook are aphorisms, sometimes for use in the plays. AMS in pencil on six pages, one of which is ripped out.

Morality is quite artificial enough. It always has been artificial. Our manners might be improved. The age as Aunt Augusta says is painfully natural.

I like manliness in women. Women are so manly that manliness looks effeminate in men.

You can't make a fool of a person unless he is a fool already.

To enter married life with a man capable of deception would augur ill for a happy future.

A woman should know nothing before marriage, and less afterwards.

I have never sowed wild oats: I have planted a few orchids.

You don't seems to realise that there are lots of people in the world who have absolutely nothing to do and don't want to be disturbed.

The husbands of beautiful women belong to the criminal classes: the husbands of plain women have married into them.

You produce a false impression—That is one of the few pleasures left to one in life.

She looks on me as a son—women of that sort are extremely dangerous.

Men forget: women forgive: that is why women are such an inferior sex intellectually.

Most people nowadays arc compelled to live within their incomes: it is a tragic sign of the times.

I don't know any Duchess who could be described as the thin edge of any wedge.

Leading a double life is the only proper preparation for marriage.

Wilde W6721M3. P611. [1890]. Bound. Finzi 2475.
[*The Picture of Dorian Gray*. Chapter III]. MS in 23 leaves. Draft with many corrections and alterations from the 1891 (not the 1890) version.

Wilde W6721M3. P6111. [1890]. Boxed. Finzi 2476.
[*The Picture of Dorian Gray*]. Typescript in 231 leaves, with extensive corrections and emendations in ink and pencil in Wilde's hand; a few are *not* in Wilde's hand. There are six leaves of MS additions to the text (at f. 27—1 leaf; at f. 162—3 leaves; at f. 164—2 leaves). The final page carries Wilde's signature. Material from the sale catalogue boxed with the MS claims that it formed the copy-text for the *Lippincott's Monthly Magazine* publication of novel in 1890.

*PR5819 P611. [1890] cop. 3.
[*The Picture of Dorian Gray*. Autograph leaf from chapter V]. Single autograph leaf with erasures and corrections from Chapter V of the 1891 version, not the 1890. Bound with the first edition of work issued separately by Lippincott (Philadelphia, 1890).

Wilde W6721M1. R389. [10 Nov. 1889]. Finzi 2477.
"Remorse; a study in saffron." [A poem]. MS in one leaf. An autograph presentation copy written, signed and dated by Oscar Wilde for Gabrielle Enthoven. See Fong, p. 300 and p. 602. Cf. Clark MS W6721M1 V58. [1888?] which contains fragments of three stanzas of the poem.

Wilde W6721M1. R427. [187–]. Boxed. Finzi 2478.
"Requiescat." AMS. Signed presentation copy of the poem in ink on 2 leaves. See Fong, p. 16 and p. 497.

Wilde W6721M3. R595. [1879?] Bound. Finzi 2479.
["The Rise of Historical Criticism"]. Original AMS of essay in ink in three lined notebooks, some with leaves removed; with corrections and deletions, sometimes in different inks. Part 1 first published in America in 1905 and reprinted in vol. VII of Ross's 1908 edition. Parts 2 and 3 were published in vol. XIV of that edition. Wilde's title is "Historical criticism among the ancients."

Wilde W6721M3. L111. [ca. 1894?]. Bound. Finzi 2480.
[*La Sainte courtisane, or The Lady Covered with Jewels*]. AMS in bound lined notebook, in 32 leaves in pencil, with deletions and corrections. At the end of the notebook there are fragments of speeches from *An Ideal Husband*. The opening stage directions of the draft of *La Sainte courtisane* correspond to Ross's edition (vol. XIV), but the remaining text has no names of characters, simply blocks of speech, and no stage directions whatsoever. The Clark catalogue claims that it is the draft of *La Sainte courtisane*, as printed in 1908 edition; but the MS text is different in places from that printed by Ross. For example, Ross rearranges the order of passages and has additional lines. So, at a local level, for example, Ross has:

> I put a figured ring on his finger and brought him to my house. I have wonderful things in my house (p. 237).

The Clark MS has:

> I put a ring figured on his finger and
> [new line]
> and brought him to my house. I have wonderful things

Ross also re-orders material to make greater sense of it. So pp. 237–38 of Ross read:

[MYRRHINA.]
The dust of the desert lies on your hair and your feet are scratched with thorns and your body is scorched by the sun. Come with me, Honorius, and I will clothe you in a tunic of silk. I will smear your body with myrrh and put spikenard on your hair. I will clothe you in hyacinth and put honey in your mouth. Love—

HONORIUS.
There is no love but the love of God.

MYRRHINA.
Who is He whose love is greater than that of mortal men?

HONORIUS.
It is He whom thou seest on the cross, Myrrhina. He is the Son of God and was born of a virgin. Three wise men who were kings brought Him offerings, and the shepherds who were lying on the hills were wakened by a great light.

The Sybils knew of His coming. The groves and the oracle spake of Him. David and the prophets announced Him. There is no love like the love of God nor any love that can be compared to it.

The body is vile, Myrrhina. God will raise thee up with a new body which will not know corruption, and thou wilt dwell in the Courts of the Lord and see him whose hair is like fine wool and whose feet are of brass.

MYRRHINA.
The beauty . . .

HONORIUS.
The beauty of the soul increases until it can see God. Therefore, Myrrhina, repent of thy sins. The robber who was crucified beside Him was brought into Paradise.*Exit.*

MYRRHINA.
How strangely he spake to me. And with what scorn did he regard me. I wonder why he spake to me so strangely.

The Clark MS, by contrast, has on f. 14, verso:

Love—
there is no love but the love of God—

The Sibyls knew of his coming. ~~and announced him.~~ The oracles spake of him[.] David and the prophets announced him.

Who is he whose love is greater than that of mortal men?

It is he whom thou seest on this cross, Myrrhina, He is the son of God and was born of a virgin. Three wise men who were Kings brought him offerings. And the shepherds who were lying on the hills were wakened by a great light.

[f. 15, recto]

The dust of the desert lies on your hair, and your feet are scratched with thorns, and your body is scorched by the sun. Come with me Honorius and I will clothe you in a tunic of silk. I will smear your body with myrrh and pour spikenard on your hair. I will clothe you in hyacinth and put honey in your mouth.

the body is vile.

[f. 15, verso]

God will raise thee up with a new body which will not know corruption, and thou wilt dwell in the Courts of the Lord—and see him whose hair is like fine wool and whose feet are of brass.

[f. 16, recto]

there is no love like the love of God. Nor any love that can be compared to it.

---

the beauty

Myrrhina

but

the beauty of the soul increases till it can see God.

Therefore Myrrhina repent of thy sins.

[f. 16, verso]

How strangely he spake to me. And with what scorn did he regard me. I wonder why he spake to me so strangely.

[The rest of this folio is written at 90° to the above text]
 the robber who was crucified beside him he brought into Paradise
and the

Wilde W6721M1. S582. [187–?]. Finzi 2481.
["Les silhouettes"]. AMS on one leaf in pencil. Fragments of early draft
of poem on recto and verso. E.g.:

   "The sky is flecked with bars of grey"
and

   "I see the dim boat on the strand"

Wilde W6721L. G646. [1878?]. Bound. Finzi 2481a.
[Sonnet. Written after hearing Mozart's "Dies Irae" sung in Magdalen
Chapel]. AMS on one leaf in ink; fair copy. Original MS of sonnet
probably written in 1877, published in *Poems* (1881) with the variant
title "On hearing the Dies Irae sung in the Sistine Chapel." (Filed with
ALS to *Good Words*.) See Fong, p. 72, pp. 381–82, and pp. 528–29.

Wilde W6721M1. S753. [1894]. Finzi 2482.
["The Sphinx"]. AMS of 3 leaves, being an original MS of several
verses, fragments and jottings for lines, with corrections and emendations.

Wilde W6721M1; S753. [1894]a. Bound. Finzi 2483.
["The Sphinx"]. AMS in 24 leaves with corrections and emendations.
Original MS of 90 stanzas of "The Sphinx," some of which is a fair
copy.

Wilde W6721M1. S753. [1894]b. Bound. Finzi 2484.
["The Sphinx"]. AMS of an early draft in 4 leaves, with corrections
and emendations; comprises fourteen verses, three of which do not
form part of published version.

Wilde W6721M1. S753. [1894]c. Bound. Finzi 2485.
["The Sphinx"]. Original typescript in 4 folio pages, with corrections
and emendations in ink in Wilde's hand. Like the manuscripts of
many of Wilde's works, those of "The Sphinx" were indiscriminately
bound together by collectors. The stemma of the poem is therefore
complex. See Fong, pp. 302–12, pp. 476–82, pp. 603–27.

Wilde W6721M1. T396. [1878?]. Finzi 2486.
["Theoretikos and Amor Intellectualis"]. AMS on one sheet, with jottings of "Theoretikos" on both sides and of "Amor Intellectualis" on one. In pencil with corrections and erasures in ink and pencil. See Fong, pp. 82–83 and pp. 536–37 for textual details.

Wilde W6721M1. T627. [187–?]. Finzi 2487.
["To Milton"]. AMS rough draft in ink on two pages of lined paper torn from a notebook. Untitled. See Fong, p. 77 and pp. 531–32 for textual details.

Wilde W6721M3. T866. [1890]. Boxed. Finzi 2488.
"The True Function and Value of Criticism; a Dialogue." Original signed AMS in 152 loose leaves, in ink on lined paper; with deletions, alterations and corrections, some on facing verso; copy, however, is clean, and probably a fair copy.

Wilde W6721M1. T974. [1874/8]. Finzi 2489.
[Two autograph poems]. AMS in ink on lined paper; recto and verso. Signed and accompanied with inscription "Magdalen College, Oxford." One side begins "And she and I are as Queen and Master"; the other "I that am only the idlest singer." See Fong, pp. 37–38 and pp. 508–509.

Wilde W6721M3. T974. [188–?]. Finzi 2490.
[Two notes]. AMS on one leaf. Jottings for a speech as follows:

> Grotesque—
> 1st lecture spoke of French art.
>
> but [was?] in the [area?] not of ideas but of execution.

Wilde W6721M1. T991. [19—] Finzi 2491.
[Typescripts of several unpublished poems and two prose essays: "Hellenism" and "Greek Women"]. Typescripts of 57 pages prepared by Robert Ross from Wilde's MSS, and bearing corrections in Ross's hands. With ALS from Methuen to A.J.A. Symons dated 18 September 1891 concerning the publication of the material, and containing the advice of E.V. Lucas that "Hellenism" and the poems should not be printed.

Typescripts include:

"She stole behind him where he lay" (see Fong, p. 32);

"Sweet, I went out in the night" (see Fong, p. 30);

"See! the gold sun has risen (see Fong, p. 28);

"Love Song" (see Fong, p. 36);

"O Golden Queen of life and joy" (see Fong, p. 204);

"Heart's Yearnings" (see Fong, p. 41);

"Choir boy" (see Fong, p. 24);

"Désespoir" (see Fong, p. 50);

"La belle Gabrielle" (see Fong, p. 168);

"The Little Ship" (see Fong, p. 43);

"La Dame Jaune" (see Fong, p. 299);

"It is for Nothing" (unpublished):

> Sweet, there is nothing left to do
>   But to kiss once again and part,
> Nay, there is nothing we should rue —
>   You have your beauty, I my art;
>   Nay, do not start,
>   One world was not enough for two
>   Like me and you.
>
> Sweet, there is nothing left to say,
>   I hold that love is never lost,
> Winter may follow after May
>   But crimson roses burst the frost.
>   Ships tempest-tossed
> Will find harbour in some bay,
>   And so we may.
>
> Look upward where the poplar trees
>   Sway and sway in the mountain air,
> Here in the valley never a breeze
>   Scathes one thistle's down, but there
>   Great winds blow fair

From the mighty murmuring mystical seas.

Oscar Wilde, from the original MS

Wilde W6721M1. U58. [187–?]. Finzi 2492.
[Unpublished fragment of poem]. AMS on one leaf in ink on lined paper, beginning: "Moonlit plain O lovely Acheron." See Dulau item 12 for a transcription.

Wilde W6721M1. U58. [187–?]a. Finzi 2493.
[Unpublished fragments of poem]. AMS on three leaves in ink on lined and unlined paper. Two fragments of poems and an address. See Dulau item 13 for further details.

Wilde W6721M1. U58. [187–?]b. Finzi 2494.
[Unpublished fragment of poem]. AMS on one leaf in pencil on lined paper. Begins: "the gurgling water leapt and fell." See Dulau item 14 for a transcription.

Wilde W6721M1. U58. [187–?]c. Finzi 2495.
[Unpublished fragment of poem]. AMS on one leaf in ink on lined paper. Begins: "They say the Cornish moon was — ". See Dulau item 15 for a transcription. See also Fong, pp. 271 and 579.

Wilde W6721M1. U58. [187–?]d. Finzi 2496.
[Unpublished poem]. Photostat of one AMS leaf of poem of three seven-line stanzas which later became incorporated into "The Burden of Itys." See Dulau item 242 (3); see also Fong, pp. 102, 541.

Wilde W6721M1. U58. [1876?]. Finzi 2497.
[Unpublished fragment of poem]. AMS on one leaf in ink on unlined paper. Writing is very unlike that of Wilde of later years and of, say, the Oxford notebooks, although Dulau and Millard (in a marginal comment) claim it as genuine. Begins: "the white narcissus break beneath my feet." See Dulau, item 20, for a transcription.

Wilde W6721M1. U58. [188–?]. Finzi 2498.
[Unpublished fragments of poem]. AMS on six leaves in ink on lined paper.

One leaf beginning: "She stole behind him where he lay." See Dulau, item 26, and p. 14 for a facsimile reproduction; see also Fong, pp. 32–33, 504–505.

Two leaves beginning: "There rose a little undertune"; and "but e're he closed the wattle door." See Dulau, item 25; Fong, pp. 32–33, 504–505.

One leaf beginning: "He rose and seized his polished crook." See Dulau, item 24; Fong, pp. 32–33, 504–505.

One leaf beginning "Topaz." See Dulau, item 22.

One leaf beginning "I love your mouth of vermilion." See Dulau, item 27.

One leaf beginning "Dusted with its stars." See Dulau, item 23.

Wilde W6721M2 V473. [1880]. Boxed. Finzi 2499.
Vera; Or, the Nihilists. Early AMS draft in 169 page notebook with lined paper. In ink and pencil with numerous revisions and additions both on copy and facing verso. Much earlier than that printed by Ross, but not the first draft. At the other end of notebook another 55 pages (on verso and recto) of drafts for a verse drama (which Rodney Shewan [1977] has called a draft of "Beatrice and Astone Manfredi") and miscellaneous writings. But see Frances Miriam Reed (1989).

Also written agreement between Wilde and Marie Prescott Perzel; and drafts for two sections of prologue to be added to 1882 version.

Wilde W6721M2 W653. [189–]. Finzi 2500.
A Wife's Tragedy. [An unfinished play]. AMS on 49 leaves, one-third in ink and two-thirds in pencil, on lined paper, often on verso. Numerous emendations and deletions; numerous jottings and unfinished lines at end. (See Shewan, 1982.)

Wilde W6721Z M533. [1881, 17 May.]
AMS on one leaf. Memorandum of agreement made between Wilde and David Bogue, the London publisher, for the publication of *Poems*, dated 17 May, 1881. Agreement gives details of costs of publication to be borne by Wilde.

Wilde, Oscar. Temp MS folio.
Author's corrected proof copy of *Salomé*, Paris: Librairie de l'art indépendent, 1892.

Second proof copy, dated 12 juillet[?] 1892. Bound. Corrections and deletions in Wilde's hand in pencil; corrections in at least one other in ink. Sale catalogue suggests that MS corrections are those of Marcel Schwob. There are both stylistic and grammatical corrections. E.g. p. 32:

> "C'est horrible, c'est infect, ton corps! . . . C'est de tes cheveux . . ."

Wilde corrects "infect" to "horrible"; and Schwob "c'est" to "il est," thus:

> "Il est horrible, il est horrible, ton corps! . . . Il est de tes cheveux . . ."

This pattern repeated elsewhere. So, on p. 35, "Ne lui dis pas des choses comme cela" is corrected by Schwob to: "Ne lui dis pas de telles choses."

| 5 |

Literary Histories

A S I indicated in the first chapter, Wilde's changing fortunes at the hands of literary historians is a fascinating topic in itself. One way of making sense of the recent revaluation of Wilde is to trace its origins to larger changes in the assumptions and methodology of literary history. That the basis and nature of literary history have changed profoundly since Wilde's contemporaries wrote about him is a point that scarcely needs mentioning. What does need emphasizing, however, is the speed and extent of the changes which have taken place over the past twenty years, in particular those associated with "post-structuralism"—that is, feminism, Marxism, gender studies, and new historicism.

In general terms, the concept of literary value has undergone a series of far-reaching changes; these have resulted in a situation where today it is no longer possible to define "literariness" separately from cultural, historical, or social concerns. The "old" literary history tended to divorce these categories, and thus to divide nineteenth-century writers into two groups: on the one hand, there were figures such as John Ruskin, William Morris, Thomas Carlyle, and Charles Dickens whose interest in literature was understood to be combined with a larger concern with contemporary culture and politics. On the other hand there were writers (generally in the last quarter of the century) whose concern with literature was generally held to be an exclusive one. Exemplary figures in this latter group included Walter Pater, Henry James and, quintessentially, Oscar Wilde. In addition, the "old" literary history ordered these two groups in a hierarchy: so a concern with social issues was held to be paramount. Hence, to value Morris necessarily implied a devaluing of Wilde. Precisely this kind of view was at the heart of the conclusions of historians such as Raymond Williams in the 1950s and 1960s.

Today, however, this kind of opposition is rarely posed. In the first place, the notion of politics has been enlarged to include all discourses of power and authority, rather than those simply of party politics. In the second place, *all* writers, by virtue of the fact that their medium is language, are now seen to be political animals, whether overtly or covertly so. Hence, the determination of the "canon" of literary works is now also held to be an essentially political process: the revaluation of Wilde's *oeuvre* which has taken place over the course of the past twenty years has therefore involved acknowledging the existence of a political agenda in his work, and discovering that the literary judgements of the past which marginalized him had their own political biasses.

A full list of works partly devoted to Wilde up to 1977 is to be found in Mikhail (1978), and the following general points about the importance of Wilde in literary history will have to be augmented by systematic reference to that work. Mikhail's bibliography testifies to the fact that, until comparatively recently, literary historians could dismiss Wilde as a figure of little significance. Indeed, Geoffrey Tillotson's posthumous *A View of Victorian Literature* (1978) does not even mention Wilde; neither does Austen Wright's collection of essays entitled *Victorian Literature* (1961).

In keeping with traditional literary history's opposition of "trivial" and "serious" work (categories and terms which Wilde himself loved to question) Raymond Chapman's *The Victorian Debate: English Literature and Society. 1832–1901* (1968) offers Wilde only a bit-part as the popularizer of the "essential Pater" (whatever such a quality might be), and devotes only a paragraph to the dramatic works. Similarly, Audrey Williamson's *Artists and Writers in Revolt* (1976) is interested in Wilde only in terms of what he borrowed from the Pre-Raphaelites. Morse Peckham in *Beyond The Tragic Vision* (1962) barely mentions Wilde. Even Raymond Williams in *Culture and Society* (1958), as I have noted, only fleetingly locates Wilde in relation to nineteenth-century debates about art and life, which he sees conducted principally by "sages" such as Matthew Arnold and

John Stuart Mill. Allan Rodway's essay on Wilde's poetry (1958) is equally perfunctory. Other works could be mentioned; obviously the pattern quickly becomes tiresome.

Nonetheless, despite the hegemony of this judgement, it is possible to trace at the same time the beginnings of a countervailing view. From as early as the mid-1950s an account of Wilde as a key transitional figure begins to emerge. Frank Kermode in *Romantic Image* (1957) sees Wilde in precisely this way, as a figure useful in concentrating "the nineteenth century for the benefit of the twentieth"; and the transitional in Wilde's work and life is also what interests Giorgio Melchiori in *The Tightrope Walkers* (1956). Lionel Trilling in *Sincerity and Authenticity* (1972) has a much surer grip on the historical significance of Wilde: "with each passing year the figure of Wilde becomes clearer and larger" is the perspicacious comment with which he begins his comparison of Wilde and Nietzsche. Wilde's commerce with his immediate literary antecedents and his contemporaries is discussed by John Dixon Hunt in *The PreRaphaelite Imagination* (1968) and Robin Spencer in *The Aesthetic Movement* (1972); and the cultural milieu of the time is well-documented by the erudite E. H. Mikhail in *The Social and Cultural Setting of the 1890s* (1969).

It should be emphasized at this point, though, that however welcome these developments were, none of the above writers (except Mikhail) saw Wilde as figure important in his own right and on his own terms. Their interest in him was part of a larger concern with revaluing the 1890s as a "transitional" decade in which the seeds of the modernist revolt against Victorian *mores* and values could be perceived: the founding of a periodical such as *English Literature in Transition* both helped to inaugurate and bore witness to this process. Wilde, however, was still only valued as a precursor of, or as a signpost to, something by implication more important. So the terms of the hierarchy of value may have changed, but in it Wilde was still in a subordinate position.

Anthologies of the writing of Aestheticism and the Decadence published in the late 1960s and 1970s tended to a reflect the beginnings of a change in Wilde's reputation. So he figures as a significant pre- or proto-modernist in, for example, Karl Beckson's *Aesthetes and Decadents of the 1890s* (1966; reprinted 1981); and in Ian Small's *The*

Aesthetes (1979); in the anthologies by Graham Hough and Eric Warner (1983) and Bernard Denvir (1986); and in Derek Stanford's *Writing of the 'Nineties* (1971). But in addition to these recent readings of the period, Holbrook Jackson's *The Eighteen Nineties* (1913), Osbert Burdett's *The Beardsley Period* (1925) and Richard Le Gallienne's *The Romantic '90s* (1925) are still essential tools for the modern critic.

The perception of Wilde as a figure centrally engaged with contemporary debates about issues such as art and morality, or gender and authority, though, had to wait until the late 1970s and 1980s—until, that is, the decisive changes which took place in literary history at that time. The kind of concerns which contemporary literary historians are beginning to find in Wilde's career and *oeuvre* are much more to do with a larger and more general interest in the politics of discourse, in the replication of ideology, and the relationship of "literary" to "popular" or mass culture.

When these approaches were applied to Wilde's work during the past decade, they enabled him to be seen as a much more important figure, in the sense that he stands as an ideal example of those writers in whose work the contradictions of contemporary politics may be glimpsed. A second and fortuitous consequence of these approaches was a reassessment of the *oeuvre* as a whole. It is now possible to see hitherto neglected parts of his work, in particular the shorter fiction, the aphorisms, the criticism, and *De Profundis*, as possessing a signficance equal to that of the society dramas and *The Picture of Dorian Gray*.

One important element in these changed concerns of literary history is to be glimpsed in the recent re-examination of Wilde's commerce with things French. The new concern with the "contexts" of literature—in this case, intellectual as well as cultural and political—has generated an interest in the notion of acculturation: in Wilde's case a revaluation and a redescription of the French influences upon his work. This subject was in itself not a new one. However, most of the pioneering work in this area, in keeping with the general pattern of literary historiography, saw Wilde as only a marginal figure in the processes involved in representing France to British culture. Typical examples include G. Turquet–Milnes (1913), Kelver Hartley's *Oscar Wilde: L'Influence française dans son oeuvre*

(1935) and Ruth Temple's *The Critic's Alchemy* (1953). Even works as informed as Christophe Campos's *The View of France from Arnold to Bloomsbury* (1965), or as recent and as comprehensive as R. K. R. Thornton's *The Decadent Dilemma* (1983) are to be included in this category. But over the past decade the balance has shifted completely.

This change is due in the first instance to new ways of thinking of acculturation (see, for example, Crossley and Small [1988] and [1989]); the exchange of ideas between Britain and France is now seen to be much more elaborate than was hitherto thought. In particular, it is now realized that the "old" model of French influence and British receptivity is simply inadequate in the sense that there were certain constraints or prohibitions which made the adoption of French ideas both complex and problematic (for more details of this process, see Guy [1991], discussed below). When Wilde's work is set against these new contexts, his appropriation of "things French" is seen to be much more subtle and sophisticated.

In this respect the best account of Wilde's transactions with French thought and French literary models is Patricia Clements's *Baudelaire and the English Tradition* (1985). (But see also Bradbury and Fletcher, 1979.) Clements describes the significance of Baudelaire's work as the originating influence of the modernist revolt in English literature. Baudelaire was constantly enlisted, Clements maintains, as an ally for the polemicists of modernism, and an account of the "transformation in the English myth of Baudelaire comprises a history of relations among generations of English poets." In this account of the literary genealogy of modernism, Wilde's Baudelaire is an ambivalent figure, but finally committed, like Wilde himself, to the inherent instability of linguistic meaning. Clements concludes her carefully argued chapter on Wilde by suggesting that in dramatizing Baudelaire's notion of the "tragic duality of man," Wilde gave the Frenchman's ideas a "wide currency" and his name a "glittering prominence" among English-speaking audiences. Also interested in Wilde's debts to French literary models is Richard Ellmann (1988). Ellmann analyzes the concept of Decadence in French thought, the ways in which Wilde used it as an organizing principle in his work and how he redefined its major concerns.

One recent account, which draws upon the developments described above, is Josephine Guy's *The British Avant-Garde: The*

Theory and Politics of Tradition (1991). Guy's principal concern is to re-theorize avant-garde politics in such a way as to give a new prominence to nineteenth-century British oppositional writers, especially Wilde. In this reading, avant-gardism becomes defined in terms of an appropriation of tradition, an activity which in Guy's view bespeaks a much more thoroughgoing engagement with politics than has hitherto been considered the case. As a consequence of this reinterpretation Wilde comes to be seen as a central figure in avant-garde history.

There are, however, other ways of measuring Wilde's growing importance for literary historians. As I have suggested, one of the issues which recent criticism has taken to be of significance in literary history is the relationship between discourse, power, and gender. In the past decade these issues have been examined much more thoroughly in terms of the relationship between power and discourse. Sima Godfrey (1982), for example, examines the phemonenon of the dandy, especially Wilde and Beau Brummel, in nineteenth-century culture, arguing that dandyism is best understood as an ironic inversion of the dominant bourgeois code of values (conclusions which can profitably be read alongside Susan Sontag's discussion of camp in Wilde in *Against Interpretation*, 1966).

The topic is also addressed in passing by Peter V. Zima in "Towards a Sociology of Fictional Texts"; Zima discusses the large issue of the sociology of texts and takes Wilde as one of his examples. He argues that "a literary text does not 'reflect' reality in some magical way, but that it should be conceived of as a response to spoken and written discourses of its time" (60–61). He uses this insight to locate Wilde's plays in the context of the "salon conversation" of the late nineteenth century and thus suggests a "functional" link between "conversationalism and dandyism": "they are both situated beyond or above productive social action" (67).

Elsewhere, both Klaus Hansen (1982) and Ernest Hess–Luttich (1984) discuss the logic of dandyism and the relationships between dandyism and Aestheticism. Indeed Aestheticism as a movement has itself undergone reassessment over the past decade, and as it has come to be seen as more central to nineteenth-century culture, so Wilde's role in it has been revalued (for further details, see Linda Dowling, Regenia Gagnier, and Ian Small, discussed below).

As I have noted, one of the most fruitful developments in literary history (as far as Wilde is concerned) has been the rise of gay studies. Wilde's homosexuality was of course discussed from the trials onwards, although, given the amount of attention his life has attracted, serious analysis has been conspicuous by its absence. Edmund Bergler briefly drew attention to Wilde's homosexuality in 1953—the same year as W. H. Auden published his famous characterization of Wilde as the "Homintern Martyr." Not surprisingly, then, Wendell Harris in his section on Wilde in the MLA's *Victorian Prose: A Guide to Research* in 1973 (which should be read alongside George Levine's and William Madden's earlier collection of essays, *The Art of Victorian Prose*, 1968) failed to find any serious discussion of the relationship between Wilde's homosexuality and his career as a writer.

Up to the mid-1970s, most accounts of Wilde's homosexuality tended to treat it as an aberration: in this view Wilde was a writer who just "happened" to be a much more interesting homosexual. Discussions of the aberrant nature of Wilde's "condition" only slowly gave way to an account of its pathology, but one which was indebted to a crude appropriation of Freudian psychoanalysis and psychopathology. The "salacious" Wilde, an easy target for moral censure, may have given way to Wilde the psychopathological curiosity, but both views ensured he remained a marginal figure in traditional literary history.

More convincing evidence for the way in which the traditional canon of literary works endorses dominant political (and dominant moral) values, and thus excludes "aberrant" figures such as Wilde, would be hard to find. Some accounts tried to rectify this situation, but only in a piecemeal and unsystematic manner. In this respect, see Noel Garde (1964) and Clifford Allen (1967), who offer more substantial analyses of Wilde's homosexuality; more recently, Rupert Croft Cooke (1967 and 1972) traces its "development." Macdonald Critchley in *The Black Hole* (1964) and A. Hoffer (1957) offer further diagnoses of Wilde's "condition."

In all these cases, however sympathetic the individual critics involved are to Wilde and to his fate, the terms and the vocabulary used to discuss his homosexuality have not changed: thus in these and similar works, oppositions such as deviant and normal, marginal and central, and so on, are still in force.

Much more alert to the subtleties of the situation is Walter Perrie's essay (1982) on the relationship between homosexuality and literature. In a closely argued piece, Perrie broaches questions about the representation of homosexuality in literature and the relationship between homosexuality and literary creativity. His essay has a brief historical preface which surveys European attitudes to homosexuality, and he suggests, following the arguments of earlier historians such as Brian Reade (1970), that "the modern homosexual," conceived as a figure articulating an "inner andogyny," is a nineteenth-century invention. Perrie traces the translation of homosexual themes on to the mode of the "aesthetic" in the careers of Swinburne and Pater. But for him it is Wilde who is the truly central figure in this transformation or invention of the "modern" homosexual.

Another writer concerned with the relationship between a homosexual consciousness and Aestheticism is Richard Dellamora. In writers such as Tennyson, Pater, Hopkins, and also Wilde, Dellamora sees homosexuality deeply implicated in attempts to formulate a new and appropriate contemporary aesthetic. In "Representation and Homophobia in *The Picture of Dorian Gray*," Dellamora develops arguments made by Eve Kosofsky Sedgwick in *Between Men* (1986) about the regulation of male bonding in nineteenth-century British society, where male intimacy was "prescribed" and male homosexuality "proscribed." Dellamora locates Wilde's treatment of male relationships in the novel by placing them against this set of tensions: "homosexual reference remains within a heterosexual discourse that focuses on male friendship and homophobic anxiety about masculine desire" (30). Dellamora has pursued this line of argument in *Masculine Desire* (1990), a challenging study of the sexual politics of Aestheticism. Sedgwick too has continued her interest in homosexuality in general and in Wilde in particular in her most recent book, *The Epistemology of the Closet* (1991). (But see also work by Ed Cohen and Lee Edelman, described below.)

The history of homosexuality in the nineteenth century is also described by Louise Crompton (1987). Jeffrey Meyers's *Homosexuality and Literature 18901930* (1977) discusses *Dorian Gray* in the context of how homosexual writers of the period were forced by the *mores* and legal restraints of the time into increasingly cautious behaviour. The argument that Wilde's trial in 1895 marked a decisive shift in British literary history is proposed by John Stokes's scholarly *In the Nineties* (1990).

It is also in terms of Wilde's homosexuality that Robert K. Martin (1983) re-opens the (by now) rather dated question of the influence of Pater's work, particularly that of *Marius the Epicurean*, upon *The Picture of Dorian Gray*. But Martin sees influence at work not simply in parody or vulgarization but in Wilde's "attempt to convert the covert homosexuality of Pater into a more openly expressed homosexuality, while at the same time exploring the morality of beauty and passion" (18).

Much more thoroughgoing in this respect is Jonathan Dollimore's suggestive essay on Wilde's subversiveness in the first number of *Textual Practice*. Dollimore argues that Wilde's "notion of individualism is inseparable from transgressive desire and a transgressive aesthetic," and that this leads to a "relinquishing" of the notion of an "essential self" (51 and 54). Dollimore establishes a series of binary oppositions to be found in Wilde's work, and lists, among other examples, the familiar oppositions of self and mask, style and authenticity, lying and truthfulness, nature and culture. He argues that Wilde's attempts to reverse those categories are the main preoccupation of his "transgressive" ethic: "deviant desire reacts against, disrupts and displaces from within; rather than seeking to escape the repressive ordering of sexuality, Wilde reinscribes himself within and relentlessly inverts the binaries upon which that ordering depends." Dollimore's essay provides compelling reasons for seeing Wilde's histrionic flamboyance, his creative and his critical work, not as separate features of a complex personality, but as aspects of his homosexuality. Wilde is also a central figure in Dollimore's comprehensive study, *Sexual Dissidence* (1991).

Ed Cohen (1987 and 1989) pursues a similar line of argument by discussing the ways in which "sex-gender ideologies shaped specific works in the late nineteenth century." For Cohen, the trials of Wilde were a spectacle in which the state "delimited legitimate male sexual practices (defining them as 'healthy,' 'natural,' or 'true') by proscribing expressions of male experience which transgressed that limit." In this sense, Cohen extends the logic of Gay's observations about the trials; and the work of both writers should thus be read alongside Baylen's and McBath's account of Wilde and Douglas in Italy (discussed above). Cohen suggests that *Dorian Gray* and *Teleny* allow us to see how texts both "reproduce and resist" dominant heterosexual ideologies and practices. (Wilde's involvement in the authorship of *Teleny: Or, The Reverse of the Medal: A Physiological Romance* is an issue which Cohen discusses but which he sees as incidental to his argument.) And in a conclusion similar to that of Hans Mayer (discussed below), Reade, Dellamora, and Cohen suggest that in *Dorian Gray*, Wilde transposes an aesthetic representation of the male body and the "sexual male body itself," and that in Wilde the erotic is therefore symbolically displaced on to the aesthetic.

Interestingly enough three editions of *Teleny* have been published over the past ten years, although Wilde's involvement in the production of that work is still disputed. H. Montgomery Hyde's *A History of Pornography* (1964) describes the source of rumours of Wilde's involvement with the book. The Frenchman Charles Hirsch opened a bookshop in London in 1889, and according to Hirsch, Wilde asked him for a copy of the MS of *Teleny* for a friend to collect. It is also worth noting that Ellmann's life of Wilde never mentions *Teleny*. For the place of *Teleny* in the history of nineteenth-century pornography, see Peter Webb, "Victorian Erotica" (1982). In a now rather dated essay in a special issue on homosexuality in *Salmagundi*, Philip Rieff asserts that in the culture of the future, "where creeds once were, therapies will be." More pertinently, for Rieff, Wilde was a "brilliant herald" of this "therapeutic culture." Jim Davidson (1989) also discusses the topic of Wilde's homosexuality. The larger subject of the relationship between the erotic and the aesthetic in Wilde's work is addressed in a study by Patricia Flanagan Behrendt (1991).

In contrast to the accounts above, Camille A. Paglia's interest in sexual issues is limited to their literary representation: she is not concerned with their relationship to cultural or social history. She examines the theme of androgyny in literature, particularly what she calls the "Androgyne of Manners—the male feminine in his careless, lounging passivity, the female masculine in her brilliant, aggressive wit." Paglia discusses the figure of the androgyne in English writing up to *The Importance of Being Earnest*, and sees in Wilde's play the most thoroughgoing expression of the androgyne, for Wilde's characters "have no sex because they have no real sexual feelings." Wilde's epicene characterizations, Paglia concludes, are intimately connected to his use of witticisms—the language of "hierarchical command in sexually aberrant or rather sexually denatured form."

Sexuality is the key, too, to Richard Ellmann's understanding of the relationship between Wilde and James in "Henry James among the Aesthetes." Ellmannn describes James's meeting with Wilde in Washington in 1882. Taking up a central theme in the biography, Ellmann constrasts James's reaction to Wilde with his reaction to Pater: "[t]he images are so steamy as to suggest that James saw in Wilde a threat which he did not find in Pater. Pater could be summed up as 'faint, pale, embarrassed, exquisite', but for Wilde James found other epithets embracing his mind, manners and probable sexual proclivities ('unclean beast')" (p. 218). Ellmann goes on to document, however, the fascination that Wilde held for James.

The relationship between the work of two writers forms the subject of a later piece by Kathryn Humphreys, who contrasts *Dorian Gray* with James's *The Sacred Fount*. Where Ellmann sees rejection but fascination, Humphreys sees similarity: "Through the resemblances and exchanges between characters and visual art in *The Picture of Dorian Gray* and *The Sacred Fount*, mimesis becomes so powerful that representations of fictional identity hollow out their own terms by calling attention to the status of characters as representations" (533).

Recent literary history has found other areas of interest, too. So in his encyclopaedic and authoritative *The Victorians and Ancient Greece* (1980), Richard Jenkyns describes the variety of uses made of Greek culture by the nineteenth century. John R. Reed in *Decadent Style* (1985) attempts to locate Wilde as a decadent writer, although his definition of decadence is as a cultural phenomenon, rather than—as with Dowling (1986), discussed below—a linguistic one. The ground covered by Frederick R. Karl in *Modern and Modernism: the Sovereignty of the Artist 1885–1925* (1985) is equally familiar, for Wilde's work is a topic treated in the context of the emergence of modernism.

Karl Miller enlists Wilde as a key figure in his encyclopaedic general history of literary duality or "doubles," but there is a sense of inevitability about Miller's decision to include him in his survey. Miller's controlling idea may be compared with that of Ralph Tymms, *Doubles in Literary Psychology* (1949) which also discusses

Wilde. Indeed, in his emphasis upon doubles, the use of the *Doppel-gänger*, and the notion of selfhood in Wilde, Miller echoes the work of Masao Miyoshi in *The Divided Self* (1969). For Miller, "dualistic fictions, in all their dream-like generic idiosyncrasy, continue to impart experiences of duplication, division, dispersal, abeyance. Many are at once alibis and apologies. They are works which can find themselves both innocent and guilty" (25). In such a thesis, *The Picture of Dorian Gray*, predictably enough, is the text of Wilde which Miller finds most useful, and he compares the uses of the motifs of the *Doppelgänger* and of masks made by Wilde in the novel with their use in works of Wilde's contemporaries. The topic of doubling is also described, if less provocatively so, by John Herdman in *The Double in Nineteenth–Century Fiction* (1990).

Similar conclusions emerge from Hans Mayer's encyclopaedic study of the theme of "otherness" in European literature, *Outsiders*. Mayer describes what he sees as a dominant feature in the history of post-Enlightenment society—the emergence of "outsiderdom" in bourgeois society, in which all forms of individuality are expressed in terms of conflict. Mayer examines in particular what Ihab Hassan in his foreword to the American edition surprisingly calls the nexus of "Woman, Sodomite and Jew." Whatever strengths Mayer's essay possesses in terms of its general account of cultural history, his arguments about Wilde (inevitably, once more, presented as the *type* of the homosexual outsider) are familiar. Thus: "What gave cause for so much umbrage in the story of Dorian Gray . . . is not to be derived from any offensive episodes but from the message it contained . . . [that] the existence of the homosexual outsider in the bourgeois society of the nineteenth century is conceivable only as an aesthetic experience" (224–25). Such a conclusion has no claims for novelty made for it—indeed students of Wilde will immediately recognize its genealogy.

More stimulating are Jerome Buckley's two studies of autobiography—his essay on the role of autobiography for Wilde and his contemporaries (1983), but more importantly his elegant and novel study of the whole genre of post-Romantic autobiography, *The Turning Key* (1984), which surveys the development of the genre within the post-Kantian (and post-Coleridgean) distinction between subject and object. Wilde is important for Buckley's thesis, because Wilde marks the moment when even the ambition for autobiographical "objectivity" ceased to be a possibility for the writer. Post-Romantic autobiographical writing, in Buckley's view, is characterized by an acceptance of the limitations of subjectivity. Here Buckley relates *De Profundis* to a nineteenth-century pattern of self-dramatization in writing.

Equally interested in Wilde as an autobiographical writer is Avrom Fleishman (1983), who describes the Western tradition of confessional and autobiographical writing as one characterized by the mixture of myth and history. Indeed, "truth-telling" is a concept which, together with those of "meaning" and "convention," Fleishman is most concerned to analyze. Autobiography, he concludes, is not to be distinguished by its truth-values, for "the intention to 'tell the truth about oneself,' like other imaginative projects, is a fictional premise which may issue in highly rewarding constructions of the self" (10). Autobiographical writing, for Fleishman, has to do with the construction of aspects of selfhood; it is not the "imitation of something already there, found or given, but the creation of a new being, a life, . . . one that exists as an aesthetic object" (13). The appropriateness of this as a prolegomenon for the study of Wilde's autobiographical writing is immediately clear, and Fleishman indeed discusses the confessional aspects of the life and the *oeuvre*, especially *De Profundis*. Fleishman suggests that the contradictions in *De Profundis*, deriving from a combination of attempted frankness and layers of self-deception, may be resolved by seeing the letter as a simultaneous "exercise in Biblical rewriting and in a typological redaction of personal experience" (286–87). The intertextual elements of Wilde's work are typological, thus connecting the biblical with the modern.

Such conclusions are perhaps best read in conjunction with those of Regenia Gagnier's work, discussed below, with an earlier essay by Jan B. Gordon (1970), and with Alick West's suggestive chapter on Wilde in *The Mountain and The Sunlight* (1958). Fleishman's comments on autobiography and fictiveness may also be profitably read alongside R. K. R. Thornton's illuminating discussion of the theme of masking in Yeats and Wilde (1989), and David Lodge's observations (1977) on the fictive elements of *The Ballad of Reading Gaol*.

Equally original in its scope and in its conclusions is Linda Dowling's pioneering study of language and the English Decadence. The observations about Wilde which she makes in *Language and Deca-*

dence in the Victorian Fin de Siècle elaborate some of the points she originally broached in an essay on "The Portrait of Mr W.H." in 1980. What is original (but finally perhaps rather limiting) in Dowling's view of the literary history of the nineteenth century is the assertion that Decadence was primarily a linguistic phenomenon rather than a cultural or even literary one. What she characterizes as a Romantic philology—the comfortable and comforting notion of language as a system securely related to, and expressive of, a teleology and an epistemology, the "outward expression" of the humanity of a human society—was threatened by the linguistic science of the nineteenth century, particularly by the work of Grimm and the Neogrammarians. For Dowling, this Neogrammarian philology suggested a schism between the idea of language as a system conforming to set of autonomous rules, and that of language as a system expressing the values of Victorian civilization; a schism which in its turn led to the characterization of literary language as a "dead language" in the last decades of the century.

Dowling argues that Wilde's response to this "post-philological moment" lies in the elevation of the spoken above the written: hence the celebration and the priorization of the spoken, the immediate utterance, within his own life, and his dramatization of self, the uses of monologual dialogues in the criticism, and the use of soliloquy in *Salomé*. However, it is perhaps worth adding that the idea of criticism in dialogue form predates Romanticism, and in this respect Wilde's revaluation of the spoken is the rediscovery of a past form.

The notion of the "spoken" plays a large part too in another important study, Regenia Gagnier's *Idylls of the Marketplace* (1987). Aestheticism, in Gagnier's view, came about with the modern idea of spectacle, and occurred at the moment when mass society was depending increasingly upon the manufacture of images and upon advertising. The idea of spectacle is used to examine both Wilde the public figure and Wilde the writer; for in spectacle, Gagnier argues, a special revolutionary value accrues to speech in the sense that signifying codes are disrupted from what is signified—and, she maintains, this is precisely what happens with Wilde's public utterances and with his society dramas. Wilde's speech subverted Victorian bourgeois ideology at a moment when that ideology was itself undergoing radical transformations.

Wilde's career, Gagnier suggests, coincided with the emergence of a service and a consumerist economy and culture, in which the devices of advertising and the construction of "personalities" began to occur. The terms of Gagnier's argument are taken explicitly from theorists such as Bakhtin and Foucault: she is concerned, that is, with the relationship between discourse, power and ideology in the manner of much of Foucault's later writing. The value of Wilde in this sense is that he provides a suitable vehicle for theory.

Gagnier's conclusions need to be read in conjunction with those of theatre historians who are beginning to direct our attention to the specificities of late nineteenth-century theatrical history, especially the conditions of dramatic authorship and details of actual audiences. In this respect, however, see "Recent Studies of Oscar Wilde" (1988), already mentioned, by Joseph Donohue. Donohue suggests that Gagnier mischaracterizes the composition of Wilde's audiences, which in its turn makes her larger arguments about ideology suspect. Gagnier's book should also be read alongside an essay by Rachel Bowlby (1987), which discusses Aestheticism and advertising, and Jonathan Freedman's persuasive account of the relationship between Aestheticism and commodity culture (1990).

Gagnier's arguments pursue ideas set out in two earlier pieces, an essay on the comedies and consumer culture (1982), and more emphatically and more substantially, an essay in *Criticism* (1984) where she offers a similarly materialist reading of *De Profundis*, the title of which, she maintains, was intended by Robert Ross to "suggest to a consumerist public" an autobiography from the "depths of a soul in pain." Gagnier details prison conditions and the changes to the British prison régime in 1877, with its new emphasis upon silence, solitary cellular confinement and labour. In Gagnier's eyes, Wilde's prison letter was an "indirect response" to the uselessness of prison labour. For Gagnier and Dowling, decadence is a profoundly different phenomenon from that invoked by other earlier literary historians such as Jan B. Gordon (1979), R. K. R. Thornton (1983), or Laurence E. Porter (1978), who connects Wilde's Decadence with that of some of his European contemporaries. Wilde's role in the Decadence, and hence his relationship to it, is changed accordingly.

A further revaluation of this period of literary history is Ian Small's *Conditions for Criticism* (1991). Small traces the specificities of late nineteenth-century literary culture to a large-scale intellectual crisis which occurred in the 1870s, and argues that the critical writing of figures such as Walter Pater, and particularly Wilde, can be seen as a rejection of new forms of intellectual authority which were produced in reaction to this crisis. In this context Wilde comes to be seen as a figure central to some of the most important intellectual debates of the late nineteenth century. Similar ideas are rehearsed in a slightly earlier piece (Small, 1990) which examined Wilde's use of intertextuality in relation to contemporary mechanisms of intellectual authority.

Bruce Haley (1985), however, in his account of the period in question, returns to the more usual definition of Decadence as a cultural phenomenon located not linguistically or via discourse, but within more empiricist notions of social history. For Haley, Decadence can be best understood as a "repudiation" of Positivism. He contrasts the declared aims of Positivism and its emphases on conformity and progress, with the anti-evolutionary and anti-social aspects of decadent thinking. Haley then sets this opposition against Wilde's ideas of personal growth and his dependence upon some of the tenets of Herbert Spencer and Auguste Comte in the essay "The Rise of Historical Criticism," where Wilde sees no disjunction between concepts of individual growth, liberty and progress.

Hilary Fraser's *Beauty and Belief: Aesthetics and Religion in Victorian Literature* (1986) is also familiar in its historiography. Fraser discusses the relationship between Christianity and "culture" in the nineteenth century and the way in which the traditional "properties and functions" of Christianity were "transferred to poetry." Fraser suggests that this process of assimilation became complete in the work of Aestheticism—in the work of Wilde and Pater in particular—and that the worship of beauty had a primacy beyond all other forms of worship: in other words, art became religion, a proposition fairly familiar to students of Aestheticism and Decadence. Indeed, Fraser's whole account of Aestheticism (and in particular of Wilde's involvement in it) inevitably has a ring of the orthodox.

Michael Steinman in *Yeats's Heroic Figures: Wilde, Parnell, Swift Casement* (1983) discusses the influence of Wilde and Wilde's family on Yeats. He suggests that Wilde was an embodiment of a "gallant recklessness" which Yeats would convert into a species of heroism.

(In this respect, see also Helen Grace Zagona [1960] and Marilyn Gaddis Rose [1967]). Wilde's relationship to Irish intellectual traditions are discussed by John Jordan (1985).

Maria Del Sapio (1984) discusses aspects of the relationship between Wilde and George Moore, and Martin Stoddard in *Art, Messianism and Crime: Sade, Wilde, Hitler, Manson and others* (1986) goes over the theme of Wilde and criminality. Grace Eckley (1989) discusses Wilde's influence on Joyce. Wilde's specific plagiarisms (rather than the generalized concept of "indebtedness") in his early poetry are given in detail by Averil Gardner (1982). Wolfgang Maier (1984) discusses the seriousness of Wilde's intentions as a literary artist. At a more local level, Alexander Stillmark (1981) and R. Bruegelmans (1984) discuss the comparisons to be drawn between Wilde and Hofmannsthal.

More recently in "The Castrating Gesture" Judith Weissman detects in *Dorian Gray* the presence (allegedly actively suppressed by Wilde) of Balzac's "Sarrasine," and perceives "deep affinities between [Wilde's] . . . story of art and Balzac's." Weissman sees in Wilde's novel a rehearsal of many of the concerns of post-structuralism and so many of the novel's "repressed sexual meanings" turn out to be oedipal in nature. A further, if less extreme, comparison between Wilde and post-structuralist interests is made by Guy Willoughby (1989). On the topic of influence, see David N. Dobrin, who finds a precise source for *Travesties* in a letter of 1894 by Wilde about the production of his plays; and Neil Sammells (1986) who also discusses the relationship between *Travesties* and *The Importance of Being Earnest,* suggesting that Wilde is the "presiding genius" of Stoppard's play, which is a "*critical* engagement" with Wilde. The "manner of that engagement is its own statement about what art can and cannot do" (377). Elsewhere John McGowan (1990) considers the the lineage of the idea of the epiphany from Pater through Wilde to Joyce, relating it to modernism's redefinitions of selfhood and identity—the dissolution of the self which is "not always experienced as a disaster, but often as a pleasure devoutly to be wished" (420). For a comprehensive discussion of Wilde's borrowings from other dramatists, see Kerry Powell's *Oscar Wilde and the Theatre of the 1890s* (1990) discussed below.

It is clear from this survey that over the last fifteen years the place of Wilde within literary history has changed dramatically and virtually beyond all recognition. Most of the judgements hitherto used to marginalize him have been reversed. So to use Wilde's favourite opposition, works once considered trivial are now seen to be serious—that is, to be thoroughly engaged with some of the most important social, cultural, political and intellectual issues of his age.

It is now no exaggeration to say that Wilde is today considered one of the central figures of the nineteenth century. To use terms which he would have appreciated and of which he would have thoroughly approved, he "sells" much better than Carlyle, Ruskin, or even Matthew Arnold (Ellmann's biography of Wilde was in the best seller lists in the United Kingdom for over a year). Most significant, however, and most promising for the future, is the fact that the recent changes in literary history which I have documented have transformed the basis of critical studies of Wilde: there is no longer any perceived opposition or tension between Wilde's sexuality and his career as a writer.

| 6 |

Major Critical Studies

WILDE'S treatment at the hands of literary critics maps very precisely on to the changes in literary history which the previous section, Literary Histories, documented. Broadly speaking, up to the Second World War critical studies of Wilde did nothing to redefine his place in literary history. The bibliographical or critical certainties of a Leavis or a Bateson, defining as they did with an unerring confidence what was to count as the literary, effectively marginalized Wilde in the canon of English literature. Oddly enough in all his voluminous writing, Leavis has nothing of significance to say about Wilde; and in Bateson's *Cambridge Bibliography of English Literature* (1940) he is dismissed as a figure of minor importance. However, as a general rule, Wilde has been treated more seriously as the century has progressed, and as a consequence the number of studies devoted to him has steadily increased.

The most noticeable feature of this change is a decreasing interest in moralizing Wilde's life. Up to the 1950s literary critics were rarely content to offer accounts of the work; rather they felt it incumbent upon themselves to judge Wilde the man, and his works were used as evidence in those judgments. Unsurprisingly, the emphasis was always upon Wilde's "immorality." As a consequence the history of Wilde criticism, certainly up to 1960, is of little interest to the modern reader. With one or two possible exceptions, Wilde has no equivalent of an A. C. Bradley or an L. C. Knights.

Good accounts of Wilde's early critical reputation are given in Karl Beckson's *Oscar Wilde: The Critical Heritage* (1970), in Fletcher and Stokes (1976), and in Mikhail (1978). Some representative contemporary reactions are also printed in Tydeman's 1982 *Casebook* volume on the comedies. The most important of these early studies—in particular Arthur Ransome's *Oscar Wilde: A Critical Study* (1912) and Arthur Symons's *A Study of Oscar Wilde* (1930)—are interesting in the manner of most of the early biographical material, in that they are written by individuals involved in some of the events which they describe, and hence are clearly partial in their judgments. In this respect, Ransome's study is far less well-known for its critical insights into Wilde's work than for the unsuccessful libel action which Lord Alfred Douglas subsequently brought against Ransome on account of his book.

The two works on Wilde by "Leonard Cresswell Ingleby" (Cyril Arthur Gull), *Oscar Wilde* (1907) and *Oscar Wilde: Some Reminiscences* (1912), Thurston Hopkins's *Oscar Wilde: A Study of the Man and his Work* (1913), and Stuart Mason's *Oscar Wilde and the Aesthetic Movement* (1920) also tell the reader more about the disposition of their respective authors than about their subject.

Studies such as these are most profitably treated as documents in the history of the relationship between literary culture and morality in the first part of the present century; what might be called their silent testimony is of more permanent interest than any insights which they offer into Wilde's work.

The best single discussion of an aspect of Wilde's *oeuvre* (interestingly, his poetry) up to the Second World War is by Douglas Bush in *Mythology and the Romantic Tradition in English Poetry* (1937). Bush writes sensitive literary criticism which is nevertheless coloured by what at the time was a familiar moral disapproval. The same is broadly true of works of the 1940s and 1950s. Although they attempted to address Wilde more seriously, they are unable to reconcile literary approbation with the (at times indignant) moral disapproval attaching to certain aspects of the life. So Edouard Roditi in *Oscar Wilde* (1947) discusses Wilde as a dandy, and thus employs, albeit programmatically and sketchily, a literary-historical methodology absent from most early works; he attempts, that is, to locate Wilde's persona within contemporary cultural debates. St. John Ervine in *Oscar Wilde: A Present Time Appraisal* (1951) also tries to locate Wilde within a context—in this case the dramatic conventions and traditions of his time. However he does so only to find him wanting in comparison with his contemporaries, particularly George Bernard Shaw. Indeed Ervine's attempts to assess Wilde's literary (rather than moral) qualities stand out against the general trend in the 1940s and 1950s; but even when Wilde is judged in literary rather than moral terms, he is still found wanting. James Agate (1947), for example, finds Wilde devoid of any artistic conscience or taste, and Louis Kronenberger (1952) attempts to explain the singularity of Wilde's comedies are only partly successful.

Even where the critic is obviously more sympathetic to Wilde's enterprises, as with Graham Hough's *The Last Romantics* (1949), Wilde is still a minor figure, sandwiched between Pater and Morris on the one hand and Yeats on the other; or he is depicted as a propagandizer of the fin de siècle, flawed by his lack of seriousness and the "unsureness of his taste." (It is only fair to add, however, that Hough's later anthology of Wilde in 1960 goes some way towards redressing the balance, and is in itself an interesting example of the change in Wilde's critical fortunes.) Aatos Ojalo's *Aestheticism and Oscar Wilde* (1954–1955) is more lenient in its judgments; however the definition of Aestheticism which it proposes (a series of tropes and styles) gives the movement only a limited significance as a literary movement and ignores its importance in a larger cultural history. James Laver (1954) offers a brief and at times superficial survey of Wilde's *oeuvre*.

Much more importantly, George Woodcock (1949) propagandizes Wilde as an anarchist—the first critic to see in Wilde those political, particularly anti-bourgeois, concerns which modern critics have been so eager to identify. But it is important to emphasize that Woodcock is not interested in reassessing Wilde's literary significance; hence, he is only interested in a part of the *oeuvre*—some of the critical essays—and that interest is a purely political one. Indeed, Woodcock's argument was taken up in his later work, *Anarchism* (1962), where Wilde is seen explicitly as a follower of William Godwin; the same topic is discussed also by Masalino D'Amico (1967); and much more recently by Michael Helfand and Philip E. Smith II (1978).

As I have indicated, it is possible to date the beginning of serious study of Wilde from the early 1960s. This change came about in two distinct phases. In the first place there was a sudden increase in the availability of scholarly materials on Wilde—principally Hart-

Davis's edition of the letters. This in turn helped provide the beginnings of serious biographical study. These developments were not surprising in the context of the general empiricist bias then dominant in British and American literary historiography which held that literary works could be best understood via their historial and cultural contexts. Thereafter in the 1960s and 1970s a series of critical monographs, devoted to tracing sympathetically the connexions between the man, the writer and his time, began to be published. Paradoxically, the second and more interesting phase in Wilde criticism occurred precisely because of a general dissatisfaction with the basis of that empiricist historiography—it coincided, that is, with the wholesale questioning of the methods and assumptions of empiricist literary history which have been described above.

Ironically, then, before students of Wilde had a chance to be provisioned with adequate empirical tools—with an accurate biography and scholarly editions, for example—their usefulness for critical judgments was being increasingly called into question. The recent assimilation of literary theory into critical practice has led to an entirely new set of priorities for critics interested in Wilde. He is now seen as a writer against whom notions of authority may be measured, and this has involved a redefinition of what is meant by an "historical context." An interest in biography or in the "background" of his work has been joined by a concern with Wilde's relationship to various nineteenth-century discourses. In other words, the first revolution of the 1960s was to overturn the dismissive judgments of a previous generation.

So the great virtue of Jacques Barzun's "Introduction: The Permanence of Wilde" (in *Oscar Wilde's De Profundis* [1964]) lies in precisely his attempt to engage Wilde as a serious writer. The same seriousness informs Charles Ryskamp's important collection of essays, *Wilde and the Nineties* (1966). A year later Epifanio San Juan, in *The Art of Oscar Wilde* (1967), reinforced these claims that Wilde's work possessed a seriousness of purpose, a view much more likely to find acceptance now than when his book was written. Kevin Sullivan (1972) and Michael Hardwick (1973) both offer less judicious, and, at times, inaccurate accounts of their subject.

Christopher Nassaar's *Into The Demon Universe* (1974) was one of the first attempts to construct a coherent critical reading by exploiting, rather than merely rehearsing, the facts of biography. Nassaar's thesis is that Wilde, from 1886 onwards, entered a world of evil, guilt, sin and atonement; and that this theme informs all his work. A companion piece, but arguing a different point of view, is Philip K. Cohen's *The Moral Vision of Oscar Wilde* (1978). Cohen's subject is that of Wilde the moralist, and his work is particularly good on some aspects of the drama. Rodney Shewan's *Oscar Wilde: Art and Egotism* (1977) is still one of the most balanced critical monographs on Wilde and his *oeuvre*. Shewan makes use of unexamined manuscript material, explores in an original manner Wilde's relationship with the intellectual currents of his time, and sees his career as an exploration of the notion of individualism. However, for a reassessment of the political consequences of individualism, see the later studies, already mentioned, by Ed Cohen (1987), Dollimore (1987), and Gagnier (1986).

The main emphasis of J. E. Chamberlin's *Ripe Was the Drowsy Hour* (1977) is to place Wilde within his intellectual, artistic, and cultural milieu; in particular his study makes interesting connexions between Wilde and contemporary scientific developments. John Stokes's informed and informative essay (1978) in the *British Council's Writers and Their Work* series is an excellent introduction to Wilde, and contains a useful, although now necessarily dated bibliography. Donald H. Ericksen's *Oscar Wilde* (1977) is a conventional introductory account which sees Wilde's artistic career finding its culmination in *The Importance of Being Earnest*.

Alan Bird's *The Plays of Oscar Wilde* (1977) was the first book to be devoted to Wilde as a dramatic author. It too is basically an introductory account, analyzing the plays (and the fragments of plays) in the order in which they were written; but the book's main emphasis is upon criticism of the plays, rather than on theatrical history. James Agate's "Oscar Wilde and the Theatre" had addressed the subject in 1947. Hesketh Pearson in *The Last Actor–Managers* (1950), *Beerbohm Tree: His Life and Laughter* (1956), and *Gilbert: His Life and Strife* (1957), all describe aspects of contemporary theatres and the staging of Wilde's plays.

Contemporary accounts of Wilde's commerce with the stage—William Archer's *"A Woman of No Importance," The Theatrical "World" of 1893*, (1894), *"An Ideal Husband," The Theatrical "World" of 1895*, (1896), *Playmaking: A Manual of Craftsmanship* (1912) and *The Old Drama and the New* (1923); Max Beerbohm's *Around Theatres* (1953) and *More Theatres, 1898-1903* (1969)—are still important secondary sources. So are A. E. W. Mason's *Sir George Alexander and the St James' Theatre* (1935), W. Macqueen–Pope's *Haymarket: Theatre of Perfection* (1948) and *St James': Theatre of Distinction* (1958).

However, until very recently, the most comprehensive account of the plays available was that by Katharine Worth (1983) in Macmillan's series on Modern Dramatists. Hers was the first full discussion of the plays since the study by Bird and in it Wilde becomes an existentialist playwright, quintessentially modern in his concerns and—like, in Worth's view, other Anglo-Irish writers of the time—cosmopolitan in the ways he assimilated European influences (but see also Clements [1985] and Guy [1991] for an account of the complexity of influence itself). Worth stresses Wilde's commerce with Symbolism, particularly with Maeterlinck's drama. In Worth's essay it is possible to detect the emergence of new ways of seeing Wilde as a dramatic author, for the *context* of his writing for the stage until this time had never been adequately described—indeed all discussions of the plays up to the 1970s have severe limitations in this respect.

As I have suggested, details such as a systematic account of the practices of dramatic authorship in the final years of the nineteenth century have been largely overlooked by critics, but they are essential tools for any proper assessment of the nature of Wilde's achievement as a commercial dramatist. A useful start in remedying this situation is Russell Jackson's comprehensive and excellently annotated anthology, *Victorian Theatre* (1989). Jackson brings together documents of what he calls the "social life of the Victorian theatre—descriptions of the audiences, the working conditions of Victorian actors and authors, the theory and practice of management, and the techniques of a theatre of elaborate scenic illusion" (1).

George Rowell (1989) provides an informed introduction to the drama of the late nineteenth century and Wilde's place in it; on this topic, see also Susan Laity (1988). Elsewhere, Walter Nelson (1989) iscusses the reviews of the social dramas and, in *From Ravenna to Salomé*, the reception of the other works. Nonetheless we still need to know how the specificities of Wilde's career fits with these general concerns—about, for instance, the collaborative nature of his work.

Up to the 1980s, issues such as these tended to be ignored by critics purporting to deal with Wilde's dramatic output. In this sense, the most lucid and comprehensive study of Wilde as a Victorian playwright is Kerry Powell's recent book, *Oscar Wilde and the Theatre of the 1890s* (1990). The emerging picture is now that of a radical Wilde (in both Worth's and Powell's view, for example, he is a devoted adherent of Ibsen) willing therefore to engage with, at least in the early plays, contemporary political subjects. Also concerned with the dramatic as the "unifying factor" in all of Wilde's work is Peter Raby's *Oscar Wilde* (1988), an intelligent and lucid, if introductory, account of its subject. Norbert Kohl's (1989) account of Wilde is systematic and scholarly, although of necessity it ignores some recent American research.

| 7 |

General Critical Studies

Collections: Critical Essays

WILLIAM Tydeman (1982) anthologizes some contemporary reviews of the plays and some of the major critical essays written since in Macmillan's Casebook series. The contemporary accounts include reviews by William Archer; the critical accounts range from essays by Max Beerbohm and St John Hankin in the first decade of this century to a selection of major modern critical writing including Ian Gregor's essay on comedy in Wilde, and extracts from Christopher Nassaar, Shewan and Ganz. Also recently reprinted is Richard Ellmann's 1969 collection of critical essays in the Twentieth Century Views series. Ellmann anthologizes from the available material in broadly the same manner as Tydeman. The critics here include Yeats, Lionel Johnson, Gide, Douglas, Joyce, Shaw and Auden—but fortunately the collections complement rather than compete with each other. In so doing they provide a convenient overview of critical trends during the past ninety years.

Meanwhile in his massive Chelsea House series, Harold Bloom (1985) provides another anthology of critical work, his emphasis being upon Wilde as a literary rather than a theatrical figure. Bloom's volume includes material by Yeats, Eric Bentley, G. Wilson Knight as well as by contemporary critics such as Ellmann, Epifanio San Juan and Nassaar; hence his selection lacks that historical perspective which characterizes Tydeman's and Ellmann's choices. More recently, Regenia Gagnier anthologizes another group of essays including those by Ed Cohen, Christopher Craft, Jonathan Dollimore,

Gerhard Joseph, Zhang Longxi, Camille A. Paglia, Philip E. Smith II and an extract from Kerry Powell's *Oscar Wilde and the Theatre of the 1890s*, all discussed elsewhere.

Individual Studies

The Criticism

In general, Wilde's criticism has been regarded in one of two ways. The first has been to set it against a tradition of nineteenth-century criticism, such as that of Matthew Arnold, John Ruskin or Walter Pater, which Wilde either exploits or rejects, depending upon the thesis of the critic. In this view of Wilde's criticism, early essays by Paul Elmer More (1910), Alice Wood (1915), and particularly, Ernst Bendz, in *The Influence of Pater and Matthew Arnold in the Prose Writings of Oscar Wilde* (1914), are clear indications of a pattern of criticism that has persisted for fifty years; a pattern which includes, for example, Leonard Brown's essay (1934) on the relationship between Wilde and Arnold, and David DeLaura (1962) or Michael S. Helfand and Philip E. Smith II (1978). Recently Bruce Bashford, in "Arnold and Wilde: Criticism as Humanistic" (1985), has picked up the threads of this familiar account of Wilde by analyzing Arnold's and Wilde's critical practices and seeing in them a fundamental humanism which he contrasts favourably with the tendencies of modern deconstructionist criticism, a proposition contested by Zhang Longxi in an essay discussed below. Edward A. Watson (1984) examines Wilde's commerce with other famous nineteenth-century statements about the function of criticism by means of a (by now) fairly familiar opposition between aesthetics and ethics. In particular, Wilde's essay "The Critic as Artist" "attempts, through knowledge, scholarship, and personality, to analyse some aspects of the theoretical foundations of literary criticism in Plato's 'Ion' and *The Republic*, Aristotle's *Poetics*, Pope's *An Essay On Criticism*, and Arnold's 'The Function of Criticism at the Present Time' " (225). In Watson's view, Wilde ultimately becomes an "iconoclast . . . a role he enjoys implicitly by taking on such legislators as Plato, Pope, and Arnold." Fuller accounts of the amount of classical reading to which Wilde would have been exposed as an Oxford undergraduate are given in Ellmann's life and in a learned and thoroughly documented essay by William Shuter (1988). Shuter examines what Pater would have been teaching to undergraduates at Oxford in the 1870s—the syllabus and texts which Wilde would have been required to follow systematically. His essay may be read as a useful complement to Ellmann's account of Wilde at Oxford simply because it provides an interesting examination of the day-to-day teaching when Wilde was an undergraduate there.

The pervasive presence of Pater, rather than of Arnold, in Wilde's critical thinking was detected somewhat later. So, for example, John Pick (1948), Ruth Temple (1960) and Wendell Harris (1971) all see, although for different reasons, Pater as the dominant influence; and hence his writing becomes the origin of the basic concepts in Wilde's criticism. Rather earlier, Ellmann, in "Overtures to *Salomé*" (1968), suggested the presence of *both* Ruskin and Pater. Other connections have also been identified. So Michael North's discussion (1985) of the themes of sculpture and poetry in Winckelmann, Pater and Yeats refers also to Wilde. He argues that in "The Critic as Artist" Wilde's celebration of Greek sculpture and his setting up of a "golden age" of Greek art is part of a strategy which emphasizes the contemporary writer's difference from society at large. More securely based, and using evidence from his and Michael Helfand's edition of the Oxford Notebooks (discussed above), is Philip E. Smith II's account (1988) of the influence of contemporary science, and especially evolutionary theory, upon Wilde's critical writing. Elsewhere, George Stavros (1978) writes on the influence of the Romantics on Wilde. Locating the writing of the late nineteenth century in relation to Romantic ideology and Romantic mythology is, of course, a long-standing feature of literary history, characteristically exemplified in works such as Graham Hough's *The Last Romantics*, Frank Kermode's *Romantic Image*, Mario Praz's *The Romantic Agony*, or Ian Fletcher's collection of essays, *Romantic Mythologies*. Speculation about other influences, particularly that of French writers such as Renan and Gautier, or German sources, such as Heinrich Heine, is documented in Fletcher and Stokes (1976, 114); although here again, as I have suggested in my discussion of literary history, detecting the presence of French influences and French paradigms in the work of late nineteenth-century British writers has been commonplace for some time.

The second way of discussing Wilde's criticism is in terms of the way it anticipates the concerns of early modernism. This line of argument can certainly be traced to Ellmann's seminal essay "The Critic as Artist as Wilde" (1967), or to the work of Jan B. Gordon (1970); there *Intentions* becomes a rejection of Victorian traditions of criticism. Such a case reinforces recent views of Wilde's exploitation of the media in late nineteenth-century consumerist culture. Hence R.J. Green (1973) notes the early modernism of *Intentions* and Hilda Schiff (1965) sees in those essays a proto-modernist programme for the autonomy of art, a topic since pursued by Herbert Sussman (1973) and Edward Said (1983). Also relevant here is Russell M. Goldfarb's essay (1962) on Victorian decadence. Related to this general interest in Wilde's arguments about the autonomy of art is an attempt to find in his varied utterances an internally coherent aesthetic. For A. E. Dyson (1965) such a synthesis is indeed possible, but for René Wellek in volume IV of *A History of Modern Criticism* (1965) Wilde's work presents only contradiction, not coherence.

Two different but related approaches to the criticism are those by J. D. Thomas (1969) and Bruce Bashford (1985). Thomas discusses intentionality in the dialogues—quintessentially a modernist concern. And more recently, Bruce Bashford looks at a more subtle aspect of this idea: he attempts to isolate in *De Profundis* a "theory of self-realization." His essay refers back to his two earlier and closely related studies of Wilde as a critic (see Bashford 1977 and 1978), for he sees the assumptions that underlie *De Profundis* to be in total opposition to the arguments which Wilde adopted in the critical dialogues. For Bashford, Wilde's concern in *De Profundis* is to outline a concept of individual development. In his essay Bashford also teases out some of the contradictions in Wilde's critical positions. In this respect his work can perhaps be profitably read as a contrast to Dollimore's essay (1987) on the same topic.

In a series of essays published in a number of periodicals, William E. Buckler discusses many of the issues rehearsed in the criticism. In "The Agnostic's Apology (1989)," he describes the formal contrivances of "The Portrait of Mr W.H." and links the themes of the essay to the other critical work; in "Antinomianism or Anarchy? A Note on Oscar Wilde's 'Pen, Pencil and Poison' " he relates the subject of that essay to Wilde's other concerns, particularly the opposition of ethics and aesthetics. In "Oscar Wilde's Quest for Utopia," Buckler discusses Wilde's attitudes towards socialism, and in "Building a Bulwark Against Despair: 'The Critic as Artist'," he examines, by means of close textual commentary, the relationship between Wilde and the persons of his dialogue, detecting the influence of Browning, Arnold, and Pater in the piece.

On the topic of influence in the critical work, Horst Schroeder (1991) detects Wilde using John Addington Symonds's *An Introduction to the Study of Dante* (1872) for a source in "The Critic as Artist" and James Robinson Planché's *Cyclopedia of Costume* (1876–1879) for "The Truth of Masks." And in a separate but related article in the same number of the same periodical, Schroeder finds echoes of Andrew Lang in "The Decay of Lying."

The subject of Wilde the early or proto-modernist has naturally been taken up most enthusiatically by recent critics. Gerhard Joseph (1987) writes briefly but stimulatingly on the topic of framing in Wilde and locates Wilde's modernity or proto-modernity initially by identifying certain repeated formal characteristics in his work. Linking Wilde and Pater, Joseph draws attention to the use of framing devices in modern and "pre-modern" authors. In this taxonomy, pre-modernists "frame or stress an 'inner' substance or field under investigation" while modernists "emphasize the very act of framing as it calls attention to itself" (61). Joseph uses this distinction to examine some of those sets of oppositions which Dollimore observes at work in Wilde's writing—particularly the opposition of the natural and the artificial, and of substance and surface. Ian Small (1985) also notes the modernity of Wilde's views about the pre-eminence of the cultural above the natural by contrasting the arguments made by modern semioticians about the signifying functions of portraits with Wilde's views on the various functions of art.

The modernity of Wilde's critical writing is also discussed in an allusive and densely argued essay by Eugenio Donato on the notion of self-awareness and its relation to representation. Donato suggests that the loss of a simple, unmediated concept of the "natural" was a feature of nineteenth-century European culture; thus the contemporary (i.e. 1979) "confrontation" between "deconstructive critical idioms and recuperative criticism" is an acute form of this nineteenth-century dilemma. Donato studies this dilemma specifically in relation to nineteenth-century metaphors for Japan, and sees in "The Decay of Lying" the first instance of the systematic distinction between the search for Japan as "original 'Natural Object' " and "Japan" as a "necessary but constructed object" (52). Later in the same periodical Marie–Rose Logan takes issue with Donato's thesis, but not with his observations about Wilde.

In a suggestive essay which picks up these themes, Zhang Longxi describes Wilde's criticism in the light of modern critical practice, suggesting that in Wilde's "creative" criticism we can witness a precursor of modern post-structuralism and deconstruction.

The Picture of Dorian Gray

Few works of Wilde have been subject to close textual scholarship: *The Picture of Dorian Gray* is one of those few. The textual problems of the novel are described in the editions listed elsewhere. Those problems and Wilde's revisions of the novel are also discussed by Donald E. Lawler (1972 and 1988) and by Isobel Murray (1972). For a debate about the reasons for Wilde's revisions to the novel, see Isobel Murray's edition and an exchange in the *TLS* (26 June–13 Sept. 1974). Details of the controversy surrounding the publication of the novel in its original periodical form are given in Stuart Mason, *Oscar Wilde: Art and Morality* (1908). But here required reading is Donald Lawler's comprehensive and informative *An Enquiry into Oscar Wilde's Revisions of The Picture of Dorian Gray* (1988). A different idea of *Dorian Gray* as text is pursued by Peter G. Christensen, who discusses the use made of Wilde's novel by Jean Cocteau in his play *Le portrait surnaturel de Dorian Gray* (1909).

Dorian Gray has been discussed most persistently in terms of the theme of the *Doppelgänger* or double. In general the notion of the double has been treated as a late nineteenth-century trope whose origins and history can be located within literary-historical culture; or it has been treated as a psychological condition, and one capable therefore of psychoanalytical exploration. Robert Rogers (1970) and C. F. Keppler (1972) examine these elements of the novel (but see also the work of Miller, Mayer, Tymms and Miyoshi discussed in other sections of this work). Martine Vieron also discusses doubling in "Le mythe du double" (1985). Jacob Korg (1967) relates duality and doubling to cultural issues such as the social consequences of the notion of identity, especially as they relate to the literary artist. Jan B. Gordon (1968) also explores the notion of duality in cultural terms, by relating it to Arnold's dialectic of human history and human nature—Hebraism and Hellenism—and in an earlier essay in *Criticism* he discusses the motif of doubling in terms of an art/life dualism. (See also, however, the reference to the notion of doubling in the section on literary history, above.) Equally prominent, and indeed related themes, those of narcissism and ageing, are discussed by Douglas Robillard Jr. (1989) and by Ellie Ragland–Sullivan (1986).

The tracing of analogues, parallels and sources has had an equally long history: and in the process striking testimony to Wilde's eclecticism has been established. Walther Fischer (1917) indicated debts to Balzac, Edgar Allen Poe and Joris–Karl Huysmans; Lucius H. Cook (1928) assembled evidence to establish the extent of those borrowings from Huysmans; Oscar Maurer (1947) saw the influence of George Sala; R.D. Brown (1956) saw sources in the work of Suetonius, Symonds and Gibbon; Houston A. Baker, Jr. (1969) compares the novel with Goethe's *Faust* (a comparison with Mephistopheles was first made by Ted R. Spivey in 1960). Dominick Rossi (1969) also sees comparisons with *Faust*; Louis J. Poteet (1971) sees sources in the Gothic novel, particularly in *Melmoth the Wanderer*; and Gerald Monsman in the same year traces the connexions and disjunctions between Pater's heroes and Dorian; William Evans Portnoy (1974) itemizes Wilde's debts to Tennyson. Apryl L. D. Heath (1988) notes an allusion to Matthew Arnold's 1879 "Wordsworth" essay.

Other critics continue to find sources for *Dorian Gray* in remoter areas. However Wolfgang Maier's account of the novel (1984) is critical of the work of most literary historians in this respect; he suggests that the overall effect of Wilde's transactions with his sources is not dependent upon a detailed knowledge of every one of them. In 1987 Isobel Murray detected the influence of Robert Louis Stevenson's *Strange Case of Dr Jekyll and Mr Hyde* upon the novel and upon other works by Wilde; and also in that year she noted the influence of William Sharp's *Children of To-morrow*. J. V. Stevenson (1979) suggests that *A Rebours* is not the book that influences Dorian Gray, and notes that Wilde's references to the chapters and to the contents of the book do not correspond to Huysmans's text. Frédéric Monneyron, looking for subtexts of a different sort, sees parallels (although not influences) between *Dorian Gray* and Nietzsche's *The Birth of Tragedy*. In particular, Monneyron discusses the relationship between Dorian's existence as an individual and his existence in portraiture. He goes on to analyze the relationship between art and death in the novel, seeing in these concerns an embodiment of Nietzsche's distinction between Apollonian and Dionysian modes of existence.

The parallels between Dionysian legend and the novel are also of interest to Terence Dawson (1987), although for other purposes. Dawson lists the parallels between the descriptions of Bacchus (Dionysus) in Ovid's *Metamorphoses* and some of Wilde's descriptions of Dorian, suggesting that Dorian is "invested with the attributes" of Dionysus; and by contrast the portrait of him stands for "Apollonian perfection." Dawson relates this double image of Dorian to Jung's definition of the self: the "god-image of the psyche." Supernatural influence of another kind is detected by Madame Eusebi (1987), who writes on "The Devil in *Dorian Gray*." More recently, but in keeping with the theological theme, Charles Swann writes on "*The Picture of Dorian Gray*, the Bible, and the Unpardonable Sin"; and Horst Schroeder (1991) finds a quotation from Mrs Humphry Ward's *Robert Elsmere* (1888).

Other critics have suggested a more generalized notion of influence and have attempted to locate the novel within Victorian literary conventions and sub-genres. Charles Altieri (1971) considers the novel in terms of a *Bildüngsroman*; and Jan B. Gordon (1967, 1970) traces the connexions to be made between the novel and contemporary writers. Kerry Powell (1978) discusses the theatrical elements in the novel. Elsewhere John Pappas (1972) examines its imagery (see also Beckson's account of the term "wild," discussed below); Robert Keefe (1973) and John E. Hart (1978) draw attention to the treatment of art and of the artist; and the wider context of the work is discussed by G. A. Cevasco (1981). Other elements in the book's reference are indicated by John Espey in Ellmann and Espey (1977). In a perceptive essay, Joyce Carol Oates (1981) emphasizes the simple, parable-like aspects of the novel and its enigmatic qualities—the sense of longing beneath its bright, epigrammatic surface, itself produced by a combination of the elements of the Gothic and of Restoration comedy.

Dorian Gray has for a long time attracted attention as a significant transitional novel. In this respect Donald R. Dickson (1983) takes issue with what he sees as a bias among literary historians in their propensity to over-emphasize the "pre-modern" or "proto-modern" elements in the novel. Elsewhere Dominic Manganiello (1983) contrasts the significance of the ethical and the aesthetic in the novel and Karl Beckson (1986) examines the occurrence of the adjective "wild" and its related forms, "wildly" and "wilder," in the final revision of the text. Beckson claims that the use of the name "shorn of the e" is a "symbolic form of self-mutilation consistent with [Wilde's] own masochistic tendencies" (30). Beckson argues that in the frequency of their occurrence and the nature of their collocations, these lexical items amount to an autobiographical "signature" in the text. (Beckson's data, though, is "raw" evidence, as a stylistician would understand the term; indeed, in this respect it would be as helpful to know whether these lexical items occur more or less frequently in Wilde's other works and how their incidence changes in the revisions to the novel.)

The generic anomolies of *Dorian Gray* is another topic which interests critics. For details of the relationship of the novel to the Gothic and to diabolism, see Fletcher and Stokes (1976, 41). Kerry Powell (1980, 1983, 1984) has written an informed and informative series of essays which attempt to draw parallels between *Dorian Gray* and various Victorian sub-genres. The general thesis in all his essays on the topic is that Wilde's works often have their origins in popular Victorian forms. So Powell notes that the sources of Wilde's novel have been sought by recent critics among genres as varied as Gothic fiction and the "decadent" novel (such as *A Rebours* and *Marius the Epicurean*), but he emphasizes that in late nineteenth-century popular literature there was a "thriving sub-genre of fiction in which the props, the themes, and even to some degree the dialogue and characterization of *Dorian Gray* are anticipated." One such sub-genre to which Powell gives particular emphasis is that of the "magic picture" novel—a tradition in which he suggests Wilde was "steeped, even to the extent of using names from other fictions in that tradition." For further reference to accounts of the haunted picture tradition, though, see Fletcher and Stokes (1976, 41). Elsewhere Powell (1984) suggests that *Dorian Gray* shares certain similarities with popular mesmeric fictions of the time. Powell's account, however, is challenged by

Nathan Cervo (1985) in a later issue of the same periodical. Cervo sees the novel presenting a fundamental antithesis between good and evil, and thus he locates it within a tradition of "spiritual autobiography." In a rejoinder Powell concedes that the novel may indeed go beyond its immediate generic origins, but he nonetheless asserts that Wilde "strangely enough, achieved his best work when he stooped to mine the worn-out veins of Victorian literature"; in this respect Powell's suggestions about Wilde's exploitation of the devices and conventions of popular forms reinforce the observations made by recent critics of the plays (including those made by Powell himself).

Finally, it should be noted that, like other aspects of Wilde's *oeuvre*, *Dorian Gray* has generated a lively academic debate among German critics in both English and German. The translated work, including Norbert Kohl, *Oscar Wilde: The Work of a Conformist Rebel* (1989), is discussed in the appropriate sections of this essay, but for an account of the work by Kohl in German—*Oscar Wilde: Leben und Werk in Daten und Bilder* (1976) and *Oscar Wilde: Das literarische Werk zwischen Provokation und Anpassung* (1980)—and Ria Omasreiter's *Oscar Wilde* (1978), see Fletcher and Stokes (1983). Wolgang Maier's account of the *The Picture of Dorian Gray* is discussed above. For details of earlier German scholarship, see Fletcher and Stokes (1976, 109).

Other Fiction

As *Dorian Gray* has allowed critics to focus attention on concepts such as genre and intertextuality, so, predictably perhaps, the other fiction has been marginalized, not the least by Ellmann (1987), who barely mentions it. Moreover the methodologies which have been been so rewarding when applied to the major works have been conspicuously absent from what little discussion there has been of the stories.

So, for example, Jean M. D'Alessandro's monograph *Hues of Mutability: The Waning Vision in Oscar Wilde's Narrative* discusses Wilde's prose fiction only in terms of its emerging complexity. The exceptions to this general pattern are as follows: the suggestive and highly original discussion of "The Portrait of Mr. W. H." (if indeed this work may be counted as fiction) by Linda Dowling (1980), who relates the story to those concerns she discusses at length elsewhere, Decadence and language; Bruce Bashford's intelligent discussion (1988) of the idea of interpretation in relation to the same story; and Horst Schroeder's instructive account of "The Canterville Ghost" (1977). Lewis L. Poteet (1970) discusses the same piece in relation to Wilde's other work, in particular to the criticism. A similar strategy is employed by Lydia Reineck Wilburn, who examines "The Canterville Ghost" by suggesting that Wilde was using the story as a means to explore "various concepts of a theory of performance," especially the artist's and the audience's role in artistic performance and she relates the novel to Wilde's account of performance in *Intentions*.

Also informative is Michael C. Kotzin (1979), who sets Wilde's fairy tales in relation to nineteenth-century fairy stories in general. Horst Schroeder (1988) gives an account of the historical and literary reference of "The Birthday of the Infanta." Elsewhere, John Allen Quintus (1977) discusses the fairy stories in terms of allegory. Robert K. Martin (1979) sees an allegory of a different nature—the emergence (and Wilde's acceptance) of homosexuality—in the same tales. On the tales as allegory and parable, see also John Updike (1962). Gisèle Sarkissian (1985) analyzes the use of ghosts in Wilde's short fiction, and Peter Cerowsky (1985) describes Wilde's treatment of fright. Elsewhere Guy Willoughby (1988) discusses "The Nightingale and the Rose."

Poems and Aphorisms

Wilde's poems and the collections of his aphorisms have not received much critical attention. In general the poems (with the exception of *The Ballad of Reading Gaol*) have not been valued highly, and from their first publication they were considered derivative to the point of plagiarism (although, as I have suggested in other parts of this work, the concept of plagiarism in a writer so careless of the authority and uniqueness of the "text" could bear a more general and more systematic examination). Jerome H. Buckley outlines the critical reception of the *Poems* in "Echo and Artifice: The Poetry of Oscar Wilde" and discusses the charges of plagiarism. He examines in particular the poems which deal with impressions, and contrasts the early work with *The Ballad of Reading Gaol*. If the poetry was condemned as unoriginal or juvenile during Wilde's life, it was virtually ignored after his death. Fletcher and Stokes (1976, 121–23) document this general disdain and, by contrast, the general and consistent admiration for the poetry in Germany (124). Bobby Fong's unpublished edition of the poems (1978) and his account of some of the manuscripts (1979) remain the best studies of textual problems.

Most critical accounts of the poetry are to be found in the general studies of Wilde, described in the previous section. See, in addition, Arthur Symons, *A Study of Oscar Wilde* (1930) and the work of Douglas Bush (1937) and A. E. Rodway (1958), all of which are discussed above; see also the discussions by Robert Louis Peters (1957), and by Kingsley Amis (1956) in his anthology of Wilde's poems and essays. At the level of individual study, J. D. Thomas (1951) discusses the composition of "The Harlot's House." *The Ballad of Reading Gaol* has in general been more favourably and more frequently discussed than the other poems. See, for example the essays by Houston A. Baker (1937) and G. Arms and J. E. Whitesell (1943). Albert Camus' remarks (1952) on the poem are interesting, if only for the fact that they are by Camus; and in a lucid discussion of Orwell and Wilde in *Modes of Modern Writing* (1977), David Lodge analyzes the fictive qualities of the poem. In "Oscar Wilde's 'Chant du cygne'," William E. Buckler (1990) discusses *The Ballad of Reading Gaol* and sets the poem against the prison letter to the *Daily Chronicle* ("The Case of Warder Martin") and *De Profundis*. He analyzes the poem and Wilde's changing attitudes to it.

Elsewhere the idea of subversion, a familiar way of discussing Wilde's other work, is central to a stimulating essay by Sandra Siegel on an unlikely part of the *oeuvre*—his aphorisms. Siegel writes briefly about the popularity of collections of aphorisms at the turn of the century—there were evidently more published then than ever before; and this popularity she connects to their function in ideology. By claiming for themselves a transhistorical nature, they seem to embody "timeless sayings which require neither context nor narrative," and are hence to be seen as confirmatory of or "compatible with the prevailing current of opinion" (16–17). Wilde's collected and uncollected aphorisms, Siegel suggests, subvert these expectations, implying a world in which words "are subject to ironic reversals of meaning." Wilde's aphorisms therefore encapsulate those ironic reversals of meaning and inversions of truths which are in many ways characteristic of the *oeuvre*. Siegel concludes by relating this aspect of Wilde's work to the then precarious nature of the colonial relationship between English and Irish culture, a line of investigation that could perhaps be usefully expanded to other aspects of Wilde's wit.

The Plays

Not surprisingly, the plays have received the most consistent critical attention. What troubled most contemporary reviewers was the relationship between what they saw as two quite disparate features—the comic elements and the "problem-play" themes. The most important reactions during the early years of this century also focused upon the related problem of generic definition. Hence essays such as those by St. John Hankin (1908), C. E. Montague (1911) and Hesketh Pearson (1921) tried to isolate what is distinctive about Wilde's drama. (Reactions to the plays in the first two decades of this century are given in fuller detail by Fletcher and Stokes, 1976, 96; contemporary reviews are listed by Mikhail, 1978; some are reprinted by Beckson, 1970).

The issue of genre definition persisted through studies in the 1950s in works by Louis Kronenberger; it was taken up in important essays by Eric Bentley (1948), Arthur Ganz (1960) and Ian Gregor (1966). The concern of all these essays is the particular nature of Wilde's comedy. Gregor's case, for example, is that *The Importance of Being Earnest* is the central play in the *oeuvre* because it succeeds in creating an arena where the values of the dandy are at a premium and may be celebrated. But Gregor's essay should be read alongside recent studies, particularly the introduction to Russell Jackson's edition (1980), which draws attention to the radicalism of the plays—more specifically to the ways in which Wilde's plots invert Victorian melodramatic conventions. (See also in this respect "Fallen Women, Lost Children: Wilde and the Theatre of the Nineties" (1984) where Wendell Stacy Johnson also discusses Wilde's relation to contemporary theatrical conventions.)

A subject not unrelated to an aspect of Gregor's essay—that of masking—is discussed by Arthur Ganz (1963) and R.K.R. Thornton (1989) and, in a penetrating and suggestive essay, by Jerusha McCormack (1976). More recently Antony Easthope (1987) discusses jokes and ideology in *Earnest*. (But on this topic compare recent work on *Salomé* discussed below.)

Another critical issue with a long pedigree is the familiar one of European influence—in this context, that of European dramatic models upon Wilde's work. Here individual studies by Stanley Schwarz (1933), Z. Raafat (1966), E. H. Mikhail (1968) and most importantly Charles B. Paul and Robert D. Pepper (1971) all draw attention to the influence of French models on Wilde—particularly the work of Scribe, Sardou, and Musset. Important, too, for the French context of Wilde's drama is Kelver Hartley's *Oscar Wilde: L'Influence française dans son oeuvre* (1935).(But, as I have already indicated, recent work has problematized the whole notion and nature of influence.) Another, more local, perceived line of influence is that of Restoration comedy. Here the issue is broached by N. W. Sawyer (1931), but the most convincing essays have been by James A. Ware (1970), Geoffrey Stone (1976) and David Parker (1974), works which should be read alongside David L. Hirst's illuminating general study, *Comedy of Manners* (1979).

Recently critics have broadened the scope of their search for sources. Emil Roy (1972) and Katharine Worth (1978) are more concerned to give Wilde's work an Irish context, while J. L. Styan (1960) compares *Earnest* with Ibsen's work, an influence seen as increasingly important in recent years. So an essay by Kerry Powell in 1985 also traces the nature of the relationship between Wilde and Ibsen. Both here and in his later book, already mentioned, Powell points out that Wilde's contemporaries usually made comparisons between his work and that of French dramatists of the 1880s and 1890s, but in so doing they failed to see the connections between Wilde's comedies and the plays of Ibsen, then being performed in Britain in private theatres. Powell describes in general terms the ways in which Ibsen's work was adapted and imitated by British playwrights in the 1890s, and he then goes on to suggest that in Wilde's case there is "undiscovered common ground" between his and Ibsen's work—in, for example, the affinities of elements of the plots in *Lady Windermere's Fan* and *Ghosts*, *The Importance of Being Earnest* and *Hedda Gabler* and most importantly, *An Ideal Husband* and *Pillars of Society*. However it should be noted that Powell's essay overlooks some British studies—particularly that of Katharine Worth (1983)—which emphasize Wilde's commerce with topical social issues and his relationship with the work of contemporary British and European playwrights.

The question of influence is pursued in a brief essay by Ali A. Al–Hejazi (1985). Al–Hejazi suggests that *The Importance of Being Earnest* is in several key ways indebted to W. S. Gilbert's *Engaged*, especially in its moral attitudes to those familiar and well-worked Victorian concerns, wealth and marriage. Influence, too, figures in an essay by Werner Vortriede (1955), who sees comparisons between *Earnest* and *Faust*. Joseph Loewenstein, following the same line of enquiry, explains the brilliance of *Earnest* by seeing Wilde's work in relation to both Sophocles's *Oedipus Rex* and to the work of Sardou. Hence for Loewenstein Wilde "flirts brilliantly" with *Oedipus Rex*, and in so doing "converts" the tragic to comedy: such dramatic tactics exemplify, in Loewenstein's view, the provisionality of all Wilde's moral positions.

Regenia Gagnier (1986), in a work already mentioned, investigates Wilde's manipulation of his theatrical audiences, and Kristin Morrison (1981) and Alan Andrews (1982) debate Wilde's stage directions, Morrison claiming that "description of external behaviour and the interpretation of motive" in Shaw's drama provided a model for Wilde's use of similar stage directions. Later Andrews points out that the text of Shaw which Wilde would have seen was an acting edition devoid of both detailed character descriptions and elaborate stage directions. Russell Jackson (1983) takes up this debate about the nature of Wilde's and Shaw's stage directions, pointing out that many of the stage directions for Wilde's last two plays were added by him to the proofs of the published versions of the plays, and in that sense are the retrospective thoughts—the "idealization of his prelapsarian self"—of the "late" Wilde.

On the plays taken individually: *Lady Windermere's Fan* is discussed by Cleanth Brooks and Robert B. Heilman (1945), by Morse Peckham (1956) and E. H. Mikhail (1968); and in the introductions to the editions by V. F. Hopper and G. B. Lahey (1960), Louis Kronenberger (1962) and Ian Small (1980). Elsewhere David Davidson (1983) discusses the film adaptation of *Lady Windermere's Fan*.

On the two middle society dramas, *A Woman of No Importance* and *An Ideal Husband*, very little has been written: however, in addition to the critical monographs described above and the work on the plays by Bird and Worth, see essays by Stanley Schwarz (1933) and E. H. Mikhail (1968) and the introduction to *Two Society Comedies* (1983) by Ian Small and Russell Jackson. Even less has been written on the minor dramatic pieces: Frances Miriam Reed (1985) provides one of the rare accounts of *Vera; or The Nihilist* (but see also Worth [1983] for an excellent discussion of the central issues of the minor plays, and the scholarly introductory material to Reed's excellent edition of the play, discussed elsewhere).

Inevitably *Earnest* has received much more detailed critical attention than the other plays. Otto Reinert (1956) discusses satire and comic inversion in the play, and E. B. Partridge (1960) relates the concept of truth-telling in the critical essays to the representation of mores in the play; and later Christopher Craft (1990) analyzes the subject of sexuality in it. The topic of *Earnest* as a dramatic text occupies Joseph Donohue (1971), who, in a ground-breaking essay, indicates the preconditions for a reconstruction of the first performance. Also good on the dramatic contexts of the play are Joseph Loewenstein (1985), and the introduction to Russell Jackson's edition (1980).

Russell Jackson (1983) describes the persistence—even up to the present day—of the image of British "Society" which Wilde invokes and exploits in his work. For Jackson, Wilde's comedy has attained a "classic" status; indeed he points out that for most audiences it is "the representative Victorian play," and as a consequence it has become "harmless." The survival of this image of Victorian society, Jackson argues, has tended to convert Wilde's radicalism into a conservatism, and hence characters such as Lady Bracknell, who were originally comic (and subversive) deviations of Victorian social and dramatic types, tend in modern productions to become indistinguishable from those types.

A tendency to see Wilde as a man of the theatre rather than as a writer-turned-dramatist is now beginning to emerge. Keith Brown (1984) finds most critical accounts of *The Importance of Being Earnest* less than adequate, simply because commentators have failed to pay proper attention to Wilde's modes of characterization. The power of the play, Brown suggests, derives from Wilde's attitude of "quiet, sympathetic, philosophic amusement" which in its turn derives from the figure of the post-Parisian Wilde of the mid-eighties, excited by the idea of evil, but able to create a mood of sustained dramatic innocence. Elsewhere Joel H. Kaplan writes illuminatingly on "Ernest Worthing's London Address." Harold Bloom (1988) devotes a whole volume in his Chelsea House series to *Earnest*.

The impact of *Salomé* on European readers has been much greater than on their English-speaking counterparts. The reason for this state of affairs is not hard to find: it is due in part, of course, to Strauss's opera and the enormous impact of its first performances, but due also in part to the fact that, more than any other of the plays, *Salomé* has explicit parallels in European literature. Early reactions to the play and to the first staging of the opera are given by Fletcher and Stokes (1976, 102), and the controversy over the first British performance of the opera (and the ensuing Pemberton Billing case in 1918) is also detailed by them (104); but in this respect see also Michael Kettle (1977).

The sources and European parallels for the plays have particularly interested critics. Ernst Bendz (1917) and Helen Grace Zagona (1960) locate the parallels to be made with Flaubert. Bertrand D'Astorg (1971) and Nicholas Joost and Franklin Court (1972) discuss the myth of Salomé and its importance for the motif of the *femme fatale*; Christopher Nassaar (1978) points out the influence of Wilde's "vision of evil" upon work by Yeats and Conrad. Marilyn Gaddis Rose (1980) briefly describes the Salomé motif in French literature in the final years of the nineteenth century and discusses the use and limitations of Wilde's Decadent language in the play. Robert C. Schweik (1987) also compares Wilde's use of the Salomé theme with its other treatments in nineteenth-century culture. For a more recent and admirably detailed account of the French influences on *Salomé*, see Peter Raby (1989).

Indeed, *Salomé* is becoming an increasingly important text for many critics with a general interest in Wilde. Because it ran foul of the constraints imposed by the Lord Chamberlain's Examiner of Plays, particularly because of its representation of sexual topics, *Salomé* is coming to be seen as a document which allows contemporary issues in the politics of gender to be glimpsed. So Kate Millett (1970) discusses the play in the context of sexual guilt and homosexual fear of women, a reading which increasingly finds favour with later critics. Edmund Bergler (1956) too, in a related essay, claims to have identified evidence of Wilde's troubled psychopathology in the play's representations of sadism and misogyny.

However, more recently such simple views of the expressive relationship between literary artefact and writer have given way to an interest in the relationship between text and ideology. So Elliot L. Gilbert's examination of *Salomé* looks at details of the play's publication, taking as its subject the question of the relationship between the text and Beardsley's illustrations for it. Gilbert argues that the two comment on each other and thus form a "notable representation of perverse sexuality" which is in turn "a devastating attack on the conventions of patriarchal culture" while at the same time expressing a "horror at the threatening female energy which is the instrument of that attack" (133–34). Gilbert maintains that Beardsley's "lurid" illustrations go well with the text and "illustrate" the subject matter and "spirit" of the play (138). These Gilbert relates to what he sees as partial attacks on patriarchal power and authority embodied in the play, which issue finally in both Beardsley's and Wilde's "undermining of clear distinctions between male and female in both play and illustrations [and] the ambivalent responses of the two artists to an aggressive female sexuality" (159). Patriarchal power, it might be noted in passing, seems to have survived the onslaught more or less unscathed.

Observations such as those of Gilbert might perhaps be usefully read alongside Ian Fletcher's accounts of the typology and sources of Beardsley's obsessive images (Fletcher 1987 and 1988); and Gilbert's conclusions about the radical nature of the representation of sexuality in Beardsley's work might also be compared with those of Linda Gertner Zatlin (1985), who argues for a view of the artist "in favour of healthy, if bawdy, sexuality, sexual education, and sexual exploration" (6). (The theme of Beardsley and sexual politics is pursued more fully in Zatlin's recent study, *Aubrey Beardsley and Victorian Sexual Politics* [1990].) For a fuller account of the relationship between Beardsley and Wilde, see Robert Langenfeld, *Reconsidering Aubrey Beardsley* (1989). Also interested in the relationship between Wilde's text and Beardsley's illustrations is Maureen T. Kravec (1983), who suggests that the "drawings strike a pose of seriousness while slyly satirizing the human folly of self-centered possessiveness by no means absent in their own society." Such effects are achieved, Kravec argues, partly by those well-known caricatures by Beardsley of Wilde himself in several of the illustrations.

Graham Good studies the first productions of *Salomé*. Seeing it as the "culminating-point" of the English Decadence, Good describes the banning of the play in Britain in 1892 and its subsequent publication in Britain, with Beardsley's illustrations, in 1894. (In passing Good maintains but does not cite any new evidence for the fairly common view that the English text was extensively revised by Wilde himself and was not the work of Douglas. But it ought to be noted in passing that such a view was in fact denied by Wilde himself in *De Profundis*). Good's description of the staging of the play is a preliminary one, and ought to be read along with the learned and suggestive observations made by Rodney Shewan (1986) on late nineteenth-century versions of *Salomé*. There is an obvious need for a full account of the first productions of all of Wilde's plays along the lines of that proposed by Joseph Donohue (1971) for *The Importance of Being Earnest*. Good's account of *Salomé* goes some way in that direction but it is, necessarily perhaps given the limitations of the means at his disposal, rather superficial in its coverage.

De Profundis

The best text of *De Profundis* is still that given by Hart–Davis in the *Letters* (1962). Reactions to the letter by contemporaries, and by those involved in its (partial) publication—particularly the reactions of Ransome, Douglas, Sherard—can be found in the works of biography listed above. Details of the circumstances of the production of the text and its textual history are given by Hart–Davis, by Ellmann (1987) and, most polemically, by Gagnier (1984). Gagnier's thesis, that the letter should read as a document written in barely tolerable prison conditions, is reinforced by Dollimore (1987) who sees in it a renunciation of Wilde's transgressive aesthetic brought about by a desire to invest suffering with meaning.

Generally speaking, *De Profundis* has tended to be discussed in relation to the biography or to the criticism. The context of the confessional tradition is a theme taken up by Jan B. Gordon (1970), Jerome H. Buckley (1983 and 1984) and Avrom Fleishman (1983), all noted above, and who, like Harvey Kail (1979) are concerned with the notion of truth-telling in the letter. Bashford (1985) contrasts some of the presuppositions of *De Profundis* with those of the critical dialogues. Works by Albert Camus (1954), Alick West (1958), Jacques Barzun (1964) and Rodney Shewan (1977), all also discussed above, suggestively relate the prison letter to other parts of the *oeuvre*; also in an essay discussed above, William E. Buckler contrasts the letter with *The Ballad of Reading Gaol*; and in "Oscar Wilde's Aesthetic of the Self" (1989) he argues that the writing of *De Profundis* was an act of self-realization. Elsewhere Steven Marcus (1982) writes a stimulating essay on Wilde's autobiographical work.

| 8 |

Editions

Collections and Selections

THERE is no satisfactory complete edition of Wilde. The only editions which have approached completeness are Robert Ross's beautifully produced 1908 edition (now a collector's item) and G. F. Maine's 1948 single volume *Works*, published by Collins and subsequently reprinted, with a changed copy-text for *Earnest*, many times. Both works, however, have their shortcomings: apart from their incompleteness, they are unsatisfactory textually. Neither, for example, has even a token textual apparatus. The grounds for Ross's omission of some of Wilde's texts (such as his exclusion of some of the journalism) have never been adequately described and offer an interesting area for study; moreover, as entries to earlier sections have indicated, the soundness of Ross's choices of copy-text needs to be carefully assessed. Maine's edition, too, although useful and widely available, is also incomplete and unsound textually. A full edition, although in hand, is still at least three years in the future. Indeed, until Wilde's journalism, reviews and occasional pieces are adequately collected, we will not have anything that amounts to a comprehensive edition of his work. Moreover, until such times as a full collation of early drafts with the performed and published texts is available, we will have no overall conception of Wilde's practices as a writer.

This general caution aside, though, since 1948 there have been useful editions for both scholar and student. Richard Aldington's *The*

Portable Oscar Wilde (1946;1977) and Isobel Murray's *Plays, Prose Writings and Poems* (1975) both remain serviceable reading editions. The old Everyman text of *Plays, Prose Writings and Poems* has recently been reissued with an introduction by Terry Eagleton (1991). Eagleton is interested in Wilde's Irishness, and he describes his career in terms of the larger context of Irish dispossession and exile.

A text more recently established is that by H. Montgomery Hyde whose usefully annotated edition of Wilde (1982) prints a large selection of the works, although it is by no means complete. In fact little attention is paid to textual matters, and for the most part Montgomery Hyde draws upon the 1948 Collins edition of the works. Despite its title, the book is not heavily annotated, although all the notes are useful and some are original. Isobel Murray's selection of texts (1989) for the Oxford Standard Authors series, although not complete, has a wide range of works, is well annotated and textually reliable, and is perhaps the best student edition so far available.

Given the absence of a collected edition, anthologies are invariably the means by which students encounter Wilde's texts. As a rule, these editions are not to be relied upon in textual matters: in general they should be regarded as working editions, useful for their introductory material and annotation, and incidentally as a means of assessing Wilde's changing fortunes and reputation. Richard Ellmann's *Oscar Wilde: Selected Writings* (1961) and *Oscar Wilde: The Artist as Critic* (1969) present useful choices of material, the latter particularly so, since it reproduces some of the little known reviews. Useful, too, are Stanley Weintraub's thoroughly annotated *The Literary Criticism of Oscar Wilde* (1968) and Hesketh Pearson's volume, *Essays by Oscar Wilde* (1950).

Eric Warner and Graham Hough (1983) anthologize an interesting and unusual, if necessarily brief, selection from the prose. The reading of Wilde which emerges from Hough's and Warner's selection is in keeping with the overall thesis of their anthology, namely that the work of late nineteenth-century writers on art and aesthetics contains the seeds of the modernist revolt—in our post-Barthesian world, a safe and fairly orthodox view of Wilde's literary pedigree. Bernard Denvir also anthologizes some of Wilde's writing, but his concern is with art and with artists on art. He sets some of Wilde's writing on art against contemporary debates, particularly those on art-education and architecture in the last decades of the century.

Much more informed, if again necessarily brief, is Ian Fletcher's introduction to his anthology *British Poetry and Prose: 1870–1905* (1987), which prints the "Preface" to *Dorian Gray* and *The Ballad of Reading Gaol*. John Wyse Jackson edits an interesting, if incomplete, anthology of the journalism, enticingly entitled *Aristotle at Afternoon Tea: The Rare Oscar Wilde* (1991).

The problems of annotating any text are of course manifold and complex: it is now clear that with Wilde's works such problems can become acute. As Wilde sought fame in the theatre, in learned and avant-garde circles and as a popular author, so he appears to have had several quite separate audiences in mind for his works. Isolating these audiences is one of the most pressing problems for the modern annotator. Moreover, Wilde's works are rich in sources and influence, the former sometimes to the point of plagiarism. So the audiences addressed by his work, and the critical responses to them, still offer rich opportunities for study despite the pioneering work of Beckson in 1970. (For a suggestive discussion of the audiences of Wilde's dramatic work, see Donohue [1988], 129ff., discussed above.)

In this respect Horst Schroeder's work, *Annotations to Oscar Wilde: "The Portrait of Mr W.H."* (1984), is an interesting study. It is a volume of painstaking and thorough annotation, and as a companion piece to Schroeder's earlier essay on the composition, publication and reception of Wilde's essay, it shows how rich and diverse Wilde's sources were. It usefully complements the essays on "The Portrait of Mr W.H." by Gerhard Joseph, Bruce Bashford and Linda Dowling—all discussed above.

Individual Works

Although we still await the *Complete Works*, Wilde has been well served with single editions of some texts. Wilfried Edener's 1964 edition of *The Picture of Dorian Gray* takes the periodical text as copy text and has textual variants and an introduction. Isobel Murray's edition of *The Picture of Dorian Gray* (1974), however, is based on the 1891 Ward Lock text and has useful annotation and some textual variants. Donald E. Lawler (1988) has produced the fullest and best edition of the work so far available, complete with a thorough textual apparatus. Isobel Murray also edits and annotates the *Complete Shorter Fiction* (1979) in which she prints the shorter version of "The Portrait of Mr W.H." John Espey (1977) reproduces photographically *The Happy Prince and Other Tales* and *A House of Pomegranates*.

The fullest editions of any of Wilde's works are the editions of the society comedies. In his edition of *The Importance of Being Earnest* (1980), Jackson uses the 1899 three-act Smithers edition as copy-text, but collates it with the manuscript and various typescript drafts, as well as with French's 1903 acting edition. (Textual revisions to *Earnest* are also discussed in a comprehensive essay by John Glavin [1987].) Ian Small's companion edition of *Lady Windermere's Fan* (1980) prints the Elkin Mathews and John Lane 1893 edition, collating that text with surviving drafts of the play. Small's and Jackson's editions of *A Woman of No Importance* and *An Ideal Husband* (1983) in the same series are companion volumes. The textual notes and apparatus give an account of the drafts, genesis and revisions of the plays and try to establish stemmas of the progress of each play from composition to performance and publication. The editors print in appendices much of the material discarded by Wilde in the course of the composition of the works and attempt to ascertain the relationships between the drafts for each act. (Some of the textual revisions to *An Ideal Husband* are further discussed by Glen E. Lich, 1986.)

Some of the missing drafts of *A Woman of No Importance* in the Beerbohm Tree Collection in the Bristol Theatre Collection have already been mentioned: see Jackson and Small (1987). Their discovery virtually trebles the number of known drafts of the play and, they argue, gives a wealth of information about the nature and extent of Wilde's collaborations with his theatre-managers.

As I have indicated, a description of a dramatic text and of its textual history has to include the history of productions; further textual research into the plays will have to take into account the particularities of performances and of audience reaction, stage-history and so forth. Ruth Berggren (1987) edits the four-act version of *The Importance of Being Earnest* (as opposed to Jackson's three-act version which takes the 1899 first edition as copy-text), as it was sent to Charles Frohman in November 1894, but which is *not* the prompt-copy for the first performance.

In recent years, one part of the "fugitive" Wilde has been given a proper edition. In an admirable piece of scholarly reconstruction, Michael Helfand and Philip E. Smith II (1989) edit the *Oxford Notebooks and Commonplace Book*. However Wilde's reviews and his journalism are the most fugitive of all his work: certainly a sizeable body of his ephemeral writing has still to be retrieved. Despite the anthology edited by John Wyse Jackson (1991) already mentioned, the full extent of what Wilde actually wrote, especially for the *Pall Mall Gazette* and the *Woman's World*, still needs to be ascertained. As with the manuscripts, a systematic census needs to be undertaken. Steps in this direction have been taken by Kevin H. F. O'Brien and John Stokes. O'Brien (1983) identifies Wilde as the author of "A Batch of Books"—an unsigned review in the *Pall Mall Gazette*, 28 (26 July 1888). O'Brien marshalls the evidence, internal and corroborative, for Wilde's authorship, lists the texts reviewed (which included Lady Wilde's *Ancient Legends of Ireland*) and reprints the text of the review. Stokes (1980) identifies Wilde's review of *Crime and Punishment* in the *Pall Mall Gazette*. There have also been some attempts at reconstructing fugitive material. Once again Kevin H. F. O'Brien (1974) has reconstructed Wilde's lecture "The House Beautiful" (see also in this respect Michael J. O'Neill, 1955). Robert D. Pepper (1972) has reconstructed Wilde's 1882 San Francisco lecture "Irish Poets and the Poetry of the Nineteenth Century." Welcome as these local studies are, they represent only a fraction of what is needed.

In an important essay, Rodney Shewan (1982) edits and reproduces the hitherto unpublished manuscript draft in the Clark Library of *A Wife's Tragedy*. He describes the state of the manuscript, and the consequent problems that arise over Wilde's inconsistent use of characters' names. He corrects the attempt made by Guillot de Saix to reconstruct the plot of the piece (which, Shewan argues, was made principally from the Dulau sale catalogue), and concludes that the fragment is important because it could mark the moment of transition from the early romantic dramas to the society comedies. Shewan (1983) goes on to discuss the significance of the sketch, seeing in it some uncomfortable "autobiographical pressures": it is precisely this nearness to Wilde's life which explains the absence of any reference to it in Wilde's correspondence, Shewan argues; and he suggests that the fragment was written just prior to the composition of *Lady Windermere's Fan*.

In a comprehensive and scholarly collation of the known MSS, the first and second printings, Frances Miriam Reed (1989) has produced an excellent edition of *Vera; Or, the Nihilist*. The collations include emendations made by Wilde for the New York performance of 1897, and those (allegedly authorial) made to Leonard Smithers' 1902 posthumous edition. The edition contains a full introduction and prints the cast of the 1883 production and extracts of reviews as appendices.

In contrast, other single works have not received such close editorial attention. There are still no proper published critical editions of the journalism, of the poems or of *Intentions* (although important editions in the form of dissertations, especially of the poems by Bobby Fong and of the journalism by Carl Markgraf, *do* exist in the University of Notre Dame, the University of California, and the University of Birmingham respectively). Fletcher and Stokes (1976, 59) list the locations of some of the poems not yet collected. An instance of the difficulties faced by editors is illuminated by Roger Lewis (1990), who, in "A Misattribution: Oscar Wilde's 'Unpublished' Sonnet on Chatterton," draws attention to the way Richard Ellmann ascribes to Wilde the authorship of a sonnet to Chatterton at the end of the (unpublished) lecture on Chatterton at the Clark Library. Lewis describes the circumstances of the lecture and points out that the sonnet is by Rossetti and not by Wilde. It is worth noting, too, that much of the text of the lecture itself is not by Wilde either.

For the apocrypha and dubia, see Guillot de Saix, *Le Chant du cygne* . . . (1942); Charles Hirsch, "Notice Bibliographique," *Teleny* (1934); see also later editions of *Teleny* (1984 and 1986); and John F. Bloxham, *The Priest and the Acolyte, with an Introductory Protest by Stuart Mason* (1907). It should be noted, however, that serious doubts remain about the provenance of all these texts: see Mikhail (1978, 32, 35, 41 and 45); Fletcher and Stokes (1976, 60).

Wilde's aphorisms and conversational *bons mots* continue, over ninety years after his death, to make good copy. Consequently selections continue to appear in print. They are listed in Fletcher and Stokes (1976, 58–59) and Fletcher and Stokes (1983, 25).

Elsewhere, Maeve Gilmore reprints Mervyn Peake's striking illustrations for some poems by Wilde, commissioned in 1945 and executed the following year. The illustrations are a revealing testimony to the way that Peake read Wilde in the last years of his life. Short illustrated editions of *The Happy Prince* (1980), *The Nightingale and the Rose* (1981) and *The Selfish Giant* (1983) have also been published.

Reprints of *The Poet and the Puppets* and *Aristophanes at Oxford*, useful contextualizing source material, are reprinted in Ian Fletcher and John Stokes, eds., *The Decadent Consciousness* (1979).

| 9 |

Bibliographies

THE first significant, and until recently the main, bibliography of Wilde was Stuart Mason (Christopher Millard), *A Bibliography of Oscar Wilde* (1914). While still containing a mine of useful information, it should be treated with caution. (For an account of some of the pitfalls awaiting the unwary, see Fletcher and Stokes [1976] 55, and Mikhail [1978] ix.)

The most complete bibliography of Wilde (listing material up to 1977) is Mikhail's. His chapter on bibliographical material in this work is excellent and is the fullest available. Other significant bibliographical material is contained in Abraham Horodisch, *Oscar Wilde's 'Ballad of Reading Gaol': A Bibliographical Study* (1954), and in Donald E. Lawler, "Oscar Wilde in *The New Cambridge Bibliography of English Literature*," *Papers of the Bibliographical Society of America* (1973). Details of specialized bibliographies are given in Mikhail (1978), 3–15.

Catalogues of the major collections at libraries are also important sources of information. See in particular Robert Ernest Cowan and William Andrews Clark, *The Library of William Andrews Clark, Jr.: Wilde and Wildeiana* (1922–1931), detailing the holdings of the Clark Library in Wilde material. The basis of that collection was the sale in 1928 of the Dulau collection; for details see A. B. Dulau and Company Ltd., *A Collection of Original Manuscripts, Letters and Books of Oscar Wilde, Including his Letters Written to Robert Ross from Reading Gaol* (1928); see also John Charles Finzi, *Oscar Wilde and his Literary Circle: A Catalog of Manuscripts and Letters in the William Andrews Clark Memorial Library* (1957).

Since the publication of Finzi's work, the Clark Library has added to its holdings; for full details of the manuscripts and letters in its possession, see the appropriate section in this work. Also useful are the following: Guillot de Saix, *Le Chant du cygne: contes parlés d'Oscar Wilde. Recuellis et redigés par Guillot de Saix* (1942); Sarah A. Dickson, "Arents Tobacco Collection," *New York Public Library Bulletin* (1950); *Handlist of the Ross Memorial Collection . . . Placed in the Bodleian on Permanent Deposit, April 1932*; and H. Montgomery Hyde, "Oscar Wilde," in Gabriel Austin, ed., *Four Oaks Library* (1967).

Sale catalogues also contain relevant information. See N. L. Munby, "Oscar Wilde" in *Sale Catalogues of Libraries of Eminent Persons* (1971) for an account of the Tite Street sale; J. B. Stetson, *The Oscar Wilde Collection of John B. Stetson* (1920); and R. B. Glaenzer, *Catalog of the Library of Richard Butler Glaenzer* (1905).

Bibliographical listings for contextualizing information may be consulted in the following: Gary H. Paterson (1980) for bibliographical material on Lord Alfred Douglas; and L. W. Connolly's and J. P. Wearing's annual bibliography in *Nineteenth-Century Theatre* (formerly *Nineteenth-Century Theatre Research*) for bibliographical material relating to nineteenth-century British theatre. Linda Dowling's *Aestheticism and Decadence: A Selective Annotated Bibliography* (1977) lists useful contextual material.

The guides to research published over the past thirty years, if used in conjunction with Mikhail (1978) and the annual bibliographies listed below, provide the most accessible way of obtaining bibliographical information about Wilde. So see: Lionel Stevenson, "Oscar Wilde" in *The Victorian Poets: A Guide to Research*, Frederic E. Faverty, ed. (1956); Wendell Harris, "Oscar Wilde" in *Victorian Prose: A Guide to Research*, David DeLaura, ed. (1973); Ian Fletcher and John Stokes, "Oscar Wilde" in *Anglo-Irish Literature: A Review of Research*, Richard J. Finneran, ed. (1976); and Ian Fletcher and John Stokes, "Oscar Wilde" in *Recent Research on Anglo-Anglo-Irish Writers: A Supplement to Anglo-Irish Literature: A Review of Research*, Richard J. Finneran, ed. (1983).

Other important sources of bibliographical information are the literary periodicals devoted to the period. The annual bibliographies in *Victorian Studies* and in the MLA *International Bibliography* are both helpful, although both have omissions: generally speaking, the MLA bibliography is best for work published outside the English-speaking countries of the world.

Apart from the bibliography in *Nineteenth–Century Theatre*, already mentioned, *English Literature in Transition*, *Modern Drama*, *Victorian Newsletter* and *The Year's Work in English Studies* all contain useful bibliographical material.

| 10 |

General Bibliography

Ackroyd, Peter. *The Last Testament of Oscar Wilde*. London: Hamish Hamilton, 1983.

Agate, James. "Oscar Wilde and the Theatre," *The Masque*, 3 (London: Curtain Press, 1947); repr. in *James Agate: An Anthology*. Herbert Van Thal, ed. London: Rupert Hart–Davis, 1961.

Ainslie, Douglas. *Adventures, Social and Literary*. London: T. Fisher Unwin, 1922.

Aldington, Richard, ed. *The Portable Oscar Wilde*. New York: Viking Press, 1946; rev. Stanley Weintraub, Harmondsworth: Penguin Books, 1977.

Al–Hejazi, Ali A., "Wilde's *The Importance of Being Earnest* and Gilbert's *Engaged*: A Comparative Study," *Journal of the College of Arts, King Saud University*, 12, 1 (1985), 107–14.

Allen, Clifford. "Homosexuality and Oscar Wilde: A Psychological Study," in *Homosexuality and Creative Genius*. Hendrik M. Ruitenbeek, ed. New York: Astor–Honor, 1967.

Altieri, Charles. "Organic and Humanist Models in Some English *Bildungsroman*," *Journal of General Education*, 23, 3 (1971), 220–40.

Amis, Kingsley, ed. *Poems and Essays by Oscar Wilde*. London: Collins, 1956.

Amor, Anne Clarke. *Mrs Oscar Wilde: A Woman of Some Importance*. London: Sidgwick and Jackson, 1983.

Anderson Galleries, The. *The Oscar Wilde Collection of John B. Stetson Jr. A Catalogue of the Original Manuscripts, Presentation Copies, First Editions and Autograph Letters of Modern Authors*. Philadelphia: The Rosenbach Co., 1933.

Andrews, Alan. "Horrible Flesh and Blood," *Theatre Notebook*, 36, 1 (1982), 34–35.

Archer, William. *"A Woman of No Importance": The Theatrical "World" of 1893*. London: Walter Scott, 1894.

———. *"An Ideal Husband": The Theatrical "World" of 1895*. London: Walter Scott, 1896.

———. *Playmaking: A Manual of Craftsmanship*. London: Chapman and Hall, 1912.

———. *The Old Drama and the New*. London: Heinemann, 1923.

Arms, G. and J. E. Whitesell. "Wilde's 'The Ballad of Reading Gaol'," *The Explicator* (March 1943): item 41.

Auden, W. H. "Playboy of the Western World: St Oscar the Homintern Martyr," in *The New Partisan Reader, 1945–1953*. William Phillips and Philip Rahv, eds. New York: Harcourt, Brace, 1953.

Austen, Zelda. "The Grasshopper and the Ant: Oscar Wilde and William Morris in the Eighties," *Journal of Pre-Raphaelite Studies*, 4, 1 (1983), 87–107.

Baker, Houston A., Jr. "'The Ballad of Reading Gaol': An Enduring Monument," *Reading and Collecting*, (27 May 1937), 11–27.

———. "A Tragedy of the Artist: *The Picture of Dorian Gray*," *Nineteenth Century Fiction*, 24, 3 (1969), 349–55.

Bartlett, Neil. *Who Was That Man?: A Present for Mr Oscar Wilde*. London: Serpent's Tail, 1988.

Barzun, Jacques, ed. *Oscar Wilde's "De Profundis"*. New York: Vintage Books, 1964.

Bashford, Bruce. "Oscar Wilde, His Criticism and His Critics," *English Literature in Transition*, 20, 4 (1977), 181–87.

_____. "Oscar Wilde and Subjectivist Criticism," *English Literature in Transition*, 21, 4 (1978), 218–34.

_____. "Arnold and Wilde: Criticism as Humanistic," *English Literature in Transition Special Series Number 3* (1985), 137–49.

_____. "Oscar Wilde as Theorist: The Case of *De Profundis*," *English Literature in Transition*, 28, 4 (1985), 395–406.

_____. "Hermeneutics in Oscar Wilde's 'The Portrait of Mr. W.H.'," *Papers in Language and Literature*, 24, 4 (1988), 412–22.

Baylen, Joseph and Robert L. McBath, "A Note on Oscar Wilde, Alfred Douglas and Lord Rosebery, 1897," *English Language Notes*, 23, 1 (1985), 42–48.

Beckson, Karl, ed. *Aesthetes and Decadents of the 1890s*. New York: Random House, 1966. (Rpt., enlarged. Chicago: Academy Chicago Publishers, 1981.)

_____. *Oscar Wilde: The Critical Heritage*. London: Routledge and Kegan Paul, 1970.

_____. *The Memoirs of Authur Symons: Life and Art in the 1890s*. London: Pennsylvania State University Press, 1977.

_____. "Oscar Wilde and the 'Almost Inhuman' Governor of Reading Gaol," *Notes & Queries*, 30, 3 (1983), 315–16.

_____. "The Importance of Being Angry: The Mutual Antagonism of Oscar and Willie Wilde," in *Blood Brothers: Siblings as Writers*. Norman Kiell, ed. New York: International University Press, 1983.

_____. "Oscar Wilde and the Masks of Narcissus," *The Psychoanalytic Study of Society*, 10 (1984), 249–67.

_____. "Wilde's Autobiographical Signature in *The Picture of Dorian Gray*," *Victorian Newsletter*, 69 (1986), 30–32.

Beerbohm, Max. *A Peep Into the Past*. New York: privately printed, 1923.

_____. *Around Theatres*. London: Rupert Hart–Davis, 1953.

_____. *More Theatres, 1898–1903*. Rupert Hart–Davis, ed. London: Rupert Hart–Davis, 1969.

Behrendt, Patricia Flangan. *Oscar Wilde: Eros and Aesthetics*. London: Macmillan, 1991.

Bendz, Ernst. *The Influence of Pater and Matthew Arnold in the Prose Writings of Oscar Wilde*. London: H. Grevel, 1914.

_____. "A propos de la *Salomé* d'Oscar Wilde," *Englische Studien*, 51, 1 (1917), 48–70.

Benson, E. F. *As We Were: A Victorian Peep Show*. London: Longmans, Green, 1930.

Bentley, Eric. *The Modern Theatre: A Study of Dramatists and the Drama*. London: Robert Hale, 1948.

Bentley, Joyce. *The Importance of Being Constance*. London: Robert Hale, 1983.

Berggren, Ruth, ed. *The Definitive Four–Act Version of "The Importance of Being Earnest: A Trivial Comedy for Serious People" by Oscar Wilde*. New York: Vanguard, 1987.

Bergler, Edmund. *Fashion and the Unconscious*. New York: Robert Brunner, 1953.

_____. *"Salomé*: The Turning Point in the Life of Oscar Wilde," *Psychoanalytic Review*, 43, 1 (1956), 97–103.

Bergonzi, Bernard. *The Turn of the Century*. London: Macmillan, 1973.

Bird, Alan. *The Plays of Oscar Wilde*. London: Vision Press, 1977.

Bloom, Harold, ed. *Oscar Wilde*. New York: Chelsea, 1985.

_____, ed. *Oscar Wilde's The Importance of Being Earnest*. New York: Chelsea, 1987.

Bloxam, John F. *The Priest and the Acolyte. With an Introductory Protest by Stuart Mason*. London: Lotus Press, 1907.

Borland, Maureen. *Wilde's Devoted Friend: A Life of Robert Ross*. Oxford: Lennard Publishing, 1990.

Bowlby, Rachel. "Promoting Dorian Gray," *Oxford Literary Review*, 9 (1987), 147–62.

Bradbury, Malcom and Ian Fletcher, eds. *Decadence and the 1890s*. London: Edward Arnold, 1979.

Brasol, Boris [Brazol', Boris L'vovich]. *Oscar Wilde: The Man, The Artist*. London: Williams and Norgate, 1938.

Braybrooke, Patrick. *Oscar Wilde: A Study*. London: Braithwaite and Miller, 1930.

_____. *Lord Alfred Douglas: His Life and His Work*. London: Cecil Palmer, 1931.

Brémont, Anna, Comtesse de. *Oscar Wilde and his Mother: A Memoir*. London: Everett, 1911.

Broad, Lewis. *The Friendships and Follies of Oscar Wilde*. London: Hutchinson, 1954.

Brooks, Cleanth and Robert B. Heilman. *Understanding Drama: Twelve Plays*. New York: H. Holt, 1945.

Brown, Keith. "Art for Ernest's Sake," *English*, 33 (1984), 235–46.

Brown, Leonard. "Arnold's Succession," *Sewanee Review*, 42 (1934), 158–79.

Brown, R. D. "Suetonius, Symonds and Gibbon in *The Picture of Dorian Gray*," *Modern Language Notes*, 71 (1956), 264.

Browne, Douglas G. *Sir Travers Humphreys: A Biography*. London: Harrap, 1960.

Bruegelmans, R. "A Comparative Examination of Oscar Wilde's and Hofmannsthal's Basic World-Views: Its Implications for the Methodology of Literary Studies," in *Proceedings of the 8th Congress of the International Comparative Literature Association*. Bela Köpeczi and Gyorgy M. Vajda, eds. Stuttgart: Bieber, 1980.

Buckler, William E. "The Agnostic's Apology: A New Reading of Oscar Wilde's 'The Portrait of Mr. W. H.'," *Victorian Newsletter*, 76 (1989), 17–23.

_____. "Building a Bulwark against Despair: 'The Critic as Artist'," *English Literature in Transition*, 32, 3, (1989), 279–89.

_____. "Oscar Wilde's Aesthetic of the Self: Art as Imaginative Self-Realization in *De Profundis*," *Biography: An Interdisciplinary Quarterly*, 12, 2 (1989), 95–115.

_____. "Oscar Wilde's Quest for Utopia: Persiflage with a Purpose in 'The Soul of Man under Socialism'," *Victorians Institute Journal*, 17 (1989), 1–12.

_____. "Antinomianism or Anarchy? A Note on Oscar Wilde's 'Pen, Pencil and Poison'," *Victorian Newsletter*, 78 (1990), 1–3.

_____. "Oscar Wilde's 'chant de cygne': 'The Ballad of Reading Gaol' in Contexual Perspective," *Victorian Poetry*, 28, 3–4 (1990), 33–41.

_____. *"The Picture of Dorian Gray*: An Essay in Aesthetic Exploration," *Victorians Institute Journal*, 18 (1990), 135–74.

Buckley, Jerome H. "Towards Early–Modern Autobiography: The Roles of Oscar Wilde, George Moore, Edmund Gosse, and Henry James," in *Modernism Reconsidered*. Robert Kiely and John Hildebidle, eds. Cambridge, MA: Harvard University Press, 1983.

_____. *The Turning Key: Autobiography and the Subjective Impulse Since 1800.* Cambridge, MA: Harvard University Press, 1984.

_____. "Echo and Artifice: The Poetry of Oscar Wilde," *Victorian Poetry*, 28, 3–4 (1990), 19–31.

Bullough, Vern L. *Sexual Variance in Society and History.* New York: Wiley, 1976; Phoenix ed. Chicago: University of Chicago Press, 1980.

Burdett, Osbert. *The Beardsley Period.* London: John Lane, 1925.

Burke, Edmund. "Oscar Wilde, The Final Scene," *The London Magazine*, 1, 2 (1951), 37–43.

Burkhart, Charles. *Ada Leverson.* New York: Twayne, 1973.

Bush, Douglas. *Mythology and the Romantic Tradition in English Poetry.* Cambridge, MA: Harvard University Press, 1937.

Byrne, Patrick. *The Wildes of Merrion Square.* London: Staples Press, 1953.

Cagle, Charles Harmon. "Oscar Wilde in Kansas," *Kansas History*, 4, 4 (1981), 227–45.

Campos, Christophe. *The View of France from Arnold to Bloomsbury.* London: Oxford University Press, 1965.

Camus, Albert. *Oscar Wilde: "Ballade de la geole de Reading"*. Paris: Falaize, 1952.

Caws, Mary Ann. *Reading Frames in Modern Fiction*. Princeton: Princeton University Press, 1985.

Cersowsky, Peter. "Das Grauen: Georg Trakl, Oscar Wilde und andere Ästhetiker das Schreckens," *Sprachkunst*, 16, 2 (1985), 231–45.

Cervo, Nathan. "Wilde's Closet Self: A Solo at One Remove," *Victorian Newsletter*, 67 (1985), 17–19.

Cevasco, G. A. "The Breviary of the Decadence," *Research Studies*, 49, 4 (1981), 193–203.

Chamberlin, J. E. *Ripe Was the Drowsy Hour*. New York: Seabury, 1977.

Chapman, Raymond. *The Victorian Debate: English Literature and Society, 1832–1901*. London: Weidenfeld and Nicholson, 1968.

Chipchase, Paul. "Truth and Legend," *Books*, 8 (1987), 19.

Christensen, Peter G. "Three Concealments: Jean Cocteau's Adaptation of *The Picture of Dorian Gray*," *Romance Notes*, 27, 1 (1986), 27–35.

Clements, Patricia. *Baudelaire and the English Tradition*. Princeton: Princeton University Press, 1985.

Cohen, Ed. "Writing Gone Wilde: Homoerotic Desire in the Closet of Representation," *Publications of the Modern Language Association*, 102, 5 (1987), 801–13.

_____. "Legislating the Norm: From Sodomy to Gross Indecency," *South Atlantic Quarterly*, 88, 1 (1989), 181–217.

Cohen, Philip K. *The Moral Vision of Oscar Wilde*. London: Associated University Press, 1978.

Cohen, William A. "Willie and Wilde: Reading 'The Portrait of Mr. W. H.'," *South Atlantic Quarterly*, 88, 1 (1989), 219–45.

Connolly, L. W. and J. P. Wearing. "Nineteenth Century Theatre Research: A Bibliography," *Nineteenth Century Theatre* [formerly *Nineteenth Century Theatre Research*], 1, 2 (1973)–to present.

Cook, Lucius H. "French Sources of Wilde's *Picture of Dorian Gray*," *Romantic Review*, 19 (1928), 25–34.

Cooke, Rupert Croft. *Bosie: The Story of Lord Alfred Douglas, His Friends and Enemies*. London: W. H. Allen, 1963.

_____. *Feasting With Panthers*. London: W. H. Allen, 1967.

_____. *The Unrecorded Life of Oscar Wilde*. London: W. H. Allen, 1972.

Cowan, Robert Ernest and William Andrews Clark. *The Library of William Andrews Clark, Jr.: Wilde and Wildeiana*. San Francisco: J. H. Nash, 1922–31.

Craft, Christopher. "Alias Bunbury: Desire and Termination in *The Importance of Being Earnest*," *Representations*, 31 (1990), 19–46.

Critchley, Macdonald. *The Black Hole and Other Essays*. London: Pitman, 1964.

Crompton, Louis. "Gay Studies: From the French Revolution to Oscar Wilde," *Nineteenth–Century Contexts*, 11 (1987), 23–32.

D'Alessandro, Jean M. Ellis. *Hues of Mutability: The Waning Vision in Oscar Wilde's Narrative*. Florence: University of Florence, 1983.

Crossley, Ceri, and Ian Small, eds. *Studies in Anglo–French Cultural Relations*. London: Macmillan, 1988.

D'Amico, Masalino. "Oscar Wilde Between 'Socialism' and Aestheticism," *English Miscellany*, 18 (1967), 111–39.

Daruwala, Maneck Homi. "Good Intentions: The Romantic Aesthetics of Oscar Wilde's Criticism," *Victorians Institute Journal*, 12 (1984), 105–32.

_____. " 'The discerning flame': Of Pater and *The Renaissance*," *Victorians Institute Journal*, 16 (1988), 85–127.

D'Astorg, Bertrand. "Le Mystère de Salomé," *Revue de deux mondes* (April 1971), 93–109.

Davidson, David. "The Importance of Being Ernst: Lubitsch and *Lady Windermere's Fan*," *Literature/ Film Quarterly*, 11, 2 (1983), 120–31.

Davidson, Jim. "A Walk on the Wilde Side," *Meanjin*, 48, 4 (1989), 785–95.

Dawson, Terence. "The Dandy in *The Picture of Dorian Gray*," *New Comparison*, 3 (1987), 133–42.

Delany, Paul. "Charles Ricketts: The Decisive Friendship of Oscar Wilde," *Antiquarian Booksellers Monthly Review*, 5 (1978), 290–93.

DeLaura, David J. "Four Arnold Letters," *Texas Studies in Literature and Language*, 4, 2 (1962), 276–84.

Dellamora, Richard. "Representation and Homophobia in *The Picture of Dorian Gray*," *Victorian Newsletter*, 73 (1988), 28–31.

_____. *Masculine Desire: The Sexual Politics of Victorian Aestheticism*. Chapel Hill: University of North Carolina Press, 1990.

Denvir, Bernard, ed. *The Late Victorians: Art, Design and Society, 1852–1910*. London: Longman, 1986.

Dickson, Donald R. " 'In a mirror that mirrors the soul': Masks and Mirrors in *Dorian Gray*," *English Literature in Transition*, 26, 1 (1983), 5–15.

Dickson, Sarah A. "Arents Tobacco Collection," *New York Public Library Bulletin*, 54 (1950), 352–53.

_____., ed. *The Importance of Being Earnest . . . In Four Acts as Originally Written by Oscar Wilde*. New York: New York Public Library: Publication no. 6 of the Arents Tobacco Collection, 1956.

Dobrin, David N. "Stoppard's *Travesties*," *Explicator*, 40, 1 (1981), 63–64.

Dollimore, Jonathan. "Different Desires: Subjectivity and Transgression in Wilde and Gide," *Textual Practice*, 1, 1 (1987), 48–67.

_____. *Sexual Dissidence: Augustine to Wilde, Freud to Foucault*. Oxford: Clarendon Press, 1991.

Donato, Eugenio. "Historical Imagination and the Idioms of Criticism," *Boundary*, 8, 1 (1979), 39–56.

Donohue, Joseph W., Jr. "The First Production of *The Importance of Being Earnest*: A Proposal for a Reconstructive Study," in *Essays on Nineteenth Century British Theatre*, Kenneth Richards and Peter Thomson, eds. London: Methuen, 1971.

_____. "Recent Studies of Oscar Wilde," *Nineteenth Century Theatre*, 16, 2 (1988), 123–36.

Douglas, Lord Alfred. *Oscar Wilde and Myself*. London: John Long, 1914.

_____. *A Letter from Lord Alfred Douglas on André Gide's Lies about Himself and Oscar Wilde. Set Forth With Comments by Robert Harborough Sherard*. Calvi, Corsica: Vindex Publishing Company, 1933.

_____. *Without Apology*. London: Martin Secker, 1938.

_____. *Oscar Wilde: A Summing–Up*. London: Duckworth, 1940.

Dowling, Linda. *Aestheticism and Decadence: A Selective Annotated Bibliography*. New York: Garland, 1977.

_____. "Imposture and Absence in Wilde's 'Portrait of Mr W.H.',"
Victorian Newsletter, 58 (1980), 26–29.

_____. *Language and Decadence in the Victorian Fin de Siècle.*
Princeton: Princeton University Press, 1986.

Dulau, A. B. and Company Ltd. *A Collection of Original Manuscripts,
Letters and Books of Oscar Wilde, Including his Letters Written to
Robert Ross from Reading Gaol.* London: Dulau, 1928.

Dyson, A. E. "Oscar Wilde: Irony of a Socialist Aesthete," *The Crazy
Fabric: Essays in Irony.* London: Macmillan, 1965.

Eagleton, Terry. "Introduction," *Oscar Wilde: Plays, Prose Writings
and Poems.* London: David Campbell, 1991.

Eakin, David B. "*In Excelsis*: Wilde's Epistolary Relationship with
Lord Alfred Douglas," in *Twilight of Dawn: Studies in English Lit-
erature in Transition*, O M Brack, Jr. ed. Tucson: University of
Arizona Press, 1987.

Easthope, Anthony. "Jokes and Ideology: 'The Frogs' and 'Earnest', "
New Comparison, 3 (1987), 117–32.

Eckardt, Wolf von, Sander L. Gilman, and Edward J. Chamberlin.
Oscar Wilde's London: A Scrapbook of Virtues and Vices 1880–1900.
Garden City, NY: Doubleday, 1987.

Eckley, Grace. "Why the Ghost of Oscar Wilde Manifests in *Fin-
negans Wake*," *Victorian Newsletter*, 75 (1989), 9–14.

Edelman, Lee. "Homographesis," *The Yale Journal of Criticism*, 3, 1
(1989), 189–207.

Edener, Wilfried, ed. *Oscar Wilde: The Picture of Dorian Gray.*
Nurnberg: Carl, 1964.

Ellis, Mary Louise. "Improbable Visitor: Oscar Wilde in Alabama,
1882," *Alabama Review*, 39, 4 (1986), 243–60.

Ellmann, Richard, ed. *Oscar Wilde: Selected Writings*. London: Oxford University Press, 1961.

_____. "The Critic as Artist as Wilde," *Encounter*, 29, 1 (1967), 28–37; repr. in *The Artist as Critic: Critical Writings of Oscar Wilde*, Richard Ellmann, ed. London: W. H. Allen, 1970.

_____. "Overtures to *Salomé*," *Yearbook of Comparative and General Literature*, 17 (1968), 17–28; repr. in *Oscar Wilde: A Collection of Critical Essays*, Richard Ellmann, ed. Englewood Cliffs, NJ: 1969; and in Richard Ellmann, *Golden Codgers: Biographical Speculations*. London: Oxford University Press, 1973.

_____. *Oscar Wilde: A Collection of Critical Essays*. Englewood Cliffs, NJ: Prentice Hall, 1969; repr. 1986.

_____, ed. *Oscar Wilde: The Artist As Critic: Critical Writings of Oscar Wilde*. London, W. H. Allen, 1970.

_____ and John J. Espey. *Oscar Wilde: Two Approaches*. Los Angeles: William Andrews Clark Memorial Library, 1977.

_____. "Henry James among the Aesthetes," *Proceedings of the British Academy*, 69 (1983), 209–28; repr. *in a long the riverrun: Selected Essays*. London: Hamish Hamilton, 1988.

_____. "Oscar at Oxford," *New York Review of Books*, 31 (29 March 1984), 23–28.

_____. "Wilde in New York: Beauty Packed Them In," *New York Times Review of Books* (1 November 1987), 15–16.

_____. "Oscar Meets Walt," *New York Review of Books* (3 December 1987), 42–44.

_____. *Oscar Wilde*. London: Hamish Hamilton, 1987.

_____. "The Uses of Decadence: Wilde, Yeats, Joyce," in *Studies in Anglo-French Cultural Relations: Imagining France*, Ceri Crossley and Ian Small, eds. London: Macmillan, 1988. (Originally delivered at Bennington College as lecture 6 in the Ben Bullitt Lectureship series and subsequently published as one of the *Bennington Chapbooks in Literature*, 1984).

Ericksen, Donald H. *Oscar Wilde*. New York: Twayne, 1977.

Ervine, St. John. *Oscar Wilde: A Present Time Appraisal*. London: George Allen and Unwin, 1951.

Eusebi, Madame. "The Devil in Dorian Gray," *Mythes, Croyances et Religion dans le Monde Anglo–Saxon*, 5 (1987), 147–62.

Evans, Jacqueline W. "A Critical Edition of Oscar Wilde's

yIntentions." Ph.D. University of Birmingham, 1987.

Farson, Daniel. *The Man Who Wrote Dracula: A Biography of Bram Stoker*. London: Michael Joseph, 1975.

Fido, Martin. *Oscar Wilde*. London: Hamlyn, 1973.

_____. *Oscar Wilde: An Illustrated Biography*. New York: Peter Bedrick, 1985.

Finger, Charles J. *The Tragic Story of Oscar Wilde's Life*. Girard, KS: Haldeman–Julius Co., 1923.

Finzi, John Charles. *Oscar Wilde and his Literary Circle: A Catalog of Manuscripts and Letters in the William Andrews Clark Memorial Library*. Berkeley and Los Angeles: University of California Press, 1957.

Fischer, Walther. "The 'Poisonous Book' in Oskar Wildes *Dorian Gray*," *Englische Studien*, 51, 1 (1917), 37–47.

Fisher, Benjamin Franklin, IV. "Guide to the Year's Work in Victorian Poetry: 1987: The Poets of the Nineties," *Victorian Poetry*, 26, 4 (1988), 464–68.

Fleishman, Avrom. *Figures of Autobiography: The Language of Self-Writing in Victorian and Modern England*. Berkeley and Los Angeles: University of California Press, 1983.

Fletcher, Ian, ed. *Romantic Mythologies*. London: Routledge and Kegan Paul, 1967.

_____, and John Stokes. "Oscar Wilde," in *Anglo–Irish Literature: A Review of Research*, Richard J. Finneran, ed. New York: MLA, 1976.

_____, and John Stokes, eds. *The Decadent Consciousness*. New York: Garland, 1979.

_____, and John Stokes. "Oscar Wilde," in *Recent Research on Anglo–Irish Writers: A Supplement to Anglo–Irish Literature: A Review of Research*, Richard J. Finneran, ed. New York: MLA, 1983.

_____. *Aubrey Beardsley*. Boston: Twayne, 1987.

_____, ed. *British Poetry and Prose: 1870–1905*. Oxford: Oxford University Press, 1987.

_____. "A Grammar of Monsters: Beardsley's Obsessive Images and Their Sources," *English Literature in Transition*, 30, 2 (1987), 141–163.

Fong, Bobby. "The Poetry of Oscar Wilde: A Critical Edition." Ph. D. University of California, Los Angeles, 1978.

_____. "Oscar Wilde: Five Fugitive Poems," *English Literature in Transition*, 22 (1979), 7–16.

Ford, Ford Madox. *Ancient Lights and Certain New Reflections*. London: Chapman and Hall, 1911.

_____. *Return to Yesterday*. London: Victor Gollancz, 1931.

Fraser, Hilary. *Beauty and Belief: Aesthetics and Religion in Victorian Literature*. Cambridge: Cambridge University Press, 1986.

Freedman, Jonathan. *Professions of Taste: Henry James, British Aestheticism, and Commodity Culture*. Stanford: Stanford University Press, 1990.

Freeman, William. *The Life of Lord Alfred Douglas, Spoilt Child of Genius*. London: Herbert Joseph, 1948.

Furnell, John. *The Stringed Lute: An Evocation in Dialogue of Oscar Wilde*. London: Rider and Co., 1955.

Furniss, Harry. *Some Victorian Women, Good, Bad, and Indifferent*. London: John Lane, 1923.

Gagnier, Regenia A. "Stages of Desire: Oscar Wilde's Comedies and the Consumer," *Genre*, 15 (1982), 315–16.

_____. *"De Profundis* as *Epistola: In Carcere et Vinculis*: A Materialist Reading of Oscar Wilde's Autobiography," *Criticism*, 26, 4 (1984), 335–54.

_____. *Idylls of the Marketplace: Oscar Wilde and the Victorian Public*. Aldershot: Scolar Press, 1987.

_____, ed. *Critical Essays on Oscar Wilde*. New York: Twayne, 1991.

Ganz, Arthur. "The Meaning of *The Importance of Being Earnest, Modern Drama*, 6, 1 (1963), 42–52.

_____. "The Divided Self in the Society Comedies of Oscar Wilde," *Modern Drama*, 3 (1960), 16–23; repr. in *British Victorian Literature: Recent Evaluations*, Shiv K. Kumar, ed. New York: New York University Press, 1969.

Garde, Noel I. *Jonathan to Gide: The Homosexual in History*. New York: Vantage Press, 1964.

Gardner, Averil. "Literary Petty Larceny: Plagiarism in Oscar Wilde's Early Poetry," *English Studies in Canada*, 8, 1 (1982), 49–61.

Gatton, John Spalding. " 'Informal Wind–Like Music': Two Unpublished Letters from Oscar Wilde," *English Language Notes*, 27, 1 (1989), 48–49.

Gay, Peter. *The Bourgeois Experience: Victoria to Freud. Vol 1: The Education of the Senses*. Oxford: Oxford University Press, 1984.

_____. *The Bourgeois Experience: Victoria to Freud. Vol 2: The Tender Passion*. Oxford: Oxford University Press, 1986.

Gide, André. *Si le grain ne meurt*. Paris: Nouvelle Revue Française, 1924.

_____. *Journal 1889–1939*. Paris: Gallimard, 1951.

Gilbert, Elliot L. " 'Tumult of Images': Wilde, Beardsley, and *Salomé*," *Victorian Studies*, 26, 2 (1983), 133–59.

Glaenzer, R. B. *Catalog of the Library of Richard Butler Glaenzer: A Remarkable Assemblage of Manuscripts, Autograph Letters, Presentation Copies, and Rare Editions of Oscar Wilde*. New York: Merwin–Clayton, 1905.

Glavin, John. "Bulgakov's Lizard and the Problems of the Playwright's Authority," *TEXT: Transactions of the Society for Textual Scholarship*, 4 (1988), 385–406.

_____. "Deadly Earnest and Earnest Revised: Oscar Wilde's Four–Act Play," *Nineteenth Century Studies*, 1 (1987), 13–24.

Godfrey, Sima. "The Dandy as Ironic Figure," *Sub–Stance*, 36 (1982), 21–33.

Going, William T. "Oscar Wilde and Wilfred Blunt: Ironic Notes on Prison, Prose, and Poetry," *Victorian Newsletter*, 13 (1958), 27–29.

Goldfarb, Russell M. "Late Victorian Decadence," *Journal of Aesthetics and Art–Criticism*, 20 (1962), 369–73.

Good, Graham. "Early Productions of Oscar Wilde's *Salomé*," *Nineteenth Century Theatre Research*, 11, 2 (1983), 77–92.

Goodman, Jonathan, ed. *The Oscar Wilde File*. London: Allison, 1989.

Gordon, Jan B. " 'Parody as Initiation': The Sad Education of Dorian Gray," *Criticism*, 9 (1967), 355–71.

_____. "Hebraism, Hellenism, and *The Picture of Dorian Gray*," *Victorian Newsletter*, 33 (1968), 36–38.

_____. "Butterflies and Gilded Cages," *Kenyon Review*, 32, 1 (1970), 152–58.

_____. "Wilde and Newman: The Confessional Mode," *Renascence*, 22 (1970), 183–91.

_____." 'Decadent Spaces': Notes for a Phenomenology of the Fin de Siècle," in *Decadence and the 1890s*, Ian Fletcher and Malcolm Bradbury, eds. London: Edward Arnold, 1979.

Gosse, Edmund. *The Life of Algernon Charles Swinburne*. London: Macmillan, 1917.

Green, R. J. "Oscar Wilde's *Intentions*: An Early Modernist Manifesto," *British Journal of Aesthetics*, 13, 4 (1973), 397–404.

Gregor, Ian. "Comedy and Oscar Wilde," *Sewanee Review*, 74, 2 (1966), 501–21.

Griffin, James D. "The Importance of Being Spurious: Gide's 'Lies', A Forged Letter, and the Emerging Wilde Biography," *Journal of Modern Literature*, 10 (1983), 166–72.

Guy, Josephine M. "The Concept of Tradition and Late Nineteenth-century British Avante–Garde Movements," *Prose Studies*, 13, 2 (1990), 250–60.

_____.*The British Avant–Garde: The Theory and Politics of Tradition*. London: Harvester–Wheatsheaf, 1991.

Habich, William. "Oscar Wilde in Louisville," *The Louisvillian*, (October 1957), 10–12.

Haley, Bruce. "Wilde's 'Decadence' and the Positivist Tradition," *Victorian Studies*, 28, 2 (1985), 215–29.

Hall, Desmond. *I Give You Oscar Wilde: A Biographical Novel*. New York: New American Library, 1965.

Handlist of the Ross Memorial Collection . . . Placed in the Bodleian on Permanent Deposit, April 1932.

Hankin, St John. "The Duchess of Padua," *Fortnightly Review*, 83 (1908), 791–802; repr. as "Wilde as a Dramatist" in *Oscar Wilde: A Collection of Critical Essays*, Richard Ellmann, ed. Englewood Cliffs, NJ: Prentice Hall, 1969; and in *Wilde: Comedies*, William Tydeman, ed. London: Macmillan, 1982.

Hansen, Klaus. "Die Anbiederung des Dandy," in *Alternative Welten*, Manfred Pfister, ed. Munich: Fink, 1982.

Hardwick, Michael. *The Osprey Guide to Oscar Wilde*. Reading: Osprey, 1973.

Harmond, Richard and G. A. Cevasco. "Another Wilde Letter," *Notes & Queries*, 34, 4 (1987), 498–99.

Harris, Frank. *Oscar Wilde: His Life and Confessions*. (New York: printed and published by the author, 1916; rev. ed. London: Constable, 1938.

Harris, Wendell. "Arnold, Pater, Wilde, and the Object as in Themselves They See It," *Studies In English Literature*, 11, 4 (1971), 733–47.

———. "The Critics," in *Victorian Prose: A Guide to Research*, David J. DeLaura, ed. New York: MLA, 1973.

Hart, John E. "Art as Hero: *The Picture of Dorian Gray*," *Research Studies*, 46 (1978), 1–11.

Hart–Davis, Rupert, ed. *The Letters of Oscar Wilde*. London: Hart–Davis, 1962.

_____. *Selected Letters of Oscar Wilde*. Oxford: Oxford University Press, 1979.

_____. *More Letters of Oscar Wilde*. London: John Murray, 1985.

Hartley, Kelver. *Oscar Wilde: l'influence française dans son oeuvre*. Paris: Librairie du Recueil Sirey, 1935.

Heath, Apryl L. D. "An Unnoted Allusion to Matthew Arnold in *The Picture of Dorian Gray*," *Notes & Queries*, 35, 3 (1988), 332.

Helfand, Michael S. and Philip E. Smith II. "Anarchy and Culture: The Evolutionary Turn of Cultural Criticism in the Works of Oscar Wilde," *Texas Studies in Literature and Language*, 20 (1978), 199–215.

Herdman, John. *The Double in Nineteenth–Century Fiction*. London: Macmillan, 1990.

Hess–Lüttich, Ernest. "Die Strategie der Paradoxie," in *Semiotics of Drama and Theatre*, Herta Schmid and Aloysius Van Kesteren, eds. Amsterdam: Benjamins, 1984.

Hirsch, Charles, ed. *Oscar Wilde, et al: Teleny: Or, The Reverse of the Medal: A Physiological Romance*. Paris: privately printed, 1934.

Hirst, David L. *Comedy of Manners*. London: Methuen, 1979.

Hoffer, A. "Oscar Wilde," *American Journal of Psychiatry*, 114 (1957), 176–77.

Holland, Merlin. "What Killed Oscar Wilde?," *Spectator*, 24 (December 1988), 34–35.

Holland, Vyvyan. *Son of Oscar Wilde*. London: Rupert Hart–Davis, 1954.

_____. *Oscar Wilde: A Pictorial Biography*. London: Thames and Hudson, 1960.

_____. *Time Remembered After Père Lachaise*. London: Gollancz, 1966.

Hopkins, Thurston. *Oscar Wilde: A Study of the Man and His Work*. London: Lynwood, 1913.

Hopper, Vincent F. and Gerald B. Lahey, eds. *Oscar Wilde: The Importance of Being Earnest*. Great Neck, NY: Barron's Educational Series, 1959.

_____. *Oscar Wilde: Lady Windermere's Fan*. Great Neck, NY: Barron's Educational Series, 1960.

Horodisch, Abraham. *Oscar Wilde's "Ballad of Reading Gaol": A Bibliographical Study*. New York: Aldus Book Co., 1954.

Hough, Graham. *The Last Romantics*. London: Duckworth, 1949.

_____, ed. *Selections from the Work of Oscar Wilde*. New York: Dell, 1960.

Humphreys, Kathryn. "The Artistic Exchange: *Dorian Gray* at the *Sacred Fount*," *Texas Studies in Literature and Language*, 32, 4 (1990), 522–35.

Hunt, John Dixon. *The Pre–Raphaelite Imagination 1848–1900*. Lincoln, NE: University of Nebraska Press, 1968.

Hyde, H. Montgomery, ed. *The Trials of Oscar Wilde*. London: Hodge, 1948.

_____. *Cases That Changed the Law*. London: Heinemann, 1951.

_____. *The Other Love*. London: Heinemann, 1970.

_____. *Oscar Wilde: The Aftermath*. London: Methuen, 1963.

_____. *A History of Pornography*. London: Heinemann, 1964.

_____. "Oscar Wilde," in *Four Oaks Library*, Gabriel Austin, ed. Somerville, NJ: privately printed, 1967.

_____. *Oscar Wilde*. New York: Farrar, Strauss, and Giroux, 1975.

_____, ed. *The Annotated Oscar Wilde*. London: Orbis, 1982.

_____. "The Riddle of *De Profundis*: Who Owns the Manuscript?" *Antigonish Review*, 54 (1983), 107–27.

_____. "Oscar Wilde and Lord Alfred Douglas," *Essays By Divers Hands*, 43 n.s. (1984), 139–60.

Hyde, Mary, ed. *Bernard Shaw and Alfred Douglas: A Correspondence*. London: John Murray, 1982.

Ingleby, Leonard Cresswell [Cyril Arthur Gull]. *Oscar Wilde*. London: T. Werner Laurie, 1907.

_____. *Oscar Wilde: Some Reminiscences*. London: T. Werner Laurie, 1912.

Jackson, Holbrook. *The Eighteen Nineties: A Review of Art and Ideas at the Close of the Nineteenth Century*. London: Grant Richards, 1913.

Jackson, John Wyse. *Aristotle at Afternoon Tea: The Rare Oscar Wilde*. London: Fourth Estate, 1991.

Jackson, Russell, ed. *Oscar Wilde, The Importance of Being Earnest*. London: Benn, 1980.

_____. "A Classic without Danger: the National Theatre's *Importance of Being Earnest*," *Critical Quarterly*, 25, 2 (1983), 73–80.

_____. "Horrible Flesh and Blood—A Rejoinder," *Theatre Notebook*, 37, 1 (1983), 29–31.

_____, ed. *Victorian Theatre*. London: A. and C. Black, 1989.

Jenkyns, Richard. *The Victorians and Ancient Greece*. Oxford: Blackwell, 1980.

Johnson, Wendell Stacy. "Fallen Women, Lost Children: Wilde and the Theatre of the Nineties," *Tennessee Studies in Literature*, 27 (1984), 196–211.

Joost, Nicholas and Franklin E. Court. "*Salomé*, the Moon, and Oscar Wilde's Aesthetics: A Reading of the Play," *Papers on Language and Literature*, 8 (Supplement) (1972), 96–111.

Jordan, John. "Shaw, Wilde, Synge and Yeats: Ideas, Epigrams, Blackberries and Cassis," in *The Irish Mind: Exploring Intellectual Traditions*, Richard Kearney, ed. Dublin: Wolfhound, 1985.

Joseph, Gerhard. "Framing Wilde," *Victorian Newsletter*, 72 (1987), 61–63.

Jullian, Phillippe. *Oscar Wilde*. Violet Wyndham, trans. London: Constable, 1969.

Kail, Harvey. "The Other Half of the Garden: Oscar Wilde's *De Profundis* and the Confessional Tradition," *Prose Studies*, 2 (1979), 141–50.

Kaplan, Joel H. "Ernest Worthing's London Address: A Reconsideration," *Canadian Journal of Irish Studies*, 11, 1 (1985), 53–54.

Karl, Frederick R. *Modern and Modernism: the Sovereignty of the Artist: 1885–1925*. New York: Macmillan, 1985.

Keefe, Robert. "Artist and Model in *The Picture of Dorian Gray*," *Studies in the Novel*, 5 (1973), 63–70.

Keppler, C. F. *The Literature of the Second Self*. Tucson: University of Arizona Press, 1972.

Kermode, Frank. *Romantic Image*. London: Routledge and Kegan Paul, 1957.

Kertzer, Adrienne. " 'The Infanta: It Was a Monster': Art in Oscar Wilde's Fairy Tales," *Victorian Studies Association of Western Canada Newsletter*, 8, 1 (1982), 23–24.

Kettle, Michael. *Salomé's Last Veil: The Libel Case of the Century*. London: Hart–Davis MacGibbon, 1977.

Klein, Alfons. "Motive und Themen in Oscar Wildes 'Lord Arthur Savile's Crime'," in *Motive und Themen in Erzahlungen des spaten 19. Jahrhunderts*, Theodor Wolpers, ed. Gottingen: Vandenhoeck and Ruprecht, 1982.

Kohl, Norbert. *Oscar Wilde: Leben und Werk in Daten und Bildern*. Frankfurt: Inscl, 1976.

_____. *Oscar Wilde: Das literarische Werk zwischen Provokation und Anpassung*. Heidelberg: Carl Winter, 1980. Translated as *Oscar Wilde: The Work of a Conformist Rebel*, D. H. Wilson. Cambridge: Cambridge University Press, 1989.

Korg, Jacob. "The Rage of Caliban," *University of Toronto Quarterly*, 37, 1 (1967), 75–89.

Kotzin, Michael C. "'The Selfish Giant' as Literary Fairy Tale," *Studies in Short Fiction*, 16 (1979), 301–309.

Kravec, Maureen T. "Wilde's *Salomé*," *Explicator*, 42, 1 (1983), 30–32.

Kronenberger, Louis. *The Thread of Laughter*. New York: Alfred Knopf, 1952.

_____. ed. *Oscar Wilde: "Lady Windermere's Fan" and "The Importance of Being Earnest"*. New York: Collier Books, 1962.

_____. *Oscar Wilde*. Boston: Little, Brown, 1976.

Laity, Susan. "The Soul of Man under Victoria: *Iolanthe, The Importance of Being Earnest,* and Bourgeois Drama," in *Oscar Wilde's The Importance of Being Earnest,* Harold Bloom, ed. New York: Chelsea, 1988.

Lambert, Eric. *Mad With Much Heart: A Life of the Parents of Oscar Wilde.* London: Muller, 1967.

Langenfeld, Robert, ed. *Reconsidering Aubrey Beardsley.* Rochester, NY: University of Rochester Press, 1989.

Langtry, Lillie. *The Days I Knew.* London: Hutchinson, 1925.

Laver, James. *Oscar Wilde: Writers and their Work Series.* London: Longman, 1954.

Lawler, Donald L. "Oscar Wilde's First Manuscript of *The Picture of Dorian Gray,*" *Studies In Bibliography: Papers of the Bibliographical Society of the University of Virginia,* 25 (1972), 125–35.

_____. "Oscar Wilde in *The New Cambridge Bibliography of English Literature,*" *Papers of the Bibliographical Society of America,* 67, 2 (1973), 172–88.

_____. "The Revisions of *Dorian Gray,*" *Victorians Institute Journal,* 3 (1974), 21–36.

_____. *An Inquiry into Oscar Wilde's Revisions of "The Picture of Dorian Gray".* New York: Garland Publishing, 1988.

_____, ed. *Oscar Wilde, The Picture of Dorian Gray.* New York: W. W. Norton, 1988.

Le Gallienne, Richard. *The Romantic '90s.* London: G. P. Putnam's Sons, 1925.

Levine, George and William Madden, eds. *The Art of Victorian Prose.* New York: Oxford University Press, 1968.

Lewis, Lloyd and Henry Justin Smith. *Oscar Wilde Discovers America*. New York: Harcourt Brace and Co., 1936.

Lewis, Roger C. "A Misattribution: Oscar Wilde's 'Unpublished Sonnet on Chatterton'," *Victorian Poetry*, 28, 2 (1990), 164–69.

Lich, Glen E. " 'Anything But a Misprint': Comments on an Oscar Wilde Typescript," *South Central Review*, 3, 2 (1986), 46–54.

Lodge, David. *Modes of Modern Writing*. London: Edward Arnold, 1977.

Loewenstein, Joseph. "Oscar Wilde and the Evasion of Principle," *South Atlantic Quarterly*, 84 (1985), 392–400.

Logan, Marie–Rose. "Deconstruction: Beyond and Back. Response To Eugenio Donato, 'Historical Imagination and the Idioms of Criticism'," *Boundary*, 8, 1 (1979), 57–63.

Longxi, Zhang. "The Critical Legacy of Oscar Wilde," *Texas Studies in Literature and Language*, 30, 1 (1988), 87–103.

Lydon, Mary. "Myself and M/others," *Sub–Stance*, 32 (1981), 6–14.

McBath, Robert Luttrell Jr. and J. O. Baylen. " 'Oh The Patriots, The Patriots!': Oscar Wilde, Georgia and the Fourth of July," *The Atlanta Historical Journal*, 27, 1 (1980), 31–41.

McCormack, Jerusha. "Masks Without Faces: the Personalities of Oscar Wilde," *English Literature in Transition*, 22 (1976), 253–69.

McGowan, John. "From Pater to Wilde to Joyce: Modernist Epiphany and the Soulful Self," *Texas Studies in Literature and Language*, 32, 3 (1990), 417–45.

Macqueen–Pope, W. *Haymarket: Theatre of Perfection*. London: W. H. Allen, 1948.

_____. *St James': Theatre of Distinction*. London: W. H. Allen, 1958.

Maier, Wolfgang. "Oscar Wilde—Maske und Wirklichkeit," *Universitas*, 39, (1984), 991–1001.

_____. *Oscar Wilde, "The Picture of Dorian Gray": Eine Kritische Analyse der anglistischen Forschung von 1962 bis 1982*. Frankfurt Am Main: Lang, 1984.

Maine, G. F., ed. *The Works of Oscar Wilde*. London: Collins, 1948.

Manganiello, Dominic. "Ethics and Aesthetics in *The Picture of Dorian Gray*," *Canadian Journal of Irish Studies*, 9, 2 (1983), 25–33.

Marcus, Steven. "Conceptions of the Self in an Age of Progress," in *Progress and Its Discontents*, Gabriel A. Almond, Marvin Chodorow, and Roy Harvey Pearce, eds. Berkeley: University of California Press, 1982.

Marjoribanks, Edward and Ian Colvin. *The Life of Lord Carson*. London: Victor Gollancz, 1932–1936.

Markgraf, Carl. *Oscar Wilde's Anonymous Criticism: An Annotated Edition*. Ph. D. University of California, Riverside, 1970.

Marlow, Louis. *Seven Friends*. London: Richards Press, 1953.

Martin, Robert K. "Oscar Wilde and the Fairy Tale: 'The Happy Prince' as Self-Dramatization," *Studies in Short Fiction*, 16 (1979), 74–77.

_____. "Parody and Homage: The Presence of Pater in *Dorian Gray*," *Victorian Newsletter*, 63 (1983), 15–18.

Mason, A. E. W. *Sir George Alexander and the St James' Theatre*. London: Macmillan, 1935.

Mason, Stuart [Christopher Millard]. *Oscar Wilde: Art and Morality: A Defence of "The Picture of Dorian Gray"*. London: J. Jacobs, 1908.

_____. *A Bibliography of Oscar Wilde*. London: T. Werner Laurie, 1914.

_____. *Oscar Wilde and the Aesthetic Movement*. Dublin: Townley Searle, 1920.

Maurer, Oscar, Jr. "A Philistine Source for *Dorian Gray?*" *Philological Quarterly*, 26 (1947), 84–86.

Mayer, Hans. *Outsiders: A Study in Life and Letters*. Denis M. Sweet, trans. Cambridge, MA: MIT Press, 1982.

Melchiori, Giorgio. *The Tightrope Walkers: Studies of Mannerism in Modern English Literature*. London: Routledge and Kegan Paul, 1956.

Merle, Robert. *Oscar Wilde*. Nouvelle édition; Paris: Librairie académique Perrin, 1984.

Meyers, Jeffrey. *Homosexuality and Literature 1890–1930*. London: Athlone Press, 1977.

Meyers, Terry L. "Oscar Wilde and Williamsburg, Virginia," *Notes & Queries*, 38, 3 (1991), 328–29.

Mikhail, E. H. "The French Influences on Oscar Wilde's Comedies," *Revue de littérature comparée*, 42, 2 (1968), 220–33.

_____. "Oscar Wilde and his First Comedy," *Modern Drama*, 10, 1 (1968), 394–96.

_____. "Self–Revelation in *An Ideal Husband*," *Modern Drama*, 11, 3 (1968), 180–86.

_____. *The Social and Cultural Setting of the 1890s*. London: Garnstone Press, 1969.

_____. *Oscar Wilde: An Annotated Bibliography of Criticism*. London: Macmillan, 1978.

_____, ed. *Oscar Wilde: Interviews and Recollections*. 2 vols. London: Macmillan, 1979.

Miller, Karl. *Doubles: Studies in Literary History.* Oxford: Clarendon Press, 1985.

Miller, Robert Keith. *Oscar Wilde.* New York: Ungar, 1982.

Millett, Kate. *Sexual Politics.* Garden City, NY: Doubleday, 1970.

Miyoshi, Masao. *The Divided Self: A Perspective on the Literature of the Victorians.* New York: New York University Press, 1969.

Moers, Ellen. *The Dandy: Brummel to Beerbohm.* London: Secker and Warburg, 1960.

Monneyron, Frédéric. "Une lecture Nietscheene de Dorian Gray," *Cahiers Victoriennes et Edwardiennes,* 16 (1982), 139–45.

Monsman, Gerald. "Pater's Aesthetic Hero," *University of Toronto Quarterly,* 40, 2 (1971), 136–51.

Montague, C. E. *Dramatic Values.* London: Methuen, 1911.

More, Paul Elmer. *Shelburne Essays.* 11 vols. New York: G. P. Putnam's Sons, 1904–21.

Morley, Sheridan. *Oscar Wilde: An Illustrated Biography.* London: Weidenfeld and Nicolson, 1976.

Morrison, Kristin. "Horrible Flesh and Blood," *Theatre Notebook,* 35, 1 (1981), 7–9.

Munby, N. L., ed. "Oscar Wilde," in *Sale Catalogues of Libraries of Eminent Persons: Poets and Men of Letters.* London and New York: Mansell, 1971. I, 371–88.

Murray, Isobel. "Some Elements in the Composition of *The Picture of Dorian Gray*," *Durham University Journal,* 33, 3 (1972), 220–31.

_____, ed. *Oscar Wilde: The Picture of Dorian Gray.* London: Oxford University Press, 1974.

_____, ed. *Oscar Wilde. Plays, Prose Writings and Poems*. London: Dent, 1975.

_____, ed. *Oscar Wilde: The Complete Shorter Fiction*. Oxford: Oxford University Press, 1979.

_____. "*Children of To-morrow*: A Sharp Inspiration for *Dorian Gray*," *Durham University Journal*, 80, 1 (1987), 69–76.

_____. "Strange Case of Dr Jekyll and Oscar Wilde," *Durham University Journal*, 79, 2 (1987), 311–19.

_____, ed. *Oscar Wilde*. Oxford: Oxford University Press, 1989.

Nassaar, Christopher. *Into The Demon Universe: A Literary Exploration of Oscar Wilde*. New Haven: Yale University Press, 1974.

_____. "Vision of Evil: The Influence of Wilde's *Salomé* on *Heart of Darkness* and *A Full Moon in March*," *Victorian Newsletter*, 53 (1978), 23–27.

Nelson, James G. *The Early Nineties: A View from the Bodley Head*. Cambridge, MA: Harvard University Press, 1971.

Nelson, Walter W. *Oscar Wilde in Sweden and Other Essays*. Dublin: Dublin University Press, 1965.

_____. *Oscar Wilde from Ravenna to Salomé: A Survey of Contemporary English Criticism*. Dublin: Dublin University Press, 1987.

_____. *Oscar Wilde and the Dramatic Critics: A Study in Victorian Theatre*. Lund: privately printed, 1989.

Nicholls, Mark [Leslie Frewin]. *The Importance of Being Oscar: The Wit and Wisdom of Oscar Wilde Set against His Life and Times*. New York: St Martin's Press, 1980. Repr. under Frewin's name; London: W. H. Allen, London, 1986.

North, Michael. *The Final Sculpture: Public Monuments and Modern Poets*. Ithaca: Cornell University Press, 1985.

Oates, Joyce Carol. "*The Picture of Dorian Gray*: Wilde's Parable of the Fall," in *Contraries: Essays*. New York: Oxford University Press, 1981.

O'Brien, Kevin H. F. *An Edition of Oscar Wilde's American Lectures*. Ph. D. University of Notre Dame, 1973.

_____. "'The House Beautiful': A Reconstruction of Oscar Wilde's American Lecture," *Victorian Studies*, 17 (1974), 395–418.

_____. *Oscar Wilde in Canada: An Apostle for the Arts*. Toronto: Personal Library, 1982.

_____. "Oscar Wilde: An Unsigned Book Review," *Notes & Queries*, 30, 4 (1983), 312–15.

_____. "Robert Sherard: Friend of Oscar Wilde," *English Literature in Transition*, 28, 1 (1985), 3–29.

Ojala, Aatos. *Aestheticism and Oscar Wilde: Pt 1: Life and Letters*. Helsinki: Suomalaisen Tiedeakatemian toimituksia, 1954.

_____. *Aestheticism and Oscar Wilde: Pt 2: Literary Style*. Helsinki: Suomalaisen Tiedeakatemian toimituksia, 1955.

Omasreiter, Ria. *Oscar Wilde: Epigone, Ästhet und wit*. Heidelberg: Carl Winter, 1978.

O'Neill, Michael J. "Irish Poets of the Nineteenth Century: Unpublished Lecture Notes of a Speech by Oscar Wilde at San Francisco," *University Review*, 1, 4 (1955), 29–33.

Ormond, Leonée. *George Du Maurier*. London: Routledge and Kegan Paul, 1969.

Page, Norman. *An Oscar Wilde Chronology*. London: Macmillan, 1991.

Paglia, Camille A. "Oscar Wilde and the English Epicene," *Raritan*, 4, 3 (1985), 85–109.

Pappas, John J. "The Flower and the Beast: A Study of Oscar Wilde's Antithetical Attitudes Toward Nature and Man in *The Picture of Dorian Gray*," *English Literature in Transition*, 15, 1 (1972), 37–48.

Parker, David. "Oscar Wilde's Great Farce: *The Importance of Being Earnest*," *Modern Language Quarterly*, 35, 2 (1974), 173–86.

Parkhill, Forbes. *The Wildest of the West*. New York: Henry Holt & Co., 1951.

Partridge, E. B. "The Importance of Not Being Earnest," *Bucknell Review*, 9, 2 (1960), 143–58.

Paterson, Gary H. "Lord Alfred Douglas: An Annotated Bibliography of Writings About Him," *English Literature in Transition*, 23, 3 (1980), 168–200.

Paul, Charles B. and Robert D. Pepper. "The Importance of Reading Alfred: Oscar Wilde's Debt to Alfred de Musset," *Bulletin of the New York Public Library*, 75 (1971), 506–42.

Peake, Mervyn and Oscar Wilde. *Extracts from the Poems of Oscar Wilde with Sixteen Illustrations by Mervyn Peake and a Foreword by Maeve Gilmore*. London: Sidgwick and Jackson, 1980.

Pearsall, Robert. *Frank Harris*. New York: Twayne, 1970.

Pearson, Hesketh. *Modern Men and Mummers*. London: George Allen and Unwin, 1921.

_____. *The Life of Oscar Wilde*. London: Methuen, 1946.

_____, ed. *Essays by Oscar Wilde*. London: Methuen, 1950.

_____. *The Last Actor–Managers*. London: Methuen, 1950.

_____. *Beerbohm Tree: His Life and Laughter*. London: Methuen, 1956.

_____. *Gilbert: His Life and Strife*. London: Methuen, 1957.

Peckham, Morse. *Beyond The Tragic Vision: The Quest for Identity in the Nineteenth Century.* New York: George Brazillier, 1962.

_____. "What Did Lady Windermere Learn?" *College English,* 18 (1956), 11–14; repr. in *The Triumph of Romanticism: Collected Essays.* Columbia: University of South Carolina Press, 1970.

Pepper, Robert D. ed. *Oscar Wilde; Irish Poets and Poetry of the Nineteenth Century. A Lecture Delivered in Platt's Hall, San Francisco on Wednesday, April fifth, 1882. Edited from Wilde's Manuscript and Reconstructed, in part, from Contemporary Newspaper Accounts.* San Francisco: Book Club of California, 1972.

_____. "San José Greets Oscar Wilde: April Third, 1882," *San José Studies,* 8, 2 (1982), 7–32.

Perrie, Walter. "Homosexuality and Literature," in *The Sexual Dimension in Literature,* Alan Bold, ed. London: Vision, 1982.

Peters, Robert Louis. "Whistler and the English Poets of the 1890s," *Modern Language Quarterly,* 18 (1957), 251–61.

Pick, John. "Divergent Disciples of Walter Pater," *Thought,* 23 (1948), 114–28.

Pincher, Chapman. *The Private World of St John Terrapin: A Novel of the Café Royal.* London: Sidgwick and Jackson, 1982.

Pine, Richard. *Oscar Wilde.* Dublin: Gill and Macmillan, 1983.

Poirier, Richard. *The Performing Self: Compositions and Decompositions in the Languages of Contemporary Life.* New York: Oxford University Press, 1971.

Porter, Laurence E. "Literary Structure and the Concept of Decadence: Huysmans, D'Annunzio and Wilde," *Centennial Review,* 22 (1978), 188–200.

Portnoy, William Evans. "Wilde's Debt to Tennyson in *Dorian Gray*," *English Literature in Transition,* 17 (1974), 259–61.

Poteet, Lewis J. "Romantic Aesthetics in Oscar Wilde's 'Mr. W. H.',"
Studies in Short Fiction, 7, 3 (1970), 458–64.

_____. "*Dorian Gray* and the Gothic Novel," *Modern Fiction Studies*, 17, 2 (1971), 239–48.

Powell, Kerry. "Oscar Wilde 'Acting': The Medium as Message in *The Picture of Dorian Gray*," *Dalhousie Review*, 58 (1978), 104–15.

_____. "Hawthorne, Arlo Bates and *The Picture of Dorian Gray*," *Papers on Language and Literature*, 16 (1980), 403–16.

_____. "Tom, Dick, and Dorian Gray: Magic–Picture Mania in Late Victorian Fiction," *Philological Quarterly*, 62 (1983), 147–70.

_____. "The Mesmerizing of Dorian Gray," *Victorian Newsletter*, 65 (1984), 10–15.

_____. "When Critics Disagree," *Victorian Newsletter*, 67 (1985), 20.

_____. "Wilde and Ibsen," *English Literature in Transition*, 28, 3 (1985), 224–42.

_____. "Who Was Basil Hallward?," *English Language Notes*, 24, 1 (1986), 84–91.

_____. *Oscar Wilde and the Theatre of the 1890s*. Cambridge: Cambridge University Press, 1990.

Powys, John Cowper. *Suspended Judgments*. New York: G. Arnold Shaw, 1916.

Poznar, Walter. "Life and Play in Wilde's *The Importance of Being Earnest*," *Midwest Quarterly*, 30, 4 (1989), 515–28.

Prescott Collection, The: Printed Books and Manuscripts sold at New York on Friday February 6, 1981. New York: Christie, Manson & Woods International Inc., 1981.

Queensberry [Francis], Marquess of, and Patrick Colson. *Oscar Wilde and the Black Douglas*. London: Hutchinson, 1949.

Quintus, John Allen. "The Moral Prerogative in Oscar Wilde: A Look at the Fairy Tales," *Virginia Quarterly Review*, 53 (1977), 708–17.

Raafat, Z. "The Literary Indebtedness of Wilde's *Salomé* to Sardou's *Théodora*," *Revue de littérature comparée*, 40 (1966), 453–66.

Raby, Peter. *Oscar Wilde*. Cambridge: Cambridge University Press, 1988.

_____. "The Making of *The Importance of Being Earnest*," *Times Literary Supplement*, no 4629 (December 1991), 13.

Raffalovich, Marc André. *Uranisme et unisexualité: étude sur différentes manifestations de l'instinct sexual*. Paris: Masson, 1896.

Ragland–Sullivan, Ellie. "The Phenomenon of Aging in Oscar Wilde's Picture of Dorian Gray: A Lacanian View," in *Memory and Desire: Aging—Literature—Psychoanalysis*, Kathleen Woodward and Murray M. Schwartz, eds. Bloomington: Indiana University Press, 1986.

Ransome, Arthur. *Oscar Wilde: A Critical Study*. London: Martin Secker, 1912.

Reade, Brian, ed. *Sexual Heretics: Male Homosexuality in English Literature from 1850 to 1900*. London: Routledge and Kegan Paul, 1970.

Reed, Frances Miriam. "Oscar Wilde's *Vera; Or, The Nihilist*: The History of a Failed Play," *Theatre Survey*, 26, 2 (1985), 163–77.

_____, ed. *Oscar Wilde. Vera; Or, the Nihilist*. Lewiston, NY; Queenston, Ontario; Lampeter, Dyfed: Edwin Mellen Press, 1989.

Reed, John R. *Decadent Style*. Athens: Ohio University Press, 1985.

Reilly, Patrick. "How Wilde Met His Death," *Guardian Weekly* (27 March 1988), 19.

Reilly, Robert. *The God of Mirrors: A Novel*. Boston and New York: Atlantic Monthly Press, 1986.

Reinert, Otto. "Satiric Strategy in *The Importance of Being Earnest*," *College English*, 18 (1956), 14–18.

Richards, Grant. *Memoirs of a Misspent Youth, 1872–1896*. London: Heinemann, 1932.

_____. *Author Hunting*. London: Hamish Hamilton, 1934.

Rieff, Philip. "The Impossible Culture: Wilde as a Modern Prophet," *Salmagundi*, 58 (1983), 406–26.

Roberts, Brian. *The Mad, Bad Line: the Family of Lord Alfred Douglas*. London: Hamish Hamilton, 1981.

Roberts, Marie. *British Poets and Secret Societies*. London: Croom Helm, 1986.

Robertson, W. Graham. *Time Was*. London: Hamish Hamilton, 1931.

Robillard, Douglas, Jr. "Self–Reflexive Art and Wilde's *The Picture of Dorian Gray*," *Essays in Arts and Sciences*, 18 (1989), 29–38.

Roditi, Edouard. *Oscar Wilde*. Norfolk, CT: New Directions Books, 1947.

Rodway, Allan, "The Last Phase," in the *Pelican Guide to English Literature, vol. 6: From Dickens to Hardy*, Boris Ford, ed. Harmondsworth: Penguin, 1958.

Rogers, Robert. *A Psychoanalytic Study of the Double in Literature*. Detroit: Wayne State University Press, 1970.

Roitinger, Anita. *Oscar Wilde's Life as Reflected in His Correspondence and His Autobiography. Salzburger Studien zur Anglistik und Amerikanistik*, 12. Salzburg: Institut fur Anglistik und Americanistik, University of Salzburg, 1980.

Rose, Marilyn Gaddis. "The Daughters of Herodias in *Hérodiade, Salomé* and *A Full Moon In March*," *Comparative Drama*, 1 (1967), 172–81.

_____. "The Synchronic Salomé," in *The Languages of Theatre: Problems in the Translation and Transposition of Drama*. Ortrun Zuber, ed. Oxford: Pergamon Press, 1980.

Ross, Margery, ed. *Robert Ross: Friend of Friends*. London: Jonathan Cape, 1952.

Ross, Robert, ed. *The First Collected Edition of the Works of Oscar Wilde*. London: Methuen, 1908.

Rossi, Dominick. "Parallels in Wilde's *The Picture of Dorian Gray* and Goethe's *Faust*," *College Language Association Journal*, 13 (1969), 188–91.

Rowell, George. "The Drama of Wilde and Pinero," in *The Cambridge Guide to the Arts in Britain: The Later Victorian Age*, Boris Ford, ed. Cambridge: Cambridge University Press, 1989.

Roy, Emil. *British Drama Since Shaw*. Carbondale: Southern Illinois University Press, 1972.

Ryals, Clyde de L. "Oscar Wilde's *Salomé*," *Notes & Queries*, 204 (1959), 56–57.

Ryskamp, Charles, ed. *Wilde and the Nineties: An Essay and an Exhibition*. Princeton: Princeton Library, 1966.

Said, Edward. *The World, The Text, And The Critic*. Cambridge, MA: Harvard University Press, 1983.

Saix, Guillot de. "Une Tragédie de Femme par Oscar Wilde," *Mercure de France*, (15 September 1938), 597–603.

_____. *Le Chant du cygne: contes parlés d'Oscar Wilde. Recuellis et redigés par Guillot de Saix*. Paris: Mercure de France, 1942.

Sammells, Neil. "Earning Liberties: *Travesties* and *The Importance of Being Earnest*," *Modern Drama*, 29, 3 (1986), 376–87.

San Juan, Epifanio. *The Art of Oscar Wilde*. Princeton: Princeton University Press, 1967.

Sarkissian, Gisèle. "Ghosts in Tales of the Fantastic," *Mythes, Croyances et Religions dans le Monde Anglo-Saxon*, 3 (1985), 155–63.

Sawyer, N. W. *The Comedy of Manners from Sheridan to Maugham*. Philadelphia: University of Pennsylvania Press, 1931.

Schiff, Hilda. "Nature and Art in Oscar Wilde's 'The Decay of Lying'," *Essays and Studies by Members of the English Association*, 18 (1965), 83–102.

Schroeder, Horst. "Oscar Wilde, The Canterville Ghost," *Literatur in Wissenschaft und Unterricht*, 10 (1977), 21–30.

_____. *Oscar Wilde, "The Portrait of Mr W.H."—Its Composition, Publication and Reception*. Braunschweig: Braunschweiger Anglistische Arbeiten, 9. 1984.

_____. "Oscar Wilde at Homburg," *Notes & Queries*, 32, 3 (1985), 361–62.

_____. *Annotations to Oscar Wilde, "The Portrait of Mr W.H."* Braunschweig: privately printed, 1986.

_____. "Some Historical and Literary References in Oscar Wilde's 'The Birthday of the Infanta'," *Literatur in Wissenschaft und Unterricht*, 21, 4 (1988), 289–92.

_____. *Additions and Corrections to Richard Ellmann's "Oscar Wilde"*. Braunschweig: privately printed, 1989.

_____. "An Echo of Andrew Lang in 'The Decay of Lying'," *Notes & Queries*, 38, 3 (1991), 326.

_____. "Two Cruces in *Intentions*: A Source Analysis," *Notes & Queries*, 38, 3 (1991), 324–26.

_____. "A Quotation in *Dorian Gray*," *Notes & Queries*, 38, 3 (1991), 327–28.

Schwarz, Stanley. "The Influence of Dumas Fils on Oscar Wilde," *French Review*, 7, 1 (1933), 5–25.

Schweik, Robert C. "Oscar Wilde's *Salomé*, the Salomé Theme in Late European Art, and a Problem of Method in Cultural History," in *Twilight of Dawn: Studies in English Literature in Transition*, O M Brack, Jr., ed. Tucson: University of Arizona Press, 1987.

Sedgwick, Eve Kosofsky. *Between Men: English Literature and Male Homosocial Desire*. New York: Columbia University Press, 1986.

_____. *The Epistemology of the Closet*. London: Harvester–Wheatsheaf, 1991.

Shaw, G. B. *Dramatic Opinions and Essays*. London: Constable, 1907.

Shelley, Andrew. "Defining Wilde," *Essays in Criticism*, 38, 2 (1988), 156–61.

Sherard, Robert Harborough. *Oscar Wilde: The Story of an Unhappy Friendship*. London: privately printed, 1902; London: Greening, 1905.

_____. *The Life of Oscar Wilde*. London: T. Werner Laurie, 1906.

_____. *André Gide's Wicked Lies About the Late Mr. Oscar Wilde in Algiers in January, 1895*. Calvi, Corisca: Vindex Publishing Company, 1933.

_____. *Oscar Wilde, "Drunkard and Swindler": A Reply to George Bernard Shaw, Dr. G. J. Renier, Frank Harris, etc.* Calvi, Corisca: Vindex Publishing Company, 1933.

_____. *Oscar Wilde Twice Defended from André Gide's Wicked Lies and Frank Harris's Cruel Libels*. Chicago: Argus, 1934.

Sherman, Stuart. *Critical Woodcuts*. New York: Scribner and Son, 1926.

Shewan, Rodney. *Oscar Wilde: Art and Egotism*. London: Macmillan, 1977.

_____, ed. *"A Wife's Tragedy*: An Unpublished Sketch for a Play by Oscar Wilde," *Theatre Research International*, 7, 2 (1982), 75–131.

_____. "Oscar Wilde and *A Wife's Tragedy*: Facts and Conjectures," *Theatre Research International*, 8, 2 (1983), 183–95.

_____. "The Artist and The Dancer in Three Symbolist *Salomés*," *Bucknell Review*, 30, 1 (1986), 102–30.

Shuter, William F. "Pater As Don," *Prose Studies*, 11, 1 (1988), 40–61.

Siegel, Sandra. "Wilde's Use and Abuse of Aphorisms," *Victorian Studies Association of Western Canada Newsletter*, 12, 1 (1986), 16–26.

Sims, George. "Son of Oscar Wilde," *Antiquarian Book Monthly Review*, 11, 2 (1984), 50–57.

Small, Ian, ed. *The Aesthetes*. London: Routledge and Kegan Paul, 1979.

_____, ed. *Oscar Wilde. Lady Windermere's Fan. A Play About a Good Woman*. London: Benn, 1980.

_____, and Russell Jackson, eds. *Oscar Wilde, Two Society Comedies: A Woman of No Importance and An Ideal Husband*. London: A. and C. Black, 1983.

_____. "Semiotics and Oscar Wilde's Accounts of Art," *British Journal of Aesthetics*, 27, 3 (1985), 50–56.

_____, and Russell Jackson. "Some New Drafts of a Wilde Play," *English Literature in Transition*, 30, 1 (1987), 7–15.

_____. "Intertextuality in Pater and Wilde," *English Literature in Transition Special Series Number 4. Essays and Poems in Memory of Ian Fletcher* (1990), 57–66.

_____. *Conditions for Criticism: Authority, Knowledge, and Literature in the Late Nineteenth Century*. Oxford: Clarendon Press, 1991.

Smith, Derek Walker and Edward Clarke. *The Life of Sir Edward Clarke*. London: Thornton Butterworth, 1939.

Smith, Ophia, D. *Fair Oxford*. Oxford, Ohio: Oxford Historical Press, 1947.

Smith, Paula V. "A Wilde Subtext for *The Awkward Age*," *Henry James Review*, 9, 3 (1988), 199–208.

Smith, Philip E. II. "Protoplasmic Hierarchy and Philosophical Harmony: Science and Hegelian Aesthetics in Oscar Wilde's Notebooks," *Victorian Newsletter*, 74 (1988), 30–33.

_____, and Michael S. Helfand. *Oscar Wilde's Oxford Notebooks: A Portrait of Mind in the Making*. New York: Oxford University Press, 1989.

Smithers, Jack. *The Early Life and Vicissitudes of Jack Smithers*. London: Martin Secker, 1939.

Sontag, Susan. *Against Interpretation and Other Essays*. New York: Farrar, Strauss, and Giroux, 1966.

Sotheby's Catalogue: English Literature and History. 22–23 July 1985.

Sotheby's Catalogue: English Literature and History. 10–11 July 1986.

Spencer, Robin. *The Aesthetic Movement: Theory and Practice*. London: Studio Vista, 1972.

Spivey, Ted R. "Damnation and Salvation in *The Picture of Dorian Gray*," *Boston University Studies in English*, 4 (1960), 162–70.

Stanford, Derek, ed. *Writing of the 'Nineties*. London: Dent, 1971.

Stanford, W. B. and R. B. MacDowell. *Mahaffy: A Biography of an Anglo-Irishman*. London: Routledge and Kegan Paul, 1971.

Stavros, George. "Oscar Wilde on the Romantics," *English Literature in Transition*, 20, 1 (1977), 35–45.

Steinman, Michael. *Yeats's Heroic Figures: Wilde, Parnell, Swift, Casement*. London: Macmillan, 1983.

Stern, Madeleine B. *Purple Passage: The Life of Mrs Frank Leslie*. Norman: University of Oklahoma Press, 1953.

Stetson, J. B. *The Oscar Wilde Collection of John B. Stetson Jr*. New York: The Anderson Galleries, 1920.

Stevenson, J. V. "The Wrong Picture of Dorian Gray," *Adam*, 419 (1979), 56–60.

Stevenson, Lionel. "Oscar Wilde," in *The Victorian Poets: A Guide to Research*, Frederic E. Faverty, ed. Cambridge: Harvard University Press, 1956.

Stillmark, Alexander. "Hofmannsthal and Oscar Wilde," in *Hugo von Hofmannsthal (1874–1929): Commemorative Essays*, W. E. Yuill and Patricia Howe, eds. London: n.p., 1981.

Stoddard, Martin. *Art, Messianism and Crime: Sade, Wilde, Hitler, Manson and Others*. New York: St. Martin's Press, 1986.

Stokes, John. *Resistible Theatres*. London: Paul Elek, 1972.

_____. *Oscar Wilde.* British Council Writers and Their Work Series. London: Longman, 1978.

_____. "Wilde on Dostoevsky," *Notes and Queries,* 27 (1980), 215–16.

_____. "Wilde at Bay: the Diaries of George Ives," *English Literature in Transition,* 26, 3 (1983), 175–86.

_____. "Foreign Correspondence: News and Notes from England," *English Literature in Transition,* 30, 2 (1987), 177–79.

_____. *In the Nineties.* London: Harvester–Wheatsheaf, 1990.

Stokes, Leslie and Sewell. *Oscar Wilde: A Play.* London: Secker and Warburg, 1937.

Stokes, Sewell. *Beyond His Means; A Novel Based on the Life of Oscar Wilde.* London: Peter Davies, 1955.

Stone, Geoffrey. "Serious Bunburyism: The Logic of *The Importance of Being Earnest,*" *Essays in Criticism,* 26 (1976), 228–41.

Styan, J. L. *The Elements of Drama.* Cambridge: Cambridge University Press, 1960.

Sullivan, Kevin. *Oscar Wilde. Columbia Essays on Modern Writers.* New York: Columbia University Press, 1972.

Sussman, Herbert. "Criticism as Art: Form in Oscar Wilde's Writings," *Studies in Philology,* 70, 1 (1973), 108–22.

Swann, Charles. "*The Picture of Dorian Gray,* The Bible, and the Unpardonable Sin," *Notes & Queries,* 38, 3 (1991), 326–27.

Symons, Arthur. *A Study of Oscar Wilde.* London: Charles J. Sawyer, 1930.

Tappe, Eric. "T. Wemyss Reid and Rumania: His *Woman's World*, Oscar Wilde and Carmen Sylva," *Slavonic and East European Review*, 64, 2 (1986), 256–60.

Temple, Ruth Z. *The Critic's Alchemy: A Study of the Introduction of French Symbolism into England*. New York: Twayne, 1953.

_____. "The Ivory Tower as Lighthouse," in *Edwardians and Late Victorians*, Richard Ellmann, ed. New York: Columbia University Press, 1960.

_____. "The Other Choice: The Worlds of John Gray, Poet and Priest," *Bulletin of Research in the Humanities*, 84, 1 (1981), 16–64.

Terry, Ellen. *The Story of My Life*. London: Hutchinson, 1908.

_____. *Ellen Terry's Memoirs*. London: Victor Gollancz, 1933.

Thomas, J. D. "The Composition of Wilde's 'The Harlot's House,'" *Modern Language Notes*, 65, 7 (1951), 485–88.

_____. " 'The Soul of Man Under Socialism': an Essay in Context," *Rice University Studies*, 51, 1 (1965) 83–95.

_____. "The Intentional Strategy In Oscar Wilde's Dialogues," *English Literature in Transition*, 12, 1 (1969), 11–20.

Thornton, R. K. R. *The Decadent Dilemma*. London: Edward Arnold, 1983.

_____. "The Mask in Wilde and Yeats," in *Die Modernisierung des Ich: Studien zur Subjektkonstitution in der Vor– und Fruhmoderne*, Manfred Pfister, ed. Passau: Rothe, 1989.

Tillotson, Geoffrey. *A View of Victorian Literature*. Oxford: Clarendon Press, 1978.

Trilling, Lionel. *Sincerity and Authenticity*. London: Oxford University Press, 1972.

Turquet–Milnes, G. *The Influence of Baudelaire in France and England*. London: Constable, 1913.

Tydeman, William. *Wilde: Comedies*. London: Macmillan, 1982.

Tymms, Ralph. *Doubles in Literary Psychology*. Cambridge: Bowes and Bowes, 1949.

Unrau, John. "Ruskin and the Wildes: the Whitelands Connection," *Notes & Queries*, 29, 4 (1982), 316–17.

Updike, John, ed. *"The Young King" and Other Fairy Tales by Oscar Wilde*. London: Macmillan, 1962.

Vieron, Martine. "Le Mythe du double dans *Le Portrait de Dorian Gray* d'Oscar Wilde," in *Mythe—Rite—Symbole*, Georges Cesbron, ed. Angers: Université d'Angers, 1985.

Vordtriede, Werner. "A Dramatic Device in *Faust* and *The Importance of Being Earnest*," *Modern Language Notes*, 70, 8 (1955), 584–85.

Ware, James M. "Algernon's Appetite: Oscar Wilde's Hero as Restoration Dandy," *English Literature in Transition*, 13 (1970), 17–26.

Warner, Eric and Graham Hough, eds. *Strangeness and Beauty: An Anthology of Aesthetic Criticism: 1840–1910*. 2 vols. Cambridge: Cambridge University Press: 1983.

Watson, Edward A. "Wilde's Iconoclastic Classicism: 'The Critic As Artist'," *English Literature in Transition*, 27, 3 (1984), 225–35.

Webb, Peter. "Victorian Erotica," in *The Sexual Dimension in Literature*, Alan Bold, ed. London: Vision, 1982.

Weintraub, Stanley. *Reggie: A Portrait of Reginald Turner*. New York: George Braziller, 1965.

_____. *Beardsley*. London: W. H.Allen, 1967.

_____, ed. *The Literary Criticism of Oscar Wilde*. Lincoln: University of Nebraska Press, 1968.

_____. *Whistler: A Biography*. London: Collins, 1974.

Weissman, Judith. " 'The Castrating Gesture' in Wilde and the Post–Structuralists," *Southern Review*, 24, 3 (1988), 520–34.

Wellek, René. *A History of Modern Criticism*. Vol. 4. New Haven: Yale University Press, 1965.

West, Alick. *The Mountain in the Sunlight: Studies in Conflict and Unity*. London: Lawrence and Wishart, 1958.

White, Nanci Jane. *An Annotated Edition of the Poems of Oscar Wilde*. See Dissertation Abstracts International, 41, 10 (1981).

White, Terence de Vere. *The Parents of Oscar Wilde*. London: Hodder and Stoughton, 1967.

Wiegler, Paul. *Genius in Love and Death*. Trans. Carl Roushenbush. New York: Albert and Charles Boni, 1929.

Wilburn, Lydia Reineck. "Oscar Wilde's 'The Canterville Ghost': The Power of an Audience," *Papers on Language and Literature*, 23, 1 (1987), 41–55.

Wilde, Oscar. *Hellenism*. Edinburgh, Tragara Press, 1979.

_____. *The Happy Prince*. Jean Claverie, illus. New York: Oxford University Press, 1980.

_____. *The Nightingale and the Rose*. Michael Foreman and Freire Wright, illus. London: Kaye and Ward, 1981.

_____. *The Selfish Giant*. Lisbeth Zwerger, illus. London: Picture Book Studio, 1984.

[Wilde, Oscar, et al.]. *Teleny: Or, The Reverse of the Medal: A Physiological Romance*. 2 vols. London: Leonard Smithers, 1893.

_____. *Teleny: Or, The Reverse of the Medal: A Physiological Romance*. Winston Leyland, intro. San Francisco: Gay Sunshine Press, 1984.

_____. *Teleny: Or, The Reverse of the Medal: A Physiological Romance*. New York: Warner Books, 1984.

_____. *Teleny: Or, The Reverse of the Medal: A Physiological Romance*. John McRae, ed. Boston: Alyson Publications, 1986.

Williams, Raymond. *Culture and Society*. London: Chatto and Windus, 1958.

Williamson, Audrey. *Artists and Writers in Revolt*. Newton Abbot: David Charles, 1976.

Willoughby, Guy. "The Marvellous Rose: Christ and the Meaning of Art in 'The Nightingale and the Rose'," *English Studies in Africa*, 31, 2 (1988), 107–17.

_____. "Oscar Wilde and Poststructuralism," *Philosophy and Literature*, 13, 2 (1989), 316–24.

Wilson, T. G. *Victorian Doctor: Being the Life of Sir William Wilde*. New York: L. B. Fischer, 1946.

Wood, Alice I. "Oscar Wilde as a Critic," *North American Review*, 202 (1915), 899–909.

Wood, Clement. *The Sensualist: A Novel of the Life and Times of Oscar Wilde*. New York: Jonathan Swift, 1942.

Woodcock, George. *The Paradox of Oscar Wilde*. London: T. V. Boardman, 1949.

_____. *Anarchism*. Gloucester, MA: Peter Smith, 1962.

Worth, Katharine. *The Irish Drama of Europe from Yeats to Beckett*. London: Athlone Press, 1978.

Oscar Wilde. London: Macmillan, 1983.

Woudhuysen, H. R. "Sales of Books and Manuscripts," *Times Literary Supplement*, 4 July 1986, 747.

_____. "Writing Types," *Times Literary Supplement*, 11 December 1987, 1376.

Wright, Austen, ed. *Victorian Literature*. New York: Oxford University Press, 1961.

Wyndham, Horace. *Speranza: A Biography of Lady Wilde*. London: T. V. Boardman, 1951.

Wyndham, Violet. *The Sphinx and Her Circle*. London: André Deutsch, 1963.

Young, Dalhousie. *Apologia Pro Oscar Wilde*. London: William Reeves, 1895.

Zagona, Helen Grace. *The Legend of Salomé and the Principle of Art for Art's Sake*. Geneva: Ambilly–Annemasse, 1960.

Zatlin, Linda Gertner. "Aubrey Beardsley Counts the Ways," *Victorian Newsletter*, 67 (1985), 1–6.

_____. *Aubrey Beardsley and Victorian Sexual Politics*. Oxford: Clarendon Press, 1990.

Zima, Peter V. "Towards a Sociology of Fictional Texts," *New Comparison*, 5 (1988), 57–74.

Appendices

Appendix 1.

Oscar Wilde's Best Sonnet

The sin was mine, I did not understand.
So now is beauty buried in her cave,
Save where some ebbing desultory wave
Frets with its restless whorls this meagre strand.
And in the withered hollow of the land
Hath summer dug herself so deep a grave,
That hardly can the silver willow crave
One leaden blossom from keen Winter's hand.

But who is this that cometh by the shore?
Nay love, look up and wonder who is this
Who cometh in dyed garments from the south?
It is thy new found lord & he shall kiss
The yet unravished roses of thy mouth.
And I shall weep and worship as before, [sic]

Appendix 2.

AMS is as follows:

PAN
A Villanelle

Ah what remains to us of thee,
    This modern world is dull and old,
O goat-foot God of Arcady!

No more the shepherd lads in glee
    Throw apples at thy wattled fold;
Ah what remains to us of thee?

Nor through the laurels can one see
    Thy soft brown limbs, thy beard of gold,
O goat-foot God of Arcady!

Yet leave the tomb of Helicé
    Though here the winds are chill and cold.
Ah what remains of us to thee?

For many an unsung elegy
    Sleep in the reeds our rivers hold,
O goat-foot God of Arcady!

And thine the silent Thames shall be
    And all the glades thou shalt behold.
Ah what remains of us to thee
    O goat-foot God of Arcady!.

The printed version is taken from the plates of the first volume of Robert Ross's 1909 *Complete Works* and retains the page numbers of that volume:

Printed by John W. Luce and Company
Boston and London 1909
19/30 numbered copies

PAN
A Double villanelle
and
DESESPOIR
A Sonnet

Hitherto Unpublished Poems
by Oscar Wilde
John Luce &Company
London and Boston

[NEW PAGE]

Pan
I

O Goat-foot God of Arcady!
This modern world is grey and old,
And what remains to us of thee?

No more the shepherd lads in glee
Throw apples at thy wattled fold.
O goat-foot God of Arcady.

Nor through the laurels can one see
    Thy soft brown limbs, thy beard of gold,
And what remains to us of thee?

And dull and dead our Thames would be,
    For here the winds are chill and cold,
O goat-foot God of Arcady!

Then keep the tomb of Helicé,
    Thine olive-woods, thy vine-clad wold,
And what remains to us of thee?

Though many an unsung elegy
    Sleeps in the reeds our rivers hold,
O goat-foot God of Arcady!
    Ah, what remains to us of thee?

APPENDIX 3: Letters of Dubious Authority

AL copy in unidentified hand to George Alexander; n.d.
Location: HRHRC; MS Wilde, O; Letters.
MS Mason, AEW; Misc.

Dear Alexander,

Come and see me tomorrow—Sunday, if you are in Chelsea, and congratulate me as I am sure you will, on the baby!

Ever yours
Oscar Wilde

ALS to [unidentified correspondent] George B–; n.d.
Location: HRHRC, Texas; MS Wilde, O; Letters.

Envelope:
Angleterre

George Bar[?]—s
Editor,
The Lancet [?]
16 John Street,
Bedford Row
London WC.

Hotel de Nice
Rue des Beaux-Arts
Paris

My dear Sir,

I must thank you very much for the books: the edition of my essays is a masterpiece of loving binding—and I was charmed to receive my

Dear father's book, and also *Salomé*, with the drawings of Max Beerbohm, in his Oxford days.

You really have been most kind to me and I *do* hope to see you.

I am worried over the sordid things of life, so cannot write—at least, intelligently—but I beg you to accept again my sincere thanks, and I hope you will review the 'Ballad of Reading Gaol' some-where—you have been so charming to the author, that you may be charming also to the work.

Yours

Oscar Wilde

ALS to Selwyn Image
Location: Clark Library
W6721L. I31. [1900?].

> Hotel d'Alsace
> Ave. des Beaux-Arts [*sic*]
> *Wednesday*

My dear Selwyn,

Thanks very much for the books and advanced copy. In your letters you have not mentioned Arthur Clifton. I cannot imagine the cause of his silence. Unless I hear from him I cannot stir. Can you send me £5? I would not worry you with my troubles but you must understand my [illegible word] position. God! When I think of it!—*Anything I think is preferable to the Hell that is in me.*

Of course *I do* expect money from Clifton but meanwhile I must have a little. It is but a small amount.

Be like a good fellow send it.

Yours

Oscar Wilde

Fragment of a draft of a letter to an unknown correspondent
Location: Clark Library.
W6721L. U58. [189–?].

[Y]ou will be glad to hear my catalogue is a great success: they have recognised my hand of course: I couldn't help it. Everybody talks of it: it's a masterpiece, though I say it myself.

Fragment of a draft of a letter to an unknown correspondent
Location: Clark Library.
W6721L. U58. [189?b].

[T]hanks for all your letters: I cannot be best-man and wear wedding-cake in my coat, or whatever one does: have written to Willie Graham.

Index of Names

| *Colophon* |

Display & Text Type
Trump Medieval

Title–Page/ Contents Page/ Text
Designed by Robert Langenfeld

Dust Jacket
Designed by David Schwartz

WordPerfect 5.1/ Ventura Publisher 4.1
Windows 3.1/ CorelDraw 2.0

Printer: Thomson–Shore, Inc.
Dexter, Michigan
Production Coordinator   Diane Nourse